Complex Situations in Coaching

Complex Situations in Coaching is a collection of 20 typical yet underdiscussed issues in coaching, ranging from value conflicts, multiple agendas, power dynamics, and emotion management, to the role of money, etc. Organized into ten chapters, they are positioned into the literature and commented on by world-class coaches, coaching researchers, educators, and program directors. This plurality of voices is designed to foster dialogue, questions, and solutions; this setting, supportive of reflexivity, critical thinking, and diversity awareness, is essential to the development and education of coaches in an increasingly complex world where ready-made solutions prove limited. Thus, beyond a "toolkit approach," this book engages in a thought-provoking and multi-perspective journey in support of the professionalization and continuous education of coaches, instructors, and/or supervisors.

Dima Louis is Assistant Professor, Department of People, Organizations & Society, Grenoble Ecole de Management, Université Grenoble Alpes ComUE, France.

Pauline Fatien Diochon is Associate Professor of Management, Innovation Academy, SKEMA Business School, Université Côte d'Azur, France.

Complex Situations in Coaching

A Critical Case-Based Approach

**Dima Louis and
Pauline Fatien Diochon**

Routledge
Taylor & Francis Group

LONDON AND NEW YORK

First published 2019
by Routledge
2 Park Square, Milton Park, Abingdon, Oxon OX14 4RN

and by Routledge
52 Vanderbilt Avenue, New York, NY 10017

Routledge is an imprint of the Taylor & Francis Group, an informa business

© 2019 Dima Louis and Pauline Fatien Diochon

British Library Cataloguing-in-Publication Data
A catalogue record for this book is available from the British Library

Library of Congress Cataloging-in-Publication Data
A catalog record for this book has been requested

ISBN: 978-0-367-17321-0 (hbk)
ISBN: 978-0-367-17323-4 (pbk)
ISBN: 978-0-429-05618-5 (ebk)

Typeset in Bembo
by Apex CoVantage, LLC

Contents

Tables

Figures

Cases

Contributors

Chapter 1. Case 1.1.

a. **Thomas Diamante, PhD**. President, Consulting Division, New York State Psychological Association, USA and EVP/Global Practice Director at CCA, Inc., a human capital consulting firm in New York. *Tom.Diamante@gmail.com*

b. **David E. Gray, PhD†**. Professor of Leadership and Organisational Behaviour, University of Greenwich, UK. *d.e.gray@gre.ac.uk*

Chapter 1. Case 1.2.

a. **Eduardo Abarzua, PhD**. Psychologist in Labor Sciences. Faculty, Alberto Hurtado University UAH, Chile, School of Economic and Business, Organizational Coaching Program Director. *Eabarzua@uahurtado.cl*

    &

    Alejandra Pallamar, MS. Psychologist and Consultant, MS in People Management for Organizations. Affiliated Faculty Alberto Hurtado University UAH, Chile, School of Economic and Business, Organizational Coaching Program. *Alejandra.pallamar@gmail.com*

b. **Ana Pliopas, PhD, MCC**. Escola de Administração de Empresas de São Paulo, Fundação Getulio Vargas, Brazil. Partner at The Hudson Institute of Coaching Brazil. *Ana.Pliopas@hudsoninstitute.com.br*

Chapter 2. Case 2.1.

a. **David Matthew Prior, MCC, BCC, MBA**. Core Facilitator Team, Columbia University Coaching Program; Principal, Getacoach.com. *david@getacoach.com*

b. **Deryk Stec, PhD**. Assistant Professor of Management, Dalhousie University, Rowe School of Business, Faculty of Management. *deryk.stec@dal.ca*

† Deceased 7 March 2019

Chapter 2. Case 2.2.

a. **Ken Otter, PhD**. Faculty, MA in Leadership. Co-director, Leadership Center, Saint Mary's College of California, USA. *kotter@stmarys-ca.edu*

b. **Hany Shoukry, PhD**. Honorary Research Associate, Oxford Brookes University. Founder, humangene.org. *hanyshoukry@me.com*

Chapter 3. Case 3.1.

a. **Clara Mandowsky Gun, PCC**. Organizational and team coach, Colombia. *cmgcoaching@yahoo.com*

b. **Konstantin Korotov, PhD**. Professor of Organizational Behavior, Director of the Center for Leadership Development Research, and Associate Dean of Executive Education, ESMT-Berlin. *konstantin.korotov@esmt.org*

Chapter 3. Case 3.2.

a. **Theo L. M. Groot, Msc. OD**. Independent Coach and Facilitator. *theogroot@icloud.com*

b. **Scarlett Salman, PhD**. Associate Professor, University Paris-Est, Marne-la-Vallée, UFR SHS (Humanities & Social Sciences), Sociology Department. Member of UMR LISIS (Laboratoire Interdisciplinaire Sciences Innovations Sociétés) (CNRS, ESIEE Paris, INRA, UPEM). *scarlett.salman@u-pem.fr*

Chapter 4. Case 4.1.

a. **Kenneth Mølbjerg Jørgensen, PhD**. Professor, Aalborg University, DK, Department of Business and Management. *kmj@business.aau.dk*

b. **Linda J. Page, PhD**. Founder and President Emerita, Adler Graduate Professional School, Toronto, Canada. *ljpage@adler.ca*

Chapter 4. Case 4.2.

a. **Bob Garvey, PhD**. Managing Partner, The Lio Partnership. *r.garvey@easynet.co.uk*

b. **Paul Stokes, PhD**. Principal Lecturer, Sheffield Hallam University, UK, Sheffield Business School, Department of Management, Director, Coaching & Mentoring Research Unit. *p.k.stokes@shu.ac.uk*

Chapter 5. Case 5.1.

a. **Sybille Persson, PhD**. Professor, ICN Business School, France, Human Resource and Organizational Behavior Department, CEREFIGE, University of Lorraine. Founder, ICN School of Coaching. *sybille.persson@icn-artem.com*

b. **Irina Todorova, PhD**. Director of Research, Institute of Coaching & Faculty, Harvard Medical School; Fellow of the European Health Psychology Society and Editor, *Health Psychology and Behavioral Medicine*. Irina_todorova@ post.harvard.edu

Chapter 5. Case 5.2.

a. **Maroussia Chanut**. Independant executive coach, Founder, Phoenix Ressources & La Science du Bonheur, France, www.phoenixressources. com, ww.la-science-du-bonheur.com, www.the-science-of-happiness.com, maroussia.chanut@gmail.com

b. **Christian J. van Nieuwerburgh, PhD**. Professor of Coaching and Positive Psychology, School of Psychology, University of East London (UK). *chrisvn@uel.ac.uk*

Chapter 6. Case 6.1.

a. **L. Felipe C. Paiva**. Partner, Artisan Consultoria. *felipe@artisanconsultoria.com*

b. **Charline S. Russo, EdD**. Affiliated Faculty, University of Pennsylvania (PA), USA, School of Arts & Sciences, Organizational Dynamics Department. Founder, The CampoMarzio Group, LLC. *campomarzio@gmail.com*

Chapter 6. Case 6.2.

a. **CB Bowman, MBA, MCEC, CMC, BCC**. Corporate Executive Coach, Speaker. CEO G-4: Association of Corporate Executive Coaches (ACEC) and the MEECO Leadership Institute. *cb@meeco-institute.org, cb@acec-association.org*

b. **Julian P. Humphreys, PhD, PCC**. Executive and Leadership Coach. Founder and Editor-in-Chief of *Philosophy of Coaching: An International Journal*. *humphreysjulian@gmail.com*

Chapter 7. Case 7.1.

a. **Brenda Dooley MA, DipPsych, FCIPD**. Executive & Leadership Coaching, Dublin, Ireland. www.brendadooley.ie

b. **David A. Lane, PhD**. Visiting Professor, Middlesex University and Canterbury Christ Church University and Director, Professional Development Foundation. *david.lane@pdf.net*

Chapter 7. Case 7.2.

a. **Geoffrey Abbott, PhD**. Director of Executive Coaching, Graduate School of Business, QUT, Australia. Founder/Director, Centre for International Business Coaching. *geoffrey.abbott@qut.edu.au*

b. **Daniel Doherty, PhD**. Chair, Critical Coaching Research Group, www. criticalcoaching.com., *dandoh123@gmail.com*

Chapter 8. Case 8.1.

a. **Tony V. Zampella, MSOL**. Coach and Researcher in Leadership Development. Faculty affiliations: Mercy College and Rutgers University in Organizational Leadership. Founder, Bhavana Learning Group. *tony@bhavanalg.com*

b. **Nadine Mendelek Theimann, PhD**. Executive Coach at Skyline Group International, Professional Certified Coach at the International Coaching Federation, New Ventures West Certified Integral Coach, IFS Certified Practitioner at the Centre for Self-Leadership. *ntheimann@hotmail.com*

Chapter 8. Case 8.2.

a. **Natalie Cunningham, PhD**. Research Associate, Gordon Institute of Business Science (GIBS), University of Pretoria, Sandton, South Africa. Founder, Origo Consultants. *natalie@origoconsultants.com*

b. **Alison Pullen, PhD**. Professor of Management and Organization Studies, Faculty of Business and Economics, Macquarie University, Sydney, Australia, and Joint Editor-in-Chief of *Gender, Work and Organization*. *alison.pullen@mq.edu.au*

&

Mojdeh Tavanayan,. PhD. candidate, Department of Management, Faculty of Business and Economics, Macquarie University, Sydney, Australia. *mojdeh.tavanayan@mq.edu.au*

Chapter 9. Case 9.1.

a. **Gilles Amado, PhD**. Psychology Dr, Emeritus Professor of Organizational Psychosociology, HEC Paris, founding member of the International Society for the Psychoanalytic Study of Organizations (ISPSO). *amado@hec.fr*

b. **Alyssa Freas, PhD**. CEO & President & Founder, Executive Coaching Network, Inc.® *alyssa@excn.com*

Chapter 9. Case 9.2.

a. **Tatiana Bachkirova, PhD**. Professor of Coaching Psychology, Oxford Brookes University, UK, Oxford Brookes Business School. Director of the International Centre for Coaching and Mentoring Studies. *tbachkirova@brookes.ac.uk*

b. **Melvin L. Smith, PhD, BCC**. Professor of Organizational Behavior and Faculty Director, Executive Education, Weatherhead School of Management, Case Western Reserve University, USA. *melvin.smith@case.edu*

Chapter 10. Case 10.1.

a. **Pascale Répécaud**. Psychoanalyst, Groupal Management Consultant and coach in France. Specializing in psychosocial risks prevention. BR&Co. Director, Founder of the Groupal Management Project. *pascale.repecaud@ outlook.fr*

b. **Andy Pendle, MSc, MA**. Senior Lecturer in Counselling, Coaching & Mentoring, York St John University, England. *a.pendle@yorksj.ac.uk*

Chapter 10. Case 10.2.

a. **Carlos Davidovich, MD**. NeuroManagement expert and Executive Coach (EMCC). Member of the Institute of Coaching at McLean Hospital, Harvard Medical School affiliate. Professor of NeuroMarketing at the University of New York in Prague (MBA program). *cdavidovich@optimumtalent.com*

b. **Olivier Piazza**. Executive Coaching, Collective Intelligence and Management Executive Education Programs Co-director, University of Cergy-Pontoise, France. *olivierpiazza@icloud.com*

&

Florence Daumarie. Executive Coaching and Collective Intelligence Executive Education Programs Co-director, University of Cergy-Pontoise, France. *florence.daumarie@u-cergy.fr*

Acknowledgments

Our heartfelt thanks first go to each of the 43 contributors to this book. Their knowledge, expertise, and passion, whether as a researcher, teacher, and/or practitioner, as well as their full engagement in the book process, contributed to achieving the objective of this book: to have an open, stimulating, and critically informed conversation around sensitive topics in coaching. Navigating their commentaries to orchestrate such a critical dialogue has been a source of enrichment for us, and hopefully for you, the reader.

We are also grateful to the 60 coaches we have interviewed over the course of various research projects these past eight years. The 20 cases presented in this book derived from these coaches' experiences will hopefully be a source of learning and growth for all of us.

We would like to express our gratitude to Natalie Tomlinson, editor at Routledge, who aided us through the proposal stage, and to our editorial assistant at Routledge, Judith Lorton, for always being available to answer our queries and for supporting us throughout the preparation of this book.

Our deep appreciation goes out to our copyeditor, Katie Flynn, for the wonderful job she has done and for the flexibility she has shown, and to our research assistant, Maria Paula Cardona. Finally, our thanks also go out to our colleagues who have accompanied us over these past years in our professional activities, as well as to our friends and families. As we are wrapping up this textbook, we are very saddened by the passing away of one of the contributors, Dr. David E. Gray. We feel indebted to David for being one of the first critical voices in the study and practice of coaching, and contributing to establishing coaching as an academic discipline.

Introduction

Though coaching is a relatively young field, it is burgeoning in organizations. Designed to support individuals and organizations to implement their objectives (from job performance to team cohesion and strategic changes), the practice is gaining momentum given the volatility and complexity of our global and diverse environment. On its way to professionalization, it suffers from a gap between the advanced stage of the practice and the lagging academic discourse surrounding the field. This book intends to answer a call for increased connectivity between practice, theory, and research in support of a more professional, impactful, and ethical practice. We chose to address this gap by constituting a collection – derived from research we personally conducted – of 20 typical, yet complex, situations that practitioners face. Organized into ten chapters, these situations are positioned into the literature and commented on by world-class coaches, coaching researchers, educators, and program directors. The goal of this text is to create conditions to foster dialogue, questions, and solutions, between you, the reader, and us, the co-authors, as well as the "experts" who commented on the cases, together with your colleagues, supervisors, and/or classmates. Typical issues include ethical dilemmas, multiple agendas, and power dynamics, rooted in real situations experienced by coaches from different cultures and backgrounds.

We believe that this orientation, supportive of reflexivity, critical thinking, and diversity awareness, is essential to the development and education of coaches in an increasingly complex world where ready-made solutions prove limited. This textbook thus contrasts with the dominant approach of most coaching textbooks, which embraces a normative and prescriptive perspective by focusing mainly on transferring coaching tools and models. In brief, we have designed this book to engage you – the reader – in a thought-provoking and multi-perspective journey in support of your professional development and continuous education as a coach, instructor, and/or supervisor.

Get ready for the journey! The chapters do not need to be read in a particular order. As part of personal development, you can choose to start with the chapter that is most relevant to your current experience, or that you feel most intrigued by.

1 Multiple agendas in coaching

Introduction

Given that most, if not all, coaching interventions involve some sort of objective, we may wonder what informs their definition, implementation, and successful attainment. This chapter depicts how the interplay between multiple stakeholders, from the coach, the coachee, to the organization, potentially generates multiple, contradictory, and hidden agendas, resulting in dilemmas and missed coaching opportunities.

Typical hidden agendas within the triadic coaching relationship include:

- *The individualization of an issue.* It is not unusual to hear that the designated coachee is not the one who really needs coaching. Indeed, the coachee can sometimes be framed as "a 'problem person'" (Tobias, 1996, p. 89), potentially leading to scapegoating while other, more holistic approaches might be more suitable to addressing the root causes of the problem. This phenomenon has been termed the individualization or psychologicalization of an issue (Amado, 2004; Fatien Diochon & Lovelace, 2015) when collective problems are rendered individual or psychological.
- *The conflicting agendas.* The various stakeholders involved in a coaching intervention expect to achieve different coaching goals, each trying to advance their own agenda without sharing it with the group (Louis & Fatien-Diochon, 2014).
- *The organization excluded.* Coachees work on an issue with the coach, without informing the organization, for example, preparing a career move away from the current organization (St John-Brooks, 2010).
- *The poisonous gift.* The organization has some intentions for the future of the executive and is using coaching as a "last resort" or an "excuse" to show that despite all their efforts, the executive still doesn't meet expectations, making the coaching a "poisonous gift" (Fatien, 2012, p. 309). A typical situation is when coaching is used to justify the coachee's firing.

In this chapter, *The organization excluded* explores the dilemma of Lisa, whose client, Peter, divulges that he wants to leave the company, a large UK publishing company, and expects Lisa to prepare him for this move. Should Lisa accept Peter's agenda or follow the initially agreed-upon agenda? In *The poisonous gift*, John realizes that in coaching the Chief Operating Officer (COO) of a large American asset management company, he has unwittingly contributed to the COO's firing.

The two cases with their commentaries below thus allow exploration of how hidden agendas can result in a number of challenges and dilemmas for coaches and can compromise the outcome of the coaching.

Case 1.1. The organization excluded

Lisa was hired by a large publishing company to coach Peter to "stop being so negative in meetings." While Lisa had noticed some friction between Peter and Daniel in the three-party meeting, they were able to agree upon a coaching agenda. Their objective was then to identify the reasons behind the perceived negativity in order to help Peter become a more positive contributor in meetings. Pretty straightforward, right?

Well, once Lisa began the coaching sessions, she quickly realized the situation was far more complicated than she originally thought. Peter explained that he was unhappy at his job, so much so that he intended to leave. On top of this, he asked for Lisa's help with his next move. He explained that rumors of a buyout by a larger publishing company had been circulating, and though he'd been unhappy for quite some time, these rumors had him rattled. Now, he was convinced to leave, and in the meantime, he was simply trying his best not to let anyone notice while he sorted things out for himself.

Peter's request put Lisa in a difficult position. She wasn't sure how to deal with it. On one hand, she thought to herself: "He's still employed by the company, and they're investing in his development, so he needs to be focused on that, or just quit." His intention to stay in the organization until he found a better job and to use the coaching assignment to prepare for the next move made her uncomfortable.

On the other hand, she thought: "If the organization is paying me to work with an employee, then the employee is my client. Therefore, if he says 'I want to leave,' then I should help him. Furthermore, he is no longer passionate about his work, he isn't invested, and he's lost the motivation to drive the business forward. It's not good for the organization to have someone in that position."

Reflexive questions

- What key issues does this case raise for Lisa? And for you?
- In this scenario, should Lisa's fundamental alliance be to her coachee or the client organization that hired her?
- When coachees leave their organization after a coaching intervention, do you consider the coaching intervention to be a failure? Why, or why not?

Ultimately, Lisa decided to help Peter with his request, using the coaching sessions to prepare him for his departure. Even though she remained uneasy about the situation, she believed it was not in her role to share this information with the company. Instead, while helping Peter, she encouraged him to be honest and transparent about his intentions. Just as he needed to prepare for his next move, the company needed to prepare to find a replacement.

Reflexive questions

- Do you agree with Lisa's decision to help Peter with his request? Why, or why not?
- Would you have handled this situation differently?

Commentary 6.1.a

Thomas Diamante

Overview of the case: points to ponder

It is clear that the coaching process in this case would benefit from structure. While there are a number of professional or psychological orientations in the literature, they more generally share a *defined* process for delivery. Coaches approach their work with varying psychological rubrics; however, the engagement is fairly predictable in terms of protocol. This is evident even on a global scale (Diamante & Primavera, 2004; Spence, Cavanagh, & Grant, 2006).

The protocol of the coach in this case, however, is somewhat elusive. It is clear that Peter has a plan and wants help executing it (i.e., departure). But what is Lisa's plan?

The incongruity between the hiring organization (client), the needs of the individual to be coached, and the professional expectations of the coach require resolution before a coaching engagement is activated. How can this occur? When should it occur? And who is responsible?

Research heavily influences the coaching profession, but it is still an evolving practice and remains unregulated in terms of licensing and oversight. This makes the profession exciting but also demands a higher level of vigilance by all practitioners to ensure standards are shared, discussed, agreed upon, and improved. Coaching can be advisory, motivational, cathartic, constructive, and educational. Regardless of its shape and form, however, clarity of goals, transparency of relationships, and the design process of the coaching experience all require consideration as they bring ethical and practical implications (London & Diamante, 2018; Spence et al., 2006). In this case, the design (approach) to the engagement and consequent goals are impacted by a degree of ambiguity apparent from the outset where the engagement plan, the organization's goals, and the coachee Peter's goals are incongruent. An agenda needs to be set with the hiring organization.

The criticality of setting mutual expectations is basic to any management consultation, and coaching is no exception. In this instance, the coach is struggling with the setting of visible goals that appear incompatible to the coachee's hidden or unrevealed goals or agenda. The client organization says stay and improve your team performance, while Peter ponders, "Get me out!" The multi-faceted nature of interpersonal and organizational dynamics in this case is not unusual. Arguably, it is the responsibility of the coach to catalyze the process of parsing out these complexities to bring clarity, understanding, and eventually action. These elements can and do intersect with personal, interpersonal, and organizational goals (Goodstone & Diamante, 2002; Diedrich, 2001).

The coaching process is an alliance. The rapport between the coach and the individual being coached (coachee) is central to progress. Rapport is earned based upon shared information, mutual openness, and authentic conversation, where confidentiality is the currency that leads to the sharing of hidden thoughts, if not their discovery, so that analysis of behavior has context. There should be a mutual "testing" where the credibility, integrity, and humanity of the helping relationship are examined – this leads to an advisory relationship that is genuine (Natale & Diamante,

2005). This alliance, however, is not limited to the coach-coachee dyad; there is also a need to involve the hiring (client) organization. Disparate treatment between coach-coachee-client can lead to confusion, conflict, and unrealized outcomes. This needs to be avoided. In this case, alliance management throughout the engagement requires attention. The coach is not attending to this alliance sufficiently and needs to take action. Why is this happening?

The psychological component that impacts the professional execution of coaching conversations is key to understanding this case (Diamante, 2013). The self-awareness of the coach who strives to catalyze positive change in others is relevant, especially because more often than not, the coach is not the target of the engagement. Still those who talk to others to counsel, coach, or otherwise engage with the goal of helping should retain keen awareness of their thoughts, beliefs, evaluations, and goals in relation to those of the client and coachee (Diamante, 2011; Leonard, 2017).

In this case the coach is needlessly conflicted between delivering a coaching engagement to "save" Peter by retaining him in the client organization or to "save" Peter by establishing a better, healthier path for him. The cognitive strain being experienced by the coach requires personal examination. The coach can benefit from reflecting on feelings toward the client organization, the request of this hiring organization, and the perception of the role (or business situation) that Peter finds himself in (Diamante & Primavera, 2004). Is the coach reading the situation based on personal feelings? Are the coach's own tendencies interfering with her analysis of how best to handle this engagement? Can this coach "push back" on the goals expressed by the hiring organization? Is this reasonable? Is it right? Is it professional?

The turbulence in this case might be exacerbated by the internal state of the coach. The coach, based on the shared business situation, views her role as either a means to retain the employee for the client organization or as a tool to help the employee escape. What is her role, as the coach? How does she add value? What are her ethics?

Total workplace dynamics are affecting behavior in this case. The coach does not need to be singularly focused on the individual. This would be a "systemic" approach to the problem, which would lead to identification of the organizational culture, the expectations (and behaviors) of leaders, the norms and values, and all the intangible elements that are so very present and often influencing the behavior of employees heavily, such as the anticipated merger. Total system analytics (e.g., open systems theory) and organizational change principles can inform the coach about the business situation, the stresses and strains that all of management is experiencing, and with that in mind, equip the coach to better help Peter sort things out cognitively, emotionally, and behaviorally (Burke, 2018; Kotter, 2012). How can parsing out these elements lead to more effective coaching?

By identifying the reasons for Peter's disengagement, it may be possible to change his behavior. How can the coach best get at the root causes? Peter must come to realize that his desire to leave is predicated on his beliefs about his life, his work, his culture, and the people with whom he works – all that impacts his performance, and he is sharing that with the world. Are these beliefs impeding his ability to relate effectively with others? Is he aware of this? How can the coach surface this issue? Peter brings fear of job loss due to a merger, and his behavior is making that unwanted possibility a likely probability. Can the coach bring this to light? What tools or gathered data might be useful to enhance self-awareness? Does Peter know the impact of his behavior on others, especially in team settings? How can that be extracted so Peter can inspect it? And change it?

Awareness of the organizational elements that influence behavior leads to enhanced self-direction (Diamante, Natale, & London, 2006; de Haan & Nilsson, 2017). To what extent can the coach define these elements, and what is the best way to present them to the coachee? How can discussing the approach to the engagement help the coach overcome the gaps between her, the client, and the coachee? How will surfacing the organizational elements that are pressing upon the individual enable all parties to clarify goals and agree to potential, desirable outcomes?

Lisa wants to help Peter. What does help look like?

In complex organizational systems, especially where uncertainty of business direction is implicated, being broad-based during an assessment (or intake) of a coaching case can be advantageous. Understanding the frame within which the picture of Peter is placed can trigger questions for the hiring organization and the coach that might not otherwise be revealed. How can the coach create an opportunity to conduct an organizational diagnostic prior to coaching? Would Peter need to be involved? Who would? How can the information gathered from such an assessment help all parties target goals for Peter? Long term, how does this reduce risk for the coach while increasing the chances of success for Peter?

The focus of the coaching, upon presentation, was improving performance on the job. The hidden agenda of desired departure and better team performance are not mutually exclusive. Peter, through coaching, can learn why his team behavior is inadequate, and the coach can help fix it. That is a key goal – it must be met. However, is that enough? Coaching is generally accepted as being focused on professional and personal development. The coachee's "hidden" agenda does not need to remain hidden if the coach can somehow connect "intent to leave" with its cause. Can Peter improve his team behavior and ready himself for departure?

The coach best serves everyone involved when she factors in her own state of mind, the psychological strain experienced by the individual being coached and the needs of the client organization. When can the coach turn this chain of strain into a dialectic self-understanding *and* organizational understanding? This can lead to better decisions by Peter, better support by the coach, and better outcomes for the organization.

The coach has responsibilities to the hiring organization and the coachee. Do you think that focusing on Peter's personal goal rather than the organizational problem will lead to failure for the coach? Will it lead to failure for Peter, as well?

Enabling professionals to chart a path toward a more productive life requires personal, interpersonal, and organizational alignment. In this case, the onus is on the coach to make certain that all parties are headed in the same direction toward mutual goals.

Commentary 1.1.b

David E. Gray

The agenda in this case is that Peter has been allocated a coach to support him to "stop being so negative in meetings." This, in itself, is often not the best start to a coach-coachee relationship since it appears to be using coaching in a remedial context – sorting out someone who is not fitting into the organization. As Reeves (2006) comments: "Coaching is not a remedial tool to help failing executives or to solve serious behavioral problems" (p. 48). If an organization persists in allocating coaching largely to those employees it sees as "a problem," it taints its own internal coaching culture with a remedial stamp: "Coaching is for problematic people." However, we will continue by assuming that the request to coach Peter is a one-off scenario. He is seen as having some problems, and Lisa has been hired to help him.

Lisa has met with Peter's direct boss, Daniel, to negotiate the coaching agenda. But quite rightly, she has also insisted on a three-party meeting to ensure that there is buy-in from all parties, reducing the dangers of what Bluckert (2006) calls misunderstandings and failed expectations in coaching. However, there is no indication in the case that these agreements were committed to any kind of formal, written document. McMahon (2010), for example, recommends that discussions should be conveyed onto a simple "terms and conditions" information sheet covering details such as the coach's cancelation policy and pricing and professional issues like confidentiality, supervision, membership of professional bodies with relevant codes of ethics and practice, and any other information the coach believes is essential for the client to know. Given that the case generates at least one major ethical dilemma – whether Lisa should divulge Peter's secret determination to quit the organization – the question is: should the boundaries between what she learns and what she tells the sponsor, Daniel, have been made more explicit from the start? Gray, Garvey, and Lane (2016) argue that there will usually be two contracts, one with the sponsor or organization and another with the coachee; however, coaches and coachees need to keep the requirements of the sponsor in mind when agreeing to individual contracts.

If the overarching goal was simply to "stop being so negative in meetings," this raises the question as to the quality of the agreed-upon goals. Jarvis, Lane, and Fillery-Travis (2006) argue that identifying achievable but challenging goals in a coaching relationship is essential. Without clear goals, coaching relationships are likely to lack focus, which can damage both the coach-coachee relationship, and the achievable results (Jarvis et al., 2006). Locke and Latham (2002), building upon over 400 experimental and field studies, have shown the importance of goal setting. As long as an individual is committed to the goal, has the requisite ability to attain it, and does not have conflicting goals, Locke and Latham (2006) argue that there is a positive, linear relationship between goal difficulty and task performance. More recent research, however, particularly within the field of neuroscience, questions the significance of goal setting. A meta-analysis of the literature, for example, found that goal intentions (e.g., "I want to be a more participative and involvement-oriented leader") have been found to be a weak predictor of acquiring new habits, accounting for only 28% of the variance in successful behavior-change efforts (Gollwitzer & Sheeran, 2009). More recently, Nowack (2017) points to the important role of the social support climate in helping coaching clients manage their emotional reactions and consequences in engaging in behavior change efforts. Within this case it is also highly questionable whether the coaching agenda to "stop being so negative" in meetings constitutes a specific, challenging goal.

This case of conflicting coaching goals reminds me of a personal experience I had some years ago, when I was involved in a coaching program for a large, global oil company. Ten coaches, including me, were recruited to help a group of 50 senior managers through a period of transition and cultural change. After a couple of meetings with one of my coachees I noticed that he talked about the organizational changes in only neutral or cautious tones. Eventually, he developed sufficient trust in me to speak his mind. He said that he disliked the oil industry intensely (despite having worked in it for many years) and was strongly committed to ecology and environmental sustainability. Indeed, he wanted to help launch a scheme in his local town for promoting the use of bicycles. The coaching conversation now turned to how I could help him quit the organization and get connected to the job of his dreams – promoting bicycle use in his hometown. I was in an ethical dilemma.

As a coaching team we had contracted with the client to help the organization through transition, but my coachee was having none of it and wanted to leave. During a coaching conference call shortly after, we discussed how our assignments were progressing, and I raised my dilemma. To my surprise (maybe I shouldn't have been surprised at all), many of my fellow coaches were experiencing exactly the same problem. In the slipstream of organizational turbulence, many managers were experiencing stress and wanted a way out. So, in terms of our contract, what was to be done? Interestingly, the leader of our team discussed the issue in broad terms with the program's sponsor, the head of human resources (HR) (describing the quitting theme while keeping all coachees' names confidential). The head of HR expressed no surprise – indeed, he admitted he was actually aware of the problem even before the program started. He reassured the coaching team, asking them to continue with the coaching, expressing confidence that the department would get through the transitional period.

Returning to our case, it seems to me that when Lisa noticed friction at the three-party meeting she held with Peter and his boss, Daniel, this should have been a warning sign. Rather than agreeing to an agenda to "fix" Peter, she could have offered a more collaborative approach, offering to coach both Peter and Daniel together (and perhaps separately), identifying the sources of the tension and helping both work towards a better relationship. Following Nowack (2017), the coach could take a more systemic stance, seeking to identify the social support mechanisms that could help both clients manage their emotional reactions and relationship. The problem, after all, may not be with Peter but with Daniel – or with neither of them, but embedded in the goals and values of the organization itself. This case is interesting because it raises the importance of hidden agendas. But these may not always come from the coachee. Sponsors and line managers have hidden agendas as well!

Case 1.2. The poisonous gift

John was hired by the HR manager of a large New York-based asset management company to coach Paul, their COO. The HR manager was very clear about the issue to be worked on in the coaching sessions: in the eyes of the Chief Executive Officer (CEO), Paul had been doing quite well in his position before facing some recent deterioration in performance.

John, being a strong believer in getting the coachee and key stakeholders involved in the coaching process, requested to see Paul's manager – who happened to be the CEO – in order to make sure that everyone was in agreement about the issues and objectives, as well as how they were to be measured.

In John's brief meeting with the very busy CEO, she concurred with the performance objectives set by the HR department and signed off on everything. Despite the difficulty of the task, John managed to keep the CEO involved in the early stages of the coaching; however, about halfway through, something changed, and the CEO began to withdraw from the process.

Reflexive questions

- When HR commissions the coaching intervention, how important is it to involve the coachee's direct manager? And why?
- How do you deal with a manager who is "too busy" to engage in the process?
- What do you make of the CEO's withdrawal from the coaching process? How would you explain it?

As is his habit, at the end of the coaching intervention, John wrote up a report for the organization. He mentioned the CEO's withdrawal and shared his concern that there might be a mismatch in expectations. Sure enough, a couple of weeks later, John found out that Paul had been let go.

That's when John realized that the CEO had used the coaching intervention to serve her own agenda. In effect, she used it as hard evidence that she'd tried to make the COO more productive, but despite her best efforts, things weren't getting better. This gave her the evidence she needed to convince the board to fire Paul. Deep down, considering the disengagement of the CEO during the coaching process, John had anticipated this outcome; however, he hadn't thought it would come right on the heels of the coaching exercise.

One of the key challenges in this particular intervention, according to John, was that the CEO and COO had a poor relationship, which kept them from seeing that they in fact had complementary skills. Looking back, John wished he'd taken the opportunity to work with them both on this relational issue.

After Paul left, the CEO eliminated the COO position and divided the role among four individuals on the board, cutting costs significantly.

Reflexive questions

- Do you agree with John's analysis of the relational dimension of this situation?
- Had he dealt with this directly, do you think he could have convinced the CEO to change her mind about firing Paul?
- Have you ever dealt with a client who conceals his/her agenda? How did this affect the coaching experience?

Commentary 1.2.a

Eduardo Abarzua and Alejandra Pallamar

The case confronts us with a not uncommon experience in organizational coaching for both beginners and more experienced coaches. This is why several authors have called attention to the fact that organizational coaching interventions occur frequently in a complex social system, where attention must be paid to dynamics of different orders.

Addressing the "complexity" of organizational coaching requires an observation point that integrates different perspectives of analysis and strategies of approach. For this we recommend three perspectives: the systemic perspective, the relational perspective, and the strategic perspective, which we will develop next.

First, several authors have drawn attention to the need to highlight the "systemic perspective" in organizational coaching (Louis & Fatien-Diochon, 2014; GSAEC, 2014). This perspective emphasizes the "contextual," leading us to include the largest number of elements dynamically interconnected in the coaching system. Peltier (2009) has raised some principles of systemic thinking that apply especially to organizational coaching. One of them is to focus the analysis on the "process" over the "content"; that is, more important than what is "said" is "how" and what is "produced" in the interactions. Another principle is the relevance of focusing on the "present," the visible interaction patterns. Finally, the idea that systems and groups tend to maintain homeostasis is also relevant, so that coaching as a change challenge can be exposed to "resistance to change" from the subsystems involved.

In the case of John, we can see that the coach lacked a systemic vision. Although he believed in the importance of involving key actors, he did not give enough relevance to visible and present interaction patterns. Thus, beyond an understanding of the content of the "agreement," with the objectives of coaching expressed by the CEO, his behavior demonstrated minimal awareness to the process both at the beginning and at the time of the "withdrawal" of the CEO. At the beginning of the process, it was essential to know the CEO's view in depth. It is always difficult to involve "very busy bosses," but starting coaching without this information can have high costs at the end of the process, as is the case here. Apparently, the coach did not configure a realistic picture of the power games that could exist between the CEO and the COO, and the role that each of them played in the board, as the latter needed to "be convinced" of the decision of the CEO.

The withdrawal could also be an alert for the coach of some "resistance" or force contrary to the coaching process present in the CEO. We are therefore constantly challenged to "see the unspoken things," to analyze them and take response options. John did not respond to this communication from the CEO in a timely manner, withdrawing to the dyadic relationship with the coachee and avoiding a confrontation with the powerful message it contained.

The second perspective would be the "Relational." Contemporary research in the field of coaching has established that the quality of the coaching relationship is the aspect that best predicts its effectiveness (de Haan, 2008; Herrera, 2011; Lai & McDowall, 2016). This is how the "relational" coaching era is framed (Lai & McDowall, 2016) and why the need for broad training in relational coaching is emphasized. Organizational coaching confronts us with a systemic complexity for which the coach needs to display relational competences at the level of multiple or triangular relationships: client, coachee, human resources, manager, boss, etc. (Louis & Fatien-Diochon, 2014). In the case at hand, a relational hypothesis was posed by the coach – that of a bad relationship between the coachee and the CEO – and John believed that intervening more actively in this could have yielded positive results. There are indications that this may have been a potential hypothesis. Since the coachee had a weak relationship with the CEO (his direct boss), and there seems to have been insufficient feedback from the boss to the collaborator, the idea of having intervened more directly with the aim of improving the relationship seems an ideal alternative, but with insufficient analysis of the relational complexity.

The coach did not develop a relationship of trust and transparency with the key stakeholders (in this case, the CEO and Human Resources), a formal relationship was observed, where the need (or the problem) was not well detected. It is important to give the necessary time to the first part of the coaching process to clarify the request of the client organization, which may involve several initial meetings, until a sufficiently clear vision of the situation is gathered and the coach is sure that coaching is the best alternative to address it. During this process, the coach can reach the conclusion that coaching is not the most appropriate tool. In this sense, in the first stage of the process of listening to the client's request, the coach needed to have "consulting" relational skills to help put all the elements involved on the table and elucidate the relevance of coaching or other interventions (outplacement, for example). On the other hand, the relational deficit was observed at the time of the CEO's withdrawal, in which case the coach could have sought a bilateral relational space with the CEO and/or human resources to try to understand what was happening, with due attention to his relationship with the coachee.

In the third place, the "strategic perspective" in organizational coaching also seems important. Although the term "strategic" has multiple meanings, it is often used to refer to a set of actions aimed at achieving a goal; as a result, the future perspective is key. The objectives of the coaching process can be oriented to impact the performance of the person in the organization or the strategy of the organization. Ideally, according to Ledgerwood (2003), for the coaching intervention to be effective, it should be oriented to both, especially when working with the management line of the organization and the CEO. Then, it becomes even more necessary to consider the context of challenges and the future goals of the organization, as well as the challenges of these on the competencies required by the different roles.

In the last decade (especially with the beginning of the new millennium), there have been major changes in the strategic paradigm. Corporate crises have incorporated several emerging problems that should be considered in the so-called strategic planning methodology: global, social, and environmental responsibility; business ethics and organizational leadership; and establishment of links with the community and various external agents.

This new perspective implies that for the coaching to be strategic, it must promote and focus on the objectives of the organization, but must also consider the appropriate balance between these (objectives), the new relevant dimensions to be considered from a sustainability perspective, and ethics (Ledgerwood, 2003, p. 48). In this sense, pursuing the organizational results and the personal growth of the coachee are two objectives recognized today as relevant in this process (Rosha & Lace, 2016). Therefore, it is also important to protect the prestige and ethics of the coaching profession.

In the case of John, we can see that the coach did not have enough information about the strategic challenges faced by the organization. Gathering more information about what was happening in the organization's environment and current and future challenges might have given the coach information about what was happening with the role of the coachee. The coach needed to understand more deeply the reasons for the change in the performance of the coachee, who had been doing his job quite well, but showed a recent deterioration in performance. It is possible that the organization had new challenges that the coachee was not prepared for or that the organization faced demands for structural changes based on future objectives or current obstacles, and the role of the coachee was seen as dispensable in the new scenario.

Whatever the answer, it seems that the coach did not sufficiently recognize this strategic perspective. He did not know what the goals of the organization were, nor the CEO's challenges, nor did he sufficiently investigate what was expected of the coachee in the future. The coaching intervention only appears as a vague request for performance improvement, without the adequate strategic contextualization of this objective. Knowing where the organization is going is essential to understanding what is expected of the coachee and also how the organization values his presence in the future.

Being able to consider this dimension of the future, with respect to both parties and how they are articulated with one another, has important ethical implications for the coaching process. It allows the coach to have a complete vision guaranteeing good results for both parties, which at the same time gives prestige to coaching as a professional activity.

Commentary 1.2.b

Ana Pliopas

Commenting on a case is like playing the engineer of an already built construction. It is much easier to see a situation from a distance, without emotional involvement, to ponder on possibilities of different actions and criticize the construction. So, I want to make clear that my comments are meant to invite reflection and propose possible different actions for coaches, since we have embraced a craft where learning never, ever ends.

This comment starts with a working definition of executive coaching from which I highlight three aspects that guide my commentary on the case. After analyzing the case through these lenses, I suggest the lessons we as coaches can reap from this situation.

After reviewing different executive coaching definitions, I chose to employ the following one: executive coaching is an **organizational** development process (de Haan, Duckworth, Birch, & Jones, 2013) conducted by a professional coach (Bozer, Sarros, & Santora, 2014), which consists of individual interactions (Reissner, 2008; Reissner & du Toit, 2011), aiming at providing **meaning-making** (Reissner & du Toit, 2011), and, from this, a change in the executives' **attitude** (Bluckert, 2006) and/ or actions (Joo, 2005). From this definition, I emphasize three important aspects that orient the subsequent comments: the organizational feature – that is, executive coaching as one of the different organizational development practices; the meaning-making dimension of coaching; and the possible change in the executive's attitude or perception.

First, building on the organizational aspect of the working definition of executive coaching, we can say that executive coaching is an organizational development process (de Haan et al., 2013) with the involvement of the organization, and consequently the formation of a triangular relationship, between the coachee, the coach, and the individuals who represent the organization, occupying each of the triangle vertices. These three actors may have different agendas, which can be explicit or not, and conscious or not (Louis & Fatien-Diochon, 2014). Also present in executive coaching are issues of power (Fatien-Diochon & Nizet, 2015; Skinner, 2012). In this case, it looks like the CEO's agenda was to fire Paul, the executive coaching client, and the coaching process was a make-believe intervention, thus doomed for failure from the start. Of course, had John known about the CEO's intentions, he probably would not have accepted the assignment. John followed best coaching practices in terms of the process, but might have neglected relationships: he was attentive and included other stakeholders in the process to make sure that everyone was in agreement about the issues and objectives, as well as how they were to be measured. What John missed was the CEO's agenda and power dynamics within this firm. The CEO's hidden agenda was to let Paul go and in terms of power, it is worth highlighting that the CEO needed the coaching process to gain evidence of her best efforts to support Paul in overcoming the recent performance deterioration. So, using power as an analytical perspective to examine this case, besides the power inherited in the CEO's position, there is also the power of the board, which had to be convinced that firing Paul was the best alternative for the asset management company.

Moving to the second concept highlighted in the executive coaching definition: Perceiving coaching as meaning-making interactions between the coachee and the coach (Reissner & Toit, 2011) places the coach-coachee relationship at the center of the coaching process, but this important feature does not seem strong in this case. This view implies that the relationship between the coachee and the coach creates opportunities where both can share the connotations, significance, and implications of what is perceived as reality (Barner & Higgins, 2005; Du Toit, 2007). The relationship between coach and coachee is one of the key elements in executive coaching processes (Gyllensten & Palmer, 2007) and seems to be lacking in this case given the absence of Paul, the coachee in the narrative. He is talked about by the HR manager, and CEO, but his voice is not present in the case. I wonder what Paul would have to say about his situation: What sense did he make of the change from a quite good performer to a not so good one? What were his alternatives to address the situation? Was there a possibility that he might be willing to leave the asset management company? How were his relationships with other members of the board? We only know there was a problem in the relationship between Paul and the CEO, but not what sense Paul made of it or if and how he decided to tackle such an issue. These questions lead to the third concept highlighted from the definition, the change on the executive's perspective towards his situation.

The third aspect of the executive coaching definition employed, a possible change regarding the coachee's attitude, is related to the objective of the coaching engagement. Instead of focusing only on the betterment of Paul's performance, the coaching engagement could be perceived, as suggested by Bluckert (2006), as a means for the coachee to take control of his own life. In the case, perceiving Paul as someone with choices and responsibilities and as an effective actor in the organizational system might not have led to a different outcome, but perhaps a more active role in his professional path. For example, as soon as Paul and John noticed the CEO withdraw, they could have considered different perspectives: Paul could have reflected on his situation, his relationships with other stakeholders, and the possible interpretations of what was going on, as well as the actions available to him. What options did Paul see for himself in this organizational system? As suggested by Skinner (2012, p. 118), any coach would be naïve to believe that they could simply establish a contract at the beginning of a process and then be left alone without interference. So, as soon as the coachee and the coach noted a change in the system, it could have been the time to recontract, either with the too busy CEO or with the HR manager. It looks like John and Paul continued the coaching process oblivious to what was happening around them and then became victims of a CEO with bad intentions.

In short, the CEO had a hidden agenda that was not perceived by John, the coach, or Paul, the coachee. We do not know if there was any kind of collusion between the CEO and the HR manager. But regardless of the relationships that are always present in organizations, the coach followed procedural aspects of the coaching process, making sure to contract with the stakeholders to ensure everyone agreed on coaching objectives. What John and Paul missed was the meaning of what was happening in the organizational system around them; with the CEO removing herself from the coaching process, they continued with the agreed-upon course of action. They also missed the opportunity to take Paul's agency into account: The senses he made about the options he had about his performance deterioration and the CEO's distancing. So, what can be learned from this case that might promote more generative executive coaching processes, even when there are hidden agendas and power issues?

One strategy coaches may consider when dealing with similar executive coaching situations is to move away from a concept of organizations as fixed structures and processes. Replacing this view, we can follow Cunliffe's (2001) perspective and see organizations as complex and dynamic relational landscapes. This perspective may invite coaches, and all stakeholders involved in the process, to be aware of the ever-changing complex dynamics where executive coaching takes place. Having this perspective as a background may alert coaches to less obvious elements in coaching processes, such as the presence of the CEO's hidden agenda. With the concept of organizations being complex relational landscapes, the coach and the coachee may be more alert to changes in the organizational system and make more deliberate choices regarding the new scenario.

Another take away from the case is remembering the coachee's agency in the process: what she wants; what meaning she makes from the situation she perceives herself in; and the possibilities she envisions for herself. Such meanings are created in the relational process between coachee and coach and are the core of coaching.

In terms of the coaching process, a coach may remember that the concept of contracting and recontracting many times during a coaching intervention also applies to the coaching program: It may be wise to contract and recontract with the organization's representatives at different times during the process. It may also be worthwhile to challenge the organization's representatives on how much they value executives' development, along with how much time they are willing to allocate in support of coaching.

As coaches we see ourselves in unforeseen situations, as happened in this case. Although it may seem obvious, it may be useful to keep in mind that the setting of executive coaching is the organization, and organizations are complex, dynamic, and relational landscapes (Cunliffe, 2001). As stakeholders change their behavior regarding the coaching engagement, coach and coachee may take the new scenario into account and make sense of what is going on, exploring possibilities with the coachee's agency in mind, and the actions that are possible. Finally, we may remember that, just as it is useful to contract and recontract with the coachee regarding her objectives for the coaching session, it is also useful to contract and recontract with the organizations' representatives.

Conclusion

When stakeholders have different needs, strategic goals, and personal expectations (Cardon, 2008), the role of multiple and hidden agendas should not be understated, but rather acknowledged and embraced. Furthermore, the boundaries between the different agendas are not always clear. It is important to clarify and re-examine them, not only at the beginning of the intervention, but also during the coaching process (Segers, Vloeberghs, & Henderickx, 2011).

Our experts have emphasized different areas that require particular attention by the coach and that will enable the alignment of the expectations and needs of the three parties involved. We will focus on three of them: 1) the coaching process, 2) the systemic perspective, and 3) the relational aspect.

First, our experts draw attention to the need for a structured coaching process as a way to clarify and align the goals of coach, coachee, and organization, and to avoid the emergence of multiple or hidden agendas left unattended. However, given the relative immaturity of the field of coaching, and the multiplicity of the different processes in practice, the profession still lacks agreement on the delineation of a unique process that would work for all coaches, in all situations. This leaves coaches to devise and improve their own strategies, keeping in mind that the coaching process is not set in stone and that coaches need to develop their awareness and adaptability.

Second, when it comes to goal setting, our experts highlight the importance of acknowledging that the coachee and organization might have different, sometimes conflicting needs and agendas, and question whether it is possible to reconcile both. A potential approach to addressing this dilemma, as suggested by three of the commentaries above, seems to be the adoption of a systemic perspective, inviting the coach to examine the whole system and its dynamics, rather than looking at the different needs and goals of the various stakeholders separately.

Finally, the relational aspect seems an important factor in dealing with multiple agendas. While both the literature and the coaching regulating bodies have addressed the importance of the quality of the coach-coachee relationship in the success of the coaching, our experts stress that the quality of the relationship with the organization is of no less importance. Accordingly, coaches need to ensure they are establishing rapport and building alliances with the different stakeholders.

References

Amado, G. (2004). Le coaching ou le retour de Narcisse? *Connexions, 1*(81), 43–51.

Barner, R., & Higgins, J. (2005). A social constructionist approach to leadership coaching. *OD Practitioner, 37*(4), 37–41.

Bluckert, P. (2006). *Psychological dimensions of executive coaching.* Maidenhead: McGraw-Hill Education.

Bozer, G., Sarros, J. C., & Santora, J. C. (2014). Academic background and credibility in executive coaching effectiveness. *Personnel Review, 43*(6), 881–897.

Burke, W. (2018). *Organizational change* (5th ed.). London: Sage Publications.

Cardon, A. (2008). *The triangular contract: Finding your way through collective contract complexity.* Retrieved from www.metasysteme.eu

Cunliffe, A. L. (2001). Managers as practical authors: Reconstructing our understanding of management practice. *Journal of Management Studies, 38*(3), 351–371.

de Haan, E. (2008). *Relational coaching: Journeys towards mastering one-to-one learning.* Chichester: John Wiley & Sons.

de Haan, E., Duckworth, A., Birch, D., & Jones, C. (2013). Executive coaching outcome research: The contribution of common factors such as relationship, personality match, and self-efficacy. *Consulting Psychology Journal: Practice and Research, 65*(1), 40–57.

de Haan, E., & Nilsson, V. O. (2017). Evaluating coaching behavior in managers, consultants, and coaches: A model, questionnaire, and initial findings. *Consulting Psychology Journal: Practice and Research, 69*, 315–333.

Diamante, T. (2011). Leadership development programs that work: Individual transformation by design. In M. London (Ed.), *Handbook of lifelong learning: The oxford library of psychology.* New York, NY: Oxford University Press.

Diamante, T. (2013). *Effective interviewing and information-gathering techniques: Proven tactics to improve your questioning skills.* New York, NY: Business Expert Collections Press (Global Distribution BEP is partner with Harvard Business Publishing).

Diamante, T., & Primavera, L. (2004). The professional practice of executive coaching: Principles, guidelines & key decisions. *International Journal of Decision Ethics, Fall*, 361–374.

Diamante, T., Natale, S., & London, M. (2006). Organizational wellness. In S. Sheinfeld-Gorin, & J. Arnold (Eds.), *Health promotion practices in industry.* San Francisco, CA: Jossey-Bass.

Diedrich, R. C. (2001). Further considerations of executive coaching as an emerging competency. *Journal of Consulting Psychology: Research and Practice, 53*, 203–204.

Du Toit, A. (2007). Making sense through coaching. *Journal of Management Development, 26*(3), 282–291.

Fatien, P. (2012). Ethical Issues in Coaching. In M. Espesito, M. Smith & P. O'Sullivan, (Eds.), *Business Ethics – A Critical Approach: Integrating Ethics Across the Business World* (pp. 302–316). Routledge.

Fatien Diochon, P., & Lovelace, K. J. (2015). The coaching continuum: Power dynamics in the change process. *International Journal of Work Innovation, 1*(3), 305–322.

Fatien Diochon, P., & Nizet, J. (2015). Ethical codes and executive coaches: One size does not fit all. *The Journal of Applied Behavioral Science, 51*(2), 277–301.

Gollwitzer, P. M., & Sheeran, P. (2009). Self-regulation of consumer decision making and behavior: The role of implementation intentions. *Journal of Consumer Psychology, 19*, 593–607.

Goodstone, M. & Diamante, T. (1998). Organizational use of therapeutic change: Strengthening multi-source feedback systems through interdisciplinary coaching. *Consulting Psychology Journal, Summer, 50*(3), 152–163.

Graduate School alliance for executive coaching (GSAEC), (2014 version). Academic standards for graduate programs in executive and organizational coaching. Executive summary. Retrieved from http://gsaec.org/wp-content/uploads/2015/10/gsaec-academic-standards-2014_executive_summary_march_2014.pdf

Gray, D. E., Garvey, B., & Lane, D. (2016). *A critical introduction to coaching & mentoring.* London: Sage Publications.

Gyllensten, K., & Palmer, S. (2007). The coaching relationship: An interpretative phenomenological analysis. *International Coaching Psychology Review, 2*(2), 168–177.

Herrera, F. (2011). *Descriptive exploratory study on coaching practices from the point of view of the coachee, in the Metropolitan Region* (Thesis for the title of Psychologist), University of Chile.

Jarvis, J., Lane, D. A., & Fillery-Travis, A. (2006). *The case for coaching*. London: CIPD.

Joo, B. K. (Brian). (2005). Executive coaching: A conceptual framework from an integrative review of practice and research. *Human Resource Development Review, 4*(4), 462–488.

Kotter, J. (2012). *Leading change*. Boston, MA: Harvard Business Review Press.

Lai, Y., & McDowall, A. (2016). Enhancing evidence-based coaching practice by developing a coaching relationship competency framework. In L. Van Zyl, A. Odendaal, & M. Stander (Eds.), *Coaching psychology: Meta-theoretical perspectives and applications in multi-cultural contexts*. New York, NY: Springer.

Ledgerwood, G. (2003). From strategic planning to strategic coaching: Evolving conceptual frameworks to enable changing business cultures. *International Journal of Evidence Based Coaching and Mentoring, 1*(1), 46–56.

Leonard, S. H. (2017). A teachable approach to leadership. *Consulting Psychology Journal: Practice and Research, 69*, 243–266.

Locke, E. A., & Latham, G. P. (2002). Building a practically useful theory of goal setting and task motivation: A 35-year odyssey. *American Psychologist, 57*, 705–717.

Locke, E. A., & Latham, G. P. (2006). New directions in goal-setting theory. *Current Directions in Psychological Science, 15*(5), 265–268.

London, M. & Diamante, T. (2018). *Learning Interventions for Consultants: Building the Talent that Drives Business*. Wash., DC: American Psychological Association.

Louis, D., & Fatien-Diochon, P. (2014). Educating coaches to power dynamics: Managing multiple agendas within the triangular relationship. *Journal of Psychological Issues in Organizational Culture, 5*(2), 31–47.

McMahon, G. (2010). *Behavioural contracting*. Retrieved from www.cognitivebehavioural coachingworks.com/wp-content/uploads/2013/01/BehaviouralContracting2010.pdf

Natale, S., & Diamante, T. (2005). Five stages of executive coaching: Better process makes better practice. *Journal of Business Ethics, 59*, 361–374.

Nowack, K. (2017). Facilitating successful change behavior: Beyond goal setting to goal flourishing. *Consulting Psychology Journal: Practice and Research, 69*(3), 153–171.

Peltier, B. (2009). *The psychology of executive coaching: Theory and application*. New York: Psychology Press.

Reeves, W. B. (2006). The value proposition for executive coaching. *Financial Executive*, December.

Reissner, S. C. (2008). *Narratives of Organisational Change and Learning Making Sense of Testing Times*. Cheltenham: Edward Edgar Publishing.

Reissner, S. C., & Toit, A. Du. (2011). Power and the tale: Coaching as storyselling. *The Journal of Management Development, 30*(3), 247–259.

Rosha, A., & Lace, N. (2016). The scope of coaching in the context of organizational change. *Journal of Open Innovation: Technology, Market, and Complexity, 2*(1), 2.

Segers, J., Vloeberghs, D., & Henderickx, E. (2011). Structuring and understanding the coaching industry: The coaching cube. *Academy of Management Learning and Education, 10*(2), 204–221.

Skinner, D. (2012). Outside forces in the coaching room: How to work with multiparty contracts. In E. de Haan, & C. Sills (Eds.), *Coaching relationships: The relational coaching field book* (Kindle ed., pp. 111–124). Faringdon, UK: Libri Publishing.

Spence, G. B., Cavanagh, M. J., & Grant, A. M. (2006). Duty of care in an unregulated industry: Initial findings on the diversity and practices of Australian coaches. *International Coaching Psychology Review, 1*, 71–85.

St John-Brooks, K. (2010). Moral support. *Coaching at Work, 5*(1), 48–51.

Tobias, L. L. (1996). Coaching executives. *Consulting Psychology Journal: Practice and Research 48*(2), 87–95.

2 Power in coaching

Introduction

Power is like the elephant in the room in coaching: it is all pervasive but rarely acknowledged. Dominant discourses indeed assume that the learner, content, and learning processes are "neutral" (Shoukry, 2017, p. 178) with the coach portrayed as a "neutral technical expert" (p. 185). This technical focus on the micro-practice distracts attention from power dynamics that can inform coaching and turns the coach into a potential "active [political] agent" (p. 185). Indeed, isn't coaching about the power of a helping figure to support change, about "responsible" executives becoming even more powerful, and about an organization strengthening its impacts?

Critical perspectives on coaching have certainly begun to tackle the issue of power in coaching, mostly by portraying it as a new practice of discipline or domination in organizations. From this perspective, coaching would be a subtle technology of the self, obtaining behavioral change through ideological brainwashing (Nielsen & Nørreklit, 2009; Reissner & Du Toit, 2011). Some critical scholars point out that coaching does not only lead to control, but can, under certain conditions, also sustain empowerment (Fatien-Diochon & Nizet, 2015; Louis & Fatien-Diochon, 2018). Our two cases explore some of the typical power dynamics in coaching.

In *Politics in the boardroom*, while Michael has been brought in to coach the CEO, he witnesses significant power issues between board members who are each trying to use him to advance their own agenda. The second case, *The coach's hidden strategy*, features Alan, hired to coach an executive become "a better manager" and "achieve team goals." Challenging this individual focus of the intervention, he uses coaching to question the whole system.

Case 2.1. Politics in the boardroom

Michael was hired to coach the CEO of a training company. Right from day one, he realized that this was going to be a complex assignment. The Board of Directors was focused on growing the business and wanted to help the CEO lead this growth. While they all agreed that the CEO needed some coaching, they had different opinions on what needed to be achieved and how to achieve it. In the initial conversation, 12 members on the board were present, and Michael wanted to make sure they all felt comfortable with him and committed to the process, hence his initial strategic focus on identifying their individual priorities and trying to find common ground.

Some of the issues that arose from that initial meeting included the Marketing Director's sour relationship with the CEO, who she found to be quite "interfering." Michael picked up on some gender issues between the two of them. Similarly, the Operations Director wanted to lead without too much involvement from the CEO. The Chief Financial Officer (CFO), on the other hand, needed more cooperation and support from the CEO. From this initial meeting, Michael sensed a complex interplay of politics, and he realized that for the coaching assignment to be a success, he would need to deal with this.

Another challenge Michael faced was the CEO's absence from that initial meeting. In fact, he didn't even know the board wanted him to be coached, and Michael worried the CEO would feel threatened if he found out. In order to gain the CEO's trust, they agreed to introduce Michael as the coach of one of the board members. After this initial introduction, Michael then explained to the CEO his approach to coaching and to leadership development. Believing that the other board member was being coached, the CEO felt comfortable giving it a try. Certainly, he had some reservations because he was aware of the politics, but Michael was able to break that initial barrier by explaining his strengthened leadership approach.

Reflexive questions

- How do you deal with a complex assignment that involves "too many cooks in the kitchen" or many, varied agendas?
- Do any ethical issues come up for you when analyzing Michael's approach to making the CEO comfortable with the coaching assignment?

During the coaching process, Michael identified what he considered to be the main issue. The CEO had founded the company, and since then, the board had developed into an essential part of the business. Ultimately, the CEO felt threatened by the growing power of the board and was afraid of losing control over his company. However, Michael eased these feelings by showing the CEO that his agenda and that of the board actually matched – they all wanted to grow the business with the CEO at the helm. Michael then suggested a small coaching session with the whole group. This group coaching session gave him the freedom to ask more sensitive questions without breaking confidentiality. The board and CEO were receptive, which helped ease some of the tension. They were able to understand Michael's approach and the importance of consensus in the leadership group, avoiding sidebar conversations that could undermine the effort.

As the coaching progressed, Michael was able to get everyone's buy-in except that of one board member who turned out to be the biggest challenge of all. He had different ideas about the direction of the coaching, but Michael handled this problem by backing off. Instead of a direct approach, he requested the help of the other members in getting this person on board. Michael then told the resistant board member: "I understand your approach, and I know you aren't comfortable with what I'm doing, or you have other things you want, but I need you to support my efforts in the direction that everyone else has agreed upon." According to Michael, this helped him "calm the ego" but he "couldn't kick it out of the room."

Reflexive questions

- What do you think of Michael's approach to the resistant board member? Would you have handled the situation differently?
- What are some strategies you might use in a coaching assignment rife with politics and power issues?

Commentary 2.1.a

David Matthew Prior

Apart from the typical one-on-one coaching relationship between the coach and the leader, executive coaches need to develop skills to work within a larger system and navigate inherent power dynamics, as illustrated in this case study. Indeed, Michael has been presented with multiple perspectives from different team members (i.e., the board of 12) as to how the coaching intervention should be designed to change the leader's (CEO) behavior. In a systems approach to organizational and executive coaching, it becomes essential practice in the early stages of contracting to clarify the nature and scope of the work, define anticipated outcomes, and align mutual expectations and account-abilities among the parties defined within the coaching engagement. A starting point is for the coach to gather critical contextual informa-tion to best assess the needs of the organization in terms of its stra-tegic vision and mission. In this case, a typical one-on-one coaching engagement would be designed to coach the leader (as being sug-gested by other board members) within the context of the organiza-tion, which could serve as a necessary, yet insufficient solution to the problem being presented.

The team as a coaching client

Probably, it could be useful for Michael to reframe and amplify the cli-ent engagement from one-on-one executive coaching to team coaching with the board as client, especially in this case where power dynamics of personalities, leadership styles, and competing agendas are both evi-dent and hidden. The familiar adage that the whole is only as good as the sum of its parts suggests that no one leader can successfully meet organizational outcomes when working apart or in isolation from their team. Pressures arise when the coach is asked to objectively assess and identify the key leadership opportunities and challenges with a pre-dominant reliance on differing story versions (qualitative data) recounted by a handful of individuals – i.e., not the whole team. Here, there's a trap that the coach can fall into by seeing the board power dynamics as an interpersonal issue. In this case, the coach may have more success working with the entire group as the unit of analysis, operating within a broader organizational system.

A team diagnostic

One way for Michael to launch the engagement could be through an initial exploratory conversation with the leader to surface the key con-textual factors for coaching, identify the critical success factors for the engagement, and explore immediate next steps to realizing the business aims. A useful step would be for the board itself, as a unit, to assess its effectiveness, using a reliable, valid, and consistent diagnostic tool, the

Team Diagnostic Survey (TDS). According to Wageman, Hackman, and Lehman (2005, pp. 376–377),

> The theory on which the TDS is based specifies that the changes for team effectiveness are higher when the following five conditions are met: (a) the people responsible for the work are a real team rather than a team in name only, (b) the team has a compelling direction for its work, (c) the team's structure facilitates rather than impedes collective work, (d) the organizational context within which the team operates provides support for task activities, and (e) the team has available and hands-on coaching to help members take the fullest advantage of their performance circumstances.

Since the publishing of this article, a sixth condition has been integrated into the framework – "Right People" – meaning that the team has both the right skills to do the work effectively, including teamwork skills, and the diversity that brings a range of perspectives needed to perform creatively and successfully.

Selective coaching interventions

The Team Diagnostic Survey is one tool that allows the coach to empower the team to assess its collective needs by identifying key strengths and weaknesses that impact overall team effectiveness. Much like an annual check-up with one's primary care physician in which a patient's overall health is objectively assessed by vital statistics (weight, height, blood pressure, blood chemistry profiles, personal narrative, and how the patient presents in person), the team diagnostic paints the picture of the overall health of the team within a snapshot of time for reflection and digestion by the coach, team, and leader. The scope of engagement in this case could be for the coach to work with the board by partnering with the CEO, to support and co-design the best intervention that would improve the board's effectiveness and learning capability in delivering the results required by its client stakeholders. As presented in the above scenario, some board members are operating on separate agendas, with a few more vocal board members attempting to convince the coach of their opinion that the real issue is an individual one – that of the failed leadership of the CEO – instead of a more likely situation, the failed responsibility, accountability, and results of the team as a whole.

With a team coaching approach, the coach can help the board determine its place along a spectrum: at one end, the board operates primarily as a work group with more individually focused work products and processes; and at the other end, it functions as a real team reliant upon shared leadership roles, collective work products and processes, and both individual and mutual accountability (Hawkins, 2014). With a clear team diagnostic, the coach can continue to work in one-on-one coaching with the leader to help the board establish norms, design a team charter, balance stakeholder engagement between internal and external environments, identify potential conflicts of interest, and review policy, strategy, operation, and governance. Additionally, it may be beneficial for the coach to work with a sub-team of the board, e.g., its Executive Committee, which when healthy, is appropriately empowered and authorized to execute on behalf of the entire board in its absence or in between meetings.

Leveraging additional resources

After administering a team diagnostic, allowing the coach to identify suitable levels of client interventions (e.g., one-on-one coaching with the leader and/or coaching the team), in this situation, Michael could leverage additional resources to help him deal with the ideological complexity of politics and power dynamics.

Supervision

In any coaching assignment, operating as a lone-ranger coach can augment self-doubt, delay critical questioning, and limit the scope of engagement possibilities and creativity. It is important that Michael be well supported by knowledge, resources, and tools through education and coaching supervision. Carroll (2001, p. 79) talks about the concept of a "supervisory life" being in touch with what is real, beyond us and still within us, which brings out the best in us. He identifies six propositions on the spirituality of supervisory life to consider: becoming reflective; learning and learning how to learn; becoming process-oriented; establishing healthy relationships; learning connectedness; and becoming an interior person.

Organizational savvy

An additional knowledge base to build is in the domain of organizational politics. In this situation, Michael is presented with a multiplicity of seemingly competing individual agendas to sort through before he can determine the most effective and impactful coaching intervention, serving the needs of the client organization and its business. Organizational savvy is a useful competency for leadership coaches to master for themselves and to develop in their coachees as they work with boards and executive teams where power plays and competition among stakeholders is not uncommon. According to Brandon and Seldman (2004, p. 1),

> Organizational politics are informal, unofficial, and sometimes behind-the-scenes efforts to sell ideas, influence an organization, increase power, or achieve other targeted objectives. Neither good or bad, the two conditions that determine whether those politics become constructive or destructive depend on whether the targeted objectives are for the company's interest or only self-interest; and, whether the influence efforts used to achieve those objectives have integrity or not.

Hence, ethical coaches do their best to maintain an apolitical stance while upholding the value of integrity in professional practice.

Gender sensitivity

In an age of increasingly sensitive social, political, and interpersonal dynamics related to gender issues, it's important for coaches to expand and deepen their knowledge base and build the capacity to work with clients through demonstrated compassion, understanding, and respect. As stated in the case: "Michael picked up on some gender issues between the two of them," which is a broad statement that doesn't provide us with enough context related to what the coach observed, how he came to that conclusion, or what he intends to do with this "information." Is the coach's observation related to gender-neutral language, male and female non-verbal communication codes, biological sex differences, social influences on psychological gender identity, cultural influences, or likely a combination thereof? As defined by Ivy (2016, pp. 21–60), "Gender communication is communication *about* and *between* men and women, and that communication becomes gendered when sex or gender overtly begins to influence your choices." How does the coach work with gender issues as they relate to the board's power dynamics, which may intersect with the coach's own unconscious biases?

Summary statement

Within complex coaching engagements, involving power dynamics, it's critical for the coach to work slowly at the beginning to clarify key contextual factors through deliberate, exploratory conversations with leadership, as well as to craft a clear understanding of the nature of the coaching, consulting, or facilitation work to be done, and with whom (leader, executive team, board, or a combination). The coach can be safely and professionally supported by a trusted and experienced coaching supervisor-practitioner who will help the coach maintain consistency in his objective observer stance and appropriately mirror back to the client, while partnering with his coaching supervisor to determine, design, and measure the most effective interventions that leverage change, action, learning, and development for both client and practitioner.

Commentary 2.1.b

Deryk Stec

Analysis

In this case, a challenge for the coach appears to involve navigating the distinction between leadership and strategic leadership, also referred to as *leading in the organization* (leadership) versus *leading of the organization* (strategic leadership), where *leadership* is viewed as a general set of behaviors that support the growth and development of employees and the organizations, while *strategic leadership* is involved in the creation of meaning and purpose for the organization (Boal & Hooijberg, 2000). There are issues of leadership in this case, but it is unclear if the issues are related to *leading in* the organization, *leading of* the organization, or both. Given that growth requires the allocation of resources and the setting of a strategic direction, this process is inherently political, and it will no doubt bring new challenges to both aforementioned dimensions of leading. For the coach in this case, it raises some questions: Does the CEO have a deficit in their approach to leading within the organization? Does the CEO possess the capacity for leading the organization by charting a path for growth? Can the CEO address the challenges that emerge in reaching for the goals one would associate with growth, especially as they pertain to leading in the organization? If the CEO, the coach, and board members have similar answers, then there is a good chance of the coaching assignment being successful.

A key issue in the case appears to be how "the CEO felt threatened by the growing power of the board and was afraid of losing control over his company" while also navigating the challenges involved in leading individuals with different functional responsibilities. The relationships with the Marketing Director (sour due to the perception of interference and potential gender issues), the Operations Director (who wants less involvement), and the CFO (who requires more support and coordination), appear particularly challenging. Kotter (1985) has described how many managers are not prepared to be dependent upon their staff, and the fear of "losing control" suggests that the CEO is struggling to manage this dependency. Over time, the CEO has become less influential and more dependent on the board. If the company is to grow, the dependency of the CEO is likely to increase. It is not uncommon for entrepreneurial founders to struggle as structures to improve efficiency and facilitate growth remove power from the CEO.

Growing an organization involves leading it through a life cycle that captures the challenges of transformation associated with going from a simple entrepreneurial organization to a more complex organization (Jones, 2006). A popular model is Greiner's (1998), which includes the following five stages: Creativity (entrepreneurial and simple), Direction (functional structure and standards), Delegation (decentralized organizational structures), Coordination (increased efforts at central planning and budgeting), and Collaboration (balance centralization with responsiveness), each of which has specific challenges for leading. In this case, the organization is facing a crisis of leadership as it shifts from the Creativity stage, simple and entrepreneurial, to the Direction stage, where it will embark upon a strategy for growth reliant upon functional structures and standards. In this instance the potential is high as the organization provides services. In contrast to organizations that provide products, where the value of the purchase is tangible, and quality is relatively easy to compare within services, the value is intangible, customer interaction is high, and individuals play a significant and valuable role in determining quality (Daft, 2001). Few people are upset with airplanes, but many are frustrated by airlines. It is likely that the CEO, when the company started, developed very personal relationships with clients. As the organization grows, areas like marketing and operations will revolve less around the personality and desires of the CEO and will require a more consistent approach, while finance, which may have never been a focus when the company began, now requires formal policies. In this sense the frustrations expressed by the Marketing Director, Operations Director, and the CFO appear to be consistent with this scenario.

Approaching the coach

The way the coach was introduced was far from ideal. If the coach is not actually coaching a board member, there is a chance that trust between the coach and the CEO could be damaged. The chances of this happening are increased if targets are not met or if the direction of the company is not aligned with the founder's values or ideas about the company. That the board was unable to create a space for outlining and discussing potential problems as a group is troubling. It suggests some combination of a lack of confidence in the CEO, a political environment, and/or deficits in leadership that extend beyond the CEO.

The resistant board member

The approach to the resistant board member appears to be appropriate. The issue the board member raises seems to be a strategic one, as the coach indicates that there had been agreement regarding the direction. However, if the company and/or CEO do not meet the targets, then, given the political nature of the board, it is likely that more members could become resistant.

Dealing with these types of situations

When faced with these situations there are many steps to be taken. First, the coach should try to understand if this is a specific case of a more general tendency, i.e., founders flounder as the company grows, or whether this CEO has a specific issue that would impede leading regardless of the context. The following matrix (See Table 2.1 below) attempts to capture the tensions that exist between the *leading of* and the *leading in* organizations at different stages of growth and should help situate the potential issue.

If, in assessing the situation, the employees and members of the board feel that the CEO was capable of the leading of the organization during the entrepreneurial stage, but new issues have arisen as it transforms into a more stable organization, then this case (Quadrant 4) probably represents a typical situation. A distinct benefit of this type of situation is that communication around sensitive topics is likely easier, as the coach is dealing with a typical situation that others have faced, suggesting it is not the CEO to blame. In this way the CEO should not feel alone and is more likely to embrace a learning process, though how they choose to respond to the situation can still produce challenges. The difficulty of these challenges is likely related to how far outside of the CEO's comfort zone are the required actions.

Table 2.1 Challenges for leading a growing organization

	Stage 1	Stage 2
Leadership of	**Q1** Was the CEO capable of providing meaning and direction to the entrepreneurial organization? Yes – Organization has increased chance of success. No – Organization will struggle.	**Q2** Does the CEO remain capable of providing meaning and direction to an organization that is increasingly reliant upon management structures and standards? Yes – Organization has increased chance of success. No – Organization will experience more politics and power plays.
Leadership in	**Q3** Was the CEO capable of leading people in the day-to-day activities associated with organizing? Yes – Organization has increased chance of success, especially as it pertains to people. No – May not be an issue if meaning is still derived from the organization, but likely not sustainable should the organization mature or decline.	**Q4** As the organization approaches stage 2, which requires leading more people and delegating more activities, is the CEO capable of leading people in the day-to-day activities associated with organizing? Yes – Organization has increased chance of success, especially as it pertains to people. No – Will increasingly be an issue, especially with managers leading employees in functional areas.

If everyone is satisfied with the leading of the organization, but issues with the leading in the organization are becoming increasingly complicated with the addition of professionals responsible for functions, then the situation (Quadrant 3) will be more difficult. An issue related to the characteristics of the CEO will be more challenging, as it will inherently deal with their identity. For the coach, it is important to understand the limits of the services they can offer; in the case of deeply personal issues, it may become appropriate to seek help from other professionals.

If there is concern regarding the leading of the organization (Quadrant 2), then there is a greater chance of power and politics playing a role. Once again, depending on what the actual problem is, it may be appropriate to seek help from other professionals.

Second, regardless of the situation facing the CEO, given the power dynamics within the company it would be important to understand the patterns of relationships within the board and the company. This would include being sensitive to the informal networks that describe how people communicate and solve problems, as well as who they trust (Krackhardt & Hanson, 1993), while also determining dependencies (Kotter, 1985) and significant interdependencies (Pfeffer, 1992a). Both Kotter (1985) and Pfeffer (1992a, 1992b) have written extensively on power, and the following steps are derived from their work to help make sense of the landscape:

1   Decide upon goals. For the CEO to be successful, determining this will be important, but not necessarily easy.
2   Diagnose the patterns of relationships. Which individuals are highly influential? Which individuals are important in achieving the goals? How would they feel about the goals? Are there individuals who might resist?
3   What are the sources of power for these individuals? Does it involve their position, relationships, expertise, control of information, etc.?
4   What are the sources of power for the CEO? Does it involve their position, relationships, expertise, control of information, etc.?
5   Work on strengthening the positive relationships, and probably more important, enhancing relationships where there is potential for resistance by developing good communication, providing necessary education, ensuring adequate resources exist, and being prepared to negotiate.
6   If resistance continues, be prepared to be courageous, as it may be necessary to design and develop more subtle or forceful methods to deal with resistance.

Third, in dealing with the reluctant board member, the coach explains, "I know you aren't comfortable with what I'm doing, or you have other things you want." It would appear vital for the success of the coaching intervention that the coach and the CEO understand if this resistance is because of what the coach is doing or because the board member wants other things. If everyone wants the same thing, and goals are achieved, then the problem may decrease. If, on the other hand, the board member wants other things, failure to achieve the stated goals is likely to cause the resistance to reemerge with more support, and even with success it is possible that other forms of resistance or resentment may appear. Thus, while challenges of the organizational lifecycle traditionally raise issues around leadership, the lifecycle of the industry may mitigate (or perhaps more accurately delay the problem) or aggravate the issue. Generally, an industry lifecycle (Hill, 2001) involves the following stages: emergent, growth, maturity, shakeout, and decline. If this industry is in an emergent and/or growth stage it is possible that leadership issues or problems with resistance can be overcome, as all companies can be profitable during these stages. However, should the growth of the industry slow-down and the meeting of targets become increasingly difficult, resistance and frustration will likely increase.

Similar experiences

I once worked with a service organization that wished to take advantage of the opportunities in the market. However, as a service organization, billable hours secure revenue. Further, the time to develop relationships and long-term service contracts detracts from the number of hours available to provide services and involves investing resources upfront. As there were enough hours available, the partners could not agree on whether the investment would produce a satisfactory return, and in the end, the partners ended their relationship. One of them went on to start a company that focused on providing services to organizations on a long-term basis, while the others continued to acquire enough work using a more ad hoc approach appropriate and common for professionals in this industry. For me, what was surprising was the lack of awareness of the economics of the situation. My role had been to coach them through this process, so I was aware of the tension. But I had no idea that the partners had not truly calculated it, for when labor is the direct source of revenue, any hours spent doing business development has a cost. Thus, upon reflection, it was apparent that the partner who wanted to grow the business had hired me as an ally who would facilitate the process; however, in outlining the costs, it became apparent that they had not been fully considered. When this was discussed during a coaching session, the tension between the partners was palpable. They wanted to enjoy the benefits of an increased client base but did not wish to pay for it. In this sense, they were comfortable with the leading in the organization but were not confident or supportive of the leading of the organization.

In another instance, I worked with an organization that wanted to grow their business. The idea was to focus on a different segment of the market and seek out long-term supply agreements with the intent to transform the business from simply selling products to providing a service that added value to customers' operations. However, while the CEO, and founder, would continually promote this idea, they had immense difficultly living with it on a day-to-day basis, especially toward the end of the month when the focus became meeting the numbers. Thus, with time, the managers in the company put less emphasis on the articulated long-term strategy and paid more attention to short-term management practices. In retrospect, more emphasis should have been placed on individually coaching the CEO and owner on their behavior and creating support structures like a board or advisory group to encourage more dialogue on the issue. In this instance, executives were generally supportive in the leading of the organization by the CEO but were frustrated by the leading in the organization, as it was frequently inconsistent with the proposed strategy.

The significance of this issue is relevant to this situation as it will likely be possible to make the CEO understand these challenges. However, it could be quite difficult to help the CEO modify how they react to challenges and to develop trust in the processes and systems of the organization. The challenges of this type of situation are captured in the research of Kisfalvi and Pitcher (2003) on the strategic leader of an organization, specifically how their character and emotions interacted with carrying out a strategy. In their study they investigated the interactions between a CEO and the advisory team and determined that while planning was formally a rational process, and everyone agreed on how to approach the future, the character and emotions of the CEO impeded the implementation of the plan. This occurred even when the process was initiated and subsequently publicly supported by the CEO and the advisors who were hired as part of the top management team that would bring the company into the 21st century. Ultimately, the CEO was unable to modify their approach because of their identity, character, and personal history. It is unlikely that this case involves as serious an issue, but it does highlight the challenge of change even when the need for change is identified and a better way is articulated.

Case 2.2. The coach's hidden strategy

Alan adopts the same strategy in every coaching assignment he takes. He feels that it is very easy to designate one person in an organization as "the problem." This is what he calls the "scapegoating process" in organizations. "Whenever there is a problem, they don't solve it," he says. "They find a scapegoat, attribute the problem to this employee, and say, 'we have to burn you down, or we have to fix you,' but this doesn't solve the real issue." According to Alan, an issue is never a person. An issue is a process, and the process is between people. As Alan says, "Very often, if you take the person out, you still have the problem."

In one case in particular, Alan was hired to coach an executive to become "a better manager" and to "achieve team goals." Alan had a number of questions to address, first to the commissioning manager: "What criteria and measuring instruments is the company using to evaluate this employee?" And he found out that the criteria were vague nearly to the point of nonexistence, mainly based on what Alan called "gossip." Other questions to the commissioning manager included: "How can you help him succeed?" "What are the measures of success?" "How can you support him?"

Then, Alan asked questions of as many people as possible before meeting with the designated coachee. For example, talking to HR, he asked about the coachee's team: "How many members are there?" "What has the boss done with this person?" "Have HR, the boss, and the coachee sat down together?" "What do you think should be done around this person instead of targeting him directly?"

These questions were important to Alan because they helped capture the big picture view of the factors influencing the coachee's performance. Every time Alan met someone from the organization related to this process, he made sure to challenge the person on what she or he could do to support the coachee. In effect, his target was the whole organization, not just the designated coachee.

After his round of questions, Alan's analysis of the situation was that the commissioning manager, as a leader, wanted a good excuse for not achieving team goals, so he identified a person on his team and said that he was not helpful at all. Because the commissioning manager could not fire the employee, he recommended coaching to help him achieve the team's goals. Further, other employees agreed that the coachee was the problem, so everybody was into this theory. Alan saw it almost as a "conspiracy" to designate a scapegoat; however, to the employees and commissioning manager, it was the reality they believed in, and they had selected information that confirmed their thinking.

Reflexive questions

- How do you feel about Alan's analysis of the "scapegoating process" and his view of the coaching assignment as an opportunity to question the whole system?
- Do you think his systemic approach to coaching is effective? Under what circumstances might this approach be more successful/more likely to fail?
- What do you do in a situation where the coaching signals underlying issues larger than the coachee's individual performance?

Alan believed his role as a coach was to challenge this group thinking. Having a designated client like this represented an excellent opportunity for him to get the whole organization to start thinking about how to function differently. His aim was not to change the coachee, but to change all the interfaces around him in order to make everyone succeed.

For every ten hours spent in the organization, Alan actually spent only two with the coaching client. In fact, most of his time was spent working with the system surrounding the coachee. His strategy was to say: "I am going to help this person, but in order to do so, I need to see the whole picture and to ask questions for the good of this individual." By asking the other employees questions, he was indirectly coaching them as well. Because they thought that it was for the good of somebody else, they didn't feel threatened, and many of them changed their behavior, which made the team more efficient as a whole.

During the process, Alan did not reveal his strategy to anyone in the organization.

Reflexive questions

- Under what circumstances, if any, would you hide your coaching strategy from your client?
- Where do you stand on the issue of "transparency" in coaches' proceedings?
- Do you think Alan used his time effectively in this coaching assignment?
- How, as a coach, might you challenge the group thinking in this scenario?

Commentary 2.2.a

Ken Otter

In reading this case, I identify six issues I think are worthy of attention. They include:

1   A whole system approach
2   The coach-client partnership
3   Transparency in coaching

4   The process of meaning-making
5   Participating in the system
6   The coach as reflective practitioner.

Given the inherent short format of the case, and related limited information, I strive to qualify many of my comments in making my points to
consider. Below I discuss each issue in turn.

A whole systems approach

According to this case description, "Alan adopts the same strategy in
every coaching assignment he takes." This strategy involves seeing a
presenting problem, in this case a particular person's actions and behavior, as embedded in and reflective of larger systemic dynamics (Senge,
Hamilton, & Kania, 2015), which others in the organization do not recognize. In the case, Alan is quoted as saying, "Very often, if you take the
person out, you still have the problem."

In other words, attention needs to be paid to the larger relational and
organizational dynamics as well as to the individual (more on this below).
Alan refers to the process of mistakenly attributing the problem to the person and not the larger dynamics in the organizational system as "scapegoating." Such scapegoating, according to Alan, is symptomatic of these
dynamics and evidence of their blindness to such dynamics. Scapegoating can also be a form of work avoidance (Heifetz, Grashow, & Linksy,
2009). It is much harder to "fix" systems dynamics than it is to "fix the
person." And much of coaching is geared more toward working with individuals as the locus of change in organizations than to addressing the
various constellations of issues in the organization, which help produce
problematic behavior in individual people.

This strategy also involves Alan as the coach focusing his attention on
the larger relational and organizational dynamics. He did this by engaging others in looking at the "bigger picture," particularly the commissioning manager and people in HR, by asking questions about the criteria
and process for evaluating the "coachee," the support and resources
provided, the team conditions, and other factors that would enhance
or hinder his performance. In fact, according to the case, Alan spent
much more time coaching the whole system than coaching his client. He
used any opportunity he could to challenge the group thinking that the
individual manager was the problem, not "the system surrounding the
coachee." Alan characterized this whole system strategy this way: "I am

going to help this person, but in order to do so, I need to see the whole picture and to ask questions for the good of this individual." According to the case description he had some success with this strategy in so far as "many of [the team members] changed their behavior, which made the team more efficient as a whole."

Alan's primary tactic in his whole system strategy was to ask critical questions to challenge people's thinking and to foster a more systemic view. If I were in Alan's shoes, I would have worked to arrange some team coaching. In my experience, this becomes a powerful means to foster greater systemic intelligence in people. Team coaching provides the opportunity to use the real-time experience as "a case in point" of systems dynamics in play, including his individual client and the commissioning manager. It also affords members the opportunity to shift problematic behaviors that reinforce these dynamics, and to gain actionable insight going forward. However, given the questionable ethical consideration, which I address below, of Alan keeping his whole systems strategy hidden, this kind of actionable insight is not possible.

The coach-client partnership

A systems approach is certainly important, but what has been lost in this case is the attention to the individual client. While Alan appears to have the interest of the coachee in mind, I see no evidence of Alan involving the individual client's needs, perspective, or input into Alan's whole system strategy and approach. Has Alan hidden it from his client as well? If so, then this undermines a core ethical and change principle in establishing a coach-client partnership.

Even the idea that the organization is Alan's client, which is implied in the case as evidenced by the statement, "his target was the whole organization," his hidden strategy does not demonstrate this partnership principle. The lack of transparency poses other problems from an ethical and learning perspective.

Transparency in coaching

There are well-established ethical precepts around honesty, establishing and maintaining clear expectations and agreements among the coach, individual client, and sponsoring organization (Maltbia & Page, 2013). Alan was contracted to provide individual coaching, and instead he engaged in systemic change work, without disclosing this or revising the contract as new data surfaced about the nature of the presenting problem. Moreover, it is unclear how transparent he was about his 1 to 4 ratio of individual coaching to coaching the organization. It is never too late to clarify expectations and agreements and revise the coaching contract (Brennan & Wildflower, 2014), but to do so would require being more transparent, something Alan seems reluctant to do.

Besides threatening the credibility and reputation of coaching as a trustworthy profession by going "rogue," not disclosing his strategy, and keeping his approach hidden, Alan undermines the development of systemic thinking to which he purports to be contributing. As mentioned above, there is a lot of value in a systemic approach. To be sure, being discerning about how much to disclose and when – especially when there is not much initial openness and readiness in the people involved as this case implies – is an important part of any learning and change strategy.

However, Alan's approach, disrupting their patterns of thinking and behaving, and shifting into more systemic thinking, appears counterproductive. To shift from patterns of "scapegoating" towards attending to and investigating the larger relational or systems dynamics in play, which undermine and enhance performance, requires one to be able to perceive and understand the current reality and to understand how to behave differently. This cognitive awareness needs to accompany the behavioral change if it is going to be sustainable. But if the strategy remains hidden throughout the engagement, this actionable insight is not likely to emerge. In other words, for systemic interventions to be effective they need to become visible to people, and without this visibility they can only go so far in changing people's thinking and acting.

In my work in organizations, I find that incorporating an educational component to other systemic interventions, particularly when doing leadership coaching for individuals and teams, accelerates the learning and change process (Otter & Paxton, 2017). For example, a short immersive learning experience, such as a workshop or a period of reflection and commentary following a team coaching session, can help to identify actionable insights with which they can explore and experiment on an ongoing basis. In this case, besides the questionable ethical issues, by keeping his strategy hidden, Alan missed an important opportunity to foster sustainable learning and change.

The process of meaning-making

Alan was contracted to coach a person to become "a better manager" and to "achieve team goals." The question of how the manager came to this conclusion, what criteria was used, and how the "coachee" was evaluated and supported was a line of inquiry Alan explored. But how much do we know about how Alan came to his conclusions, what criteria did he use, and what methods did he use to evaluate the data he was getting? For example, in the case Alan concludes: "The commissioning manager, as a leader, wanted a good excuse for not achieving team goals, so he identified a person on his team and said that *he* was not helpful at all." I am uncomfortable with such a claim without knowing more about the data and Alan's meaning-making process. I would be more comfortable using this as a hypothesis to explore, rather than a conclusion.

But this does not appear to be how Alan operates. It appears that Alan enters his coaching engagements with a strong bias: "Alan adopts the same strategy in every coaching assignment he takes." This leaves me quite suspicious that he is not very attentive to diagnosing the situation anew, and to how he arrives at his conclusions, allowing his biases to influence how he makes sense of the situation. I cannot help but think that he may be mirroring the very tendencies of the people in the organization he is criticizing.

Participating in the system

When we coach inside of an organization, it is quite likely we become entangled in the dynamics of the system. On one hand, they can provide us with an empathic understanding of what organizational members experience, assuming we are able to "get on the balcony" (Heifetz et al., 2009, pp. 7–8), to get a perspective of the system in which we are engaged. Without this ability to gain a perspective of the experience of the organizational dynamics, which can ensnare a coach as well, what Heifetz Grashow and Linksy refer to as being "on the dance floor" (pp. 7–8), Alan runs the risk of participating in and even perpetuating the very system dynamics he strives to change.

While Alan concluded that the commissioning manager, the coachee's team members, and others in the organization had selected information that confirmed their own biases toward scapegoating the "coachee," demonstrating a lack of critical self-reflection, might Alan be doing the same thing? Given his preferred theory that organizations automatically adopt a systems approach and his assumption that scapegoating is going on, was he also susceptible to selecting information to confirm his own biases, identifying "a 'conspiracy' to designate a scapegoat" in the organization? It is hard to tell without knowing more about how Alan addressed the tendency to get entangled in the very system dynamics he sought to change.

Another type of system entanglement involves the use of coercive power. While this case does not explicitly frame the scapegoating and other system dynamics in play as coercive social power, the commissioning manager and others in the organization appear to be exercising their authority over the "coachee" in problematic ways, in so far as this manager is not part of the assessing and framing of the problem with his apparent performance issues. Similarly, by keeping his strategy hidden Alan is not including others in how to frame the problem and what approach to take in addressing it, thus mirroring similar misuse of the power available to him in this engagement.

As was the case for the organization, it is possible that in keeping his strategy hidden, he was also engaged in his own form of work avoidance (Heifetz et al., 2009). In other words, it is hard work to engage people and the organization in owning up to their current reality and to actively participating in cultivating a healthier, more ethical, and more productive future. To engage the organization in generating actionable insights and a commitment to change requires a commitment to the partnership in the contracting and re-contracting process, in negotiating the learning and change approach, and in engaging in honest and constructive communication, something which appears to be missing in this case.

The coach as reflective practitioner

All of the issues named above would be better addressed if Alan were involved in a committed practice of critical and creative self-reflection – individually, in a community of practice, and/or in a mentor or coaching relationship. Following Schon (1983), coaches enact their professional expertise in contexts rife with complexity, ambiguity, uncertainty, and dynamic change. Because practitioners acquire a good part of their expertise in more controlled situations, such as their education and training, the shift to practice in changing circumstances requires ongoing, in-the-midst-of-action inquiry and learning, which Schon refers to as professional knowing. On this point he writes, "many practitioners . . . find nothing in the world of practice to occasion reflection. They have become too skillful at techniques of selective inattention, junk categories, and situational control" (p. 69).

In this case, I saw no indication that Alan engaged in this kind of professional knowing. Given his whole systems approach, and his coaching expertise, it would not be a big leap for him to apply the same approach to himself. After all, unlike many other professions, coaching clients and reflecting on one's coaching practice are mirror images of themselves – what we seek to develop in others is predicated on what we practice with ourselves. For Alan if he were to engage in such an in-the-midst-of-action inquiry, to help surface assumptions, identify learning edges, and to recognize unbiased data gathering and meaning-making processes, it would not only contribute to his effectiveness as a coach but also contribute to being a more ethical one as well.

In closing

Throughout this commentary, I have tried to show the intimate coupling between ethics and effective practice. Establishing agreements in the contracting and re-contracting process and ongoing transparent communication, as well as avoiding coercive power, sharing power, and co-facilitating learning and change, not only help to produce actionable insights and the necessary commitment to and direction toward change, but they are also a means by which coaching upholds ethical principles and practice. Keeping his strategy hidden was only one issue out of many in this case. If Alan had made it more visible as an explicit part of his approach, many other issues I discuss here would have been addressed. In this way, engaging ethical principles and practices such as honesty, transparency, and partnership will make an effective systemic change more likely to take root in the organization.

Commentary 2.2.b

Hany Shoukry

This case highlights three distinct – though interlinked – dimensions that are important to reflect upon, namely Alan's coaching philosophy, approach, and strategy. Alan's coaching philosophy is built on a systemic view of organizations, one that encourages the interpretation of individual and relational issues as part of a wider organizational context. Alan's approach to coaching follows his philosophy: He implements a form of systemic or group coaching, where different members and stakeholders in the system are involved in reflecting on what is not working, and their collective contribution to creating a better environment. However, Alan perceives a blocker; he believes that the organization would not be receptive to his approach. Alan's response to the assumed organizational rejection is described as his coaching strategy. The strategy is to hide the coaching approach from the organization, and to coach the whole group under the guise of coaching a single individual.

I believe that Alan's philosophy can bring real value to the coaching process. I also believe that systemic approaches to coaching could be extremely effective in many situations. Meanwhile, I would argue that Alan's strategy of hiding his approach is highly problematic and incongruent with his philosophy and approach. I will discuss the three dimensions in the following paragraphs.

First, I examine the choice of systemic interpretation of organizational problems. Organizations are complex social systems that cannot be reduced to the sum of the individuals in the organization. Many researchers argue that cultural and institutional systems have a bigger impact on organizational outcomes than the choices and capabilities of individuals. For example, O'Connor and Cavanagh (2017) argue that while the individual is often used as the unit of analysis in most Western coaching approaches, systems theory suggests that the individual is only one possible level of analysis that may not necessarily deserve to be the privileged focus. They suggest, "A focus on the individual (or even the relationships between individuals) is unlikely to meet the need for developing high performing groups and teams" (p. 488).

Coaching in organizations takes place against the backdrop of organizational politics, cultural biases, structural inequalities, and a set of unique processes that describe how things get done inside the organization. In order to appreciate this complexity, Hopper (2013) suggests that we need to shift focus from the individual to the social systems, and to the roles and properties of these social systems, such as cultures and power structures. He notes: "Persons must be seen primarily, if not exclusively, in terms of their personifications of and valences to systemic processes, and great attention must be given to the interpretation of contextual societal social system with the social system of the organization itself" (p. 268). The environment, or the current systemic reality, is what gives rise to the probability of the coachee growing and performing in the organization (Kahn, 2011).

So, I share with Alan the appreciation of the importance of context and structure. Understanding systemic factors may be a key ingredient in the success of almost any coaching process. Meanwhile, I am questioning who should, ideally, construct this systemic understanding. In Alan's case, he seems to be the only one trying to critically understand the system, a privilege he doesn't seem to share with his coachees. Thus, Alan seems to be investigating and analyzing the organization in order to reach a view of reality that informs his approach, rather than facilitating a process whereby individuals in the organization can construct a systemic view of the reality they are living.

Next, I explore Alan's systemic coaching approach. In line with his coaching philosophy, Alan believes that dysfunctional organizations need to be the target for improvement, rather than individual coachees within the organization. O'Connor and Cavanagh (2017) argue that when considering the failure of particular team members to behave in a way that is functional for the team, it is tempting to resort to an individual-level explanation, which leads to scapegoating, but "from a systems perspective, individual performance is typically a function of team dynamics, rather than vice versa" (p. 491). Similarly, Whittington (2012) argues that when the symptoms are an expression of something in the system, as they very often are, then only a systemic approach will have an enduring effect. He notes: "Working only at the level of the individual means you may be able to remove the symptom, but the dynamic, if it belongs at the level of the system, will simply re-emerge and be expressed through someone or something else" (p. 8).

Systemic or group coaching approaches may well prove to be more effective than individual coaching in many cases. However, in my experience, systemic approaches are only effective when the system chooses to engage with them. Organizational systems can be changed, but very rarely would an external approach be able to produce sustainable change in the system unless it has been invited to do so. Whittington (2012) argues that you need to ask permission to work in a systemic way, and more importantly, you need to establish that the person being coached feels they have permission and agency to access and influence the system. Alan does not seem to ask for such permission from his coachee or the organization, as they are unaware that they are part of a systemic coaching approach. Consequently, I am questioning the sustainability of the coaching outcomes. As there is no shared understanding of what the purpose of the coaching intervention is, the change in the behaviors of the individuals interviewed may help to mitigate the issue of the designated coachee, but is unlikely to change the scapegoating culture, or to challenge the inherent structural issues that are the root cause of the problem.

This leads us nicely to what is perhaps the most controversial dimension in this case, Alan's strategy. Alan decides to hide his systemic approach from everyone in the organization. He does so because he believes that scapegoating is embedded in the organizational culture, to the extent that no one would be receptive to the idea that the system needs to change. It needs to be said that there is some truth to Alan's belief. Organizations often suffer from a cultural lock-in, a "gradual stiffening of the invisible architecture of the corporation" (Foster & Kaplan, 2001, p. 16). Scapegoating plays an important role in group dynamics that "emerges in response to the group's need to avoid task-related anxiety and is intricately connected to issues of group survival" (McRae & Short, 2009, p. 88).

However, Alan's response to the perceived organizational stiffness is problematic, for two main reasons: First, Alan adopts the same strategy in every assignment. He seems to be making an assumption about whom to trust, and deciding only to trust himself, in the sense that no one else could come to understand the importance of examining the organizational system. I would argue that having any pre-meditated strategy in coaching may lead to a disconnect between the coach and the reality of the people and organization he/she is coaching. Second, by choosing to hide his approach, Alan gets some form of leverage or power over the system, while at the same time disempowering the people whom he is coaching. This is perhaps my biggest concern: There is a general theme that the coach is the real protagonist, the one analyzing the system, challenging it, and evaluating the success of his approach. There is a "Savior" feeling around Alan's strategy, secretly trying to change organizations without invitation, while the coachee has almost no part to play in that journey.

The purpose of a critical coaching philosophy and a systemic coaching approach is to help the agents of a system to uncover and change the structural issues that affect them. By reclaiming agency, they can co-create new structures that deliver better outcomes for the organization and the individuals. The question then becomes: Who is/are the agent(s)? If the agent is deemed to be the coachee, the commissioning manager, or any number of people inside the organization, it follows that it should be their prerogative and their task to challenge and improve the system of which they are the agents. Drake and Pritchard (2017) argue that if coaching is to play a systemic role in developing the whole organization, critical questions need to be answered, such as: Whose agenda is being served? How much of this agenda is explicitly acknowledged? And how compatible are the different agendas? In a typical organizational setup, where individual and organizational agendas may collide, supporting people's agency does not fit with manipulating them as part of a hidden strategy.

There is a lot to learn from reflecting on the three dimensions of this case (philosophy, approach, and strategy). To conclude, I summarize below the key lessons, from my point of view:

1   A coach would benefit from keeping an open mind with regards to which strategy or approach to use. This allows the coach to connect with the reality of the situation and to respond in the most adequate way.

2   It is valuable to incorporate a critical perspective into the coaching philosophy and approach, by questioning the impact and validity of taken-for-granted assumptions, goals, and systems in the organization. Critical perspectives and systemic approaches may be more effective in supporting organizational change, but it is important to understand how to propose them to the organization and get buy-in from the different stakeholders.

3   It is essential to identify the real agents in the coaching intervention, and to empower them at every stage: analyzing the system, defining what success would look like, deciding how change may take place, and taking action. Systemic and group coaches may benefit from understanding how some relatively older approaches, like participative inquiry (Heron & Reason, 2008), have dealt with issues of agency and empowerment.

4   Empowerment requires disclosure of goals, and in the case of conflicting agendas, a level of transparent dialogue that would support a shared understanding among all participants.

Conclusion

By tackling the issue of multiple agendas, Chapter 1 introduces some power-loaded situations, such as conflicting agendas and the poisonous gift, and Chapter 2 delves into the individualization of issues, and explores agency and sources of power in coaching. Overall, based on the commentaries presented by the experts and the literature review, we want to draw attention to the following questions:

What are the sources of a coach's power? And of power in coaching more generally? Building on French and Ravens' typology (1959), our experts invite us to consider both formal (coercive, reward, and legitimate), as well as informal (expert and referent) bases for power. Table 2.2

Table 2.2 Bases of power in coaching

Power bases	Examples in coaching
Coercive	Constraining contracts; restrictive contract perimeters
Reward	Money: Positive and appreciative feedback; client's change
Legitimate	Degrees; Positions
Expert	Skills; Experience
Referent	Similar interests; Personal aura

identifies multiple bases for power in coaching, which can stem from all the stakeholders involved. How do coaches leverage these sources, and with what (ethical) consequences? In particular, as suggested by our experts, coaches should ask themselves what they have to "gain" through the intervention, especially in terms of the benefits obtained through helping another person.

What power are we talking about? Building on the commentaries, we suggest distinguishing between power "over people" and "over one's acts" in coaching. Indeed, traditionally, power is approached in terms of power "over people," where individuals, be it the coach or the coachee, are forced by others into things they do not totally agree with; this would fall into the prevalent criticism of coaching as a new practice of domination. Power "over one's acts" however offers a more outcome-oriented approach, where the focus lies on how individuals can actually impact their lives and their environment, reclaiming agency, as discussed by our experts. This relates to the concept of "poweract" (*actepouvoir* in French) coined by French psychiatrist and psychoanalyst Gérard Mendel (Arnaud, 2007), describing the possibility to "act upon one's own acts in order to modify something" (p. 414). Through a focus on the activity, Mendel suggests locating power in the appropriation of one's acts. This focus on activity stands for Mendel as an essential condition to avoid work alienation, i.e., situations where individuals are prevented from participating in the full realization of a task, or the "regression" of organizational structural issues to psychological ones. Calling for non-psychologized interpretations in organizations, Arnaud's wish echoes the recommendations of our experts who emphasize the role of critical systemic approaches in coaching where an issue is used as a symptom to question the organization.

References

Arnaud, G. (2007). Poweract and organizational work: Gérard Mendel's socio-psychoanalysis. *Organization Studies, 28*, 409–428.

Boal, K. B., & Hooijberg, R. (2000). Strategic leadership research: Moving on. *The Leadership Quarterly, 11*(4), 515–549.

Brandon, R., & Seldman, M. (2004). *Survival of the savvy*. New York, NY: Free Press.

Brennan, D., & Wildflower, L. (2014). Ethics in coaching. In E. Cox, T. Bachkirova, & D. A. Clutterbuck (Eds.), *The complete handbook of coaching* (pp. 430–484). London: Sage Publications.

Carroll, M. (2001). The spirituality of supervision (Chapter 6). In M. Carroll, & M. Tholstrup (Eds.), *Integrative approaches to supervision*. London: Jessica Kingsley Publishers.

Daft, R. L. (2001). *Organization theory and design* (7th ed.). Cincinnati, OH: South-Western College Publishing.

Drake, D., & Pritchard, J. (2017). Coaching for organisation development. In T. Bachkirova, G. Spence, & D. Drake (Eds.), *The sage handbook of coaching* (pp. 159–175). London: Sage Publications.

Fatien Diochon, P., & Nizet, J. (2015). Ethical codes and executive coaching: One size does not fit all. *The Journal of Applied Behavioral Science, 51*(2), 277–301.

Foster, R. N., & Kaplan, S. (2001). *Creative destruction: Why companies that are built to last underperform the market and how to successfully transform them*. New York, NY: Currency.

French, J. R. P., & Raven, B. (1959). The bases of social power. In D. Cartwright (Ed.), *Studies in social power* (pp. 150–167). Ann Arbor, MI: University of Michigan, Institute for Social Research.

Greiner, L. E. (1998). Evolution and revolution as organizations grow. 1972. *Harvard Business Review, 76*(3), 55–68.

Hawkins, P. (2014). *Leadership team coaching: Developing collective transformational leadership* (2nd ed.). London: Kogan Page Limited.

Heifetz, R., Grashow, A., & Linksy, M. (2009). *The practice of adaptive leadership*. Boston, MA: Harvard Business Press.

Heron, J., & Reason, P. (2008). The practice of co-operative inquiry: Research 'with' rather than 'on' people. In P. Reason, & H. Bradbury (Eds.), *The sage handbook of action research: participative inquiry and practice* (pp. 179–188). London: Sage Publications.

Hill, C. W. L. (2001). *Strategic management: An integrated approach, Annual update* (5th ed.). Boston: Houghton Mifflin.

Hopper, E. (2013). Consulting in/to organizations/societies as traumatized living human social systems. *International Journal of Group Psychotherapy, 63*(2), 267–272.

Ivy, D. (2016). *Gender speak: Communicating in a gendered world*. Dubuque, IA: Kendall Hunt Publishing Company.

Jones, G. R. (2006). *Organizational theory, design, and change* (4th Canadian ed.). Toronto: Pearson Prentice Hall.

Kahn, M. S. (2011). Coaching on the axis: An integrative and systemic approach to business coaching. *International Coaching Psychology Review, 6*(2), 194–210.

Kisfalvi, V., & Pitcher, P. (2003). Doing what feels right: The influence of CEO character and emotions on top management team dynamics. *Journal of Management Inquiry, 12*(1), 42–66.

Kotter, J. P. (1985). *Power and influence*. New York, NY: Free Press.

Krackhardt, D., & Hanson, J. (1993). Informal networks: The company behind the chart. *Harvard Business Review, 74*(4), 104–111.

Louis, D., & Fatien-Diochon, P. (2018). The coaching space: A production of power relationships in organizational settings. *Organization* (Paper conditionally accepted).

Maltbia, T. E., & Page, L. J. (2013). *Academic standards for graduate programs in executive and organizational coaching: Graduate school alliance for executive coaching*. Retrieved from www. gsaec.org/curriculum.html

McRae, M. B., & Short, E. L. (2009). *Racial and cultural dynamics in group and organizational life: Crossing boundaries*. London: Sage Publications.

Nielsen, A. E., & Nørreklit, H. (2009). A discourse analysis of the disciplinary power of management coaching. *Society and Business Review, 4*(3), 202–214.

O'Connor, S., & Cavanagh, M. (2017). Group and team coaching. In T. Bachkirova, G. Spence, & D. Drake (Eds.), *The sage handbook of coaching* (pp. 486–504). London: Sage Publications.

Otter, K., & Paxton, D. (2017). A journey into collaborative leadership: Toward innovation and adaptability in turbulent times. In C. Etmanski, K. Bishop, & B. Page (Eds.), *Adult learning through collaborative leadership: New directions for adult & continuing education* (p. 156). San Francisco, CA: Jossey-Bass.

Pfeffer, J. (1992a). *Managing with power: Politics and influence in organizations.* Boston, MA: Harvard Business School Press.

Pfeffer, J. (1992b). Understanding power in organizations. *California Management Review, 34*(2), 29–50.

Reissner, S. C., & Du Toit, A. (2011). Power and the tale: Coaching as storyselling. *Journal of Management Development, 30*(3), 247–259.

Schon, D. A. (1983). *The reflective practitioner.* New York, NY: Basic Books.

Senge, P., Hamilton, H., & Kania, J. (2015). The dawn of system leadership. *Stanford Social Innovation Review, 13*, 27–33.

Shoukry, H. (2017). Coaching for social change. In T. Bachkirova, G. Spence, & D. D. Drake (Eds.), *The sage handbook of coaching* (pp. 176–194). London: Sage Publications.

Wageman, R., Richard Hackman, J., & Lehman, E. (2005). Team diagnostic survey: Development of an instrument. *The Journal of Applied Behavioral Science, 41*(4), 373–398.

Whittington, J. (2012). *Systemic coaching and constellations: An introduction to the principles, practices and applications.* London: Kogan Page.

3 Boundaries in coaching

Introduction

Executive coaching is a practice that involves different boundaries. From a spatial perspective, coaching takes place at the boundary of the organization, at its borders, neither totally inside, nor totally outside (Louis & Fatien Diochon, 2018). From a discipline point of view, executive coaching also stands at the boundary of several practices such as management consulting, psychotherapy, mentoring, and training (Kilburg, 1996). From a relational perspective, the coach is in a boundary position supposedly at an equal distance between the coachee and the organization, working towards achieving objectives that are in the best interest of both parties (Fatien Diochon & Louis, 2015).

What are boundaries? Do they define territories, including or excluding people? Inadvertently, boundaries get blurred, making it difficult for the coach to know where to stand or how to act, even to the point that the coach might be forced to cross boundaries in one direction or the other.

Chapter 3 examines the issue of boundaries specifically in relation to the coach's role as a supposedly neutral third party between the coachee and the organization. Indeed, as seen in other chapters, the "ideal" position of the coach is often portrayed as one of neutrality, as an intermediary position between the different stakeholders (Fatien Diochon & Louis, 2015). However, in various situations, this ideal neutral position gets challenged. On the one hand, the coach runs the risk of becoming a "puppet" when instrumentalized by the organization, feeling helpless or even disengaged. On the other hand, the coach can wear Zorro's cape, taking the side of one of the stakeholders and sacrificing herself to protect the interests of this stakeholder.

This chapter's cases look at situations where the coach leaves the supposedly ideal neutral position to take the side of one of the stakeholders (the coachee in the first case, and the organization in the second). In *The coach wears Zorro's cape* Lucy, a seasoned coach with over 15 years of experience in executive coaching and leadership development, is contracted by an oil and gas company to coach an executive who was fairly new to the organization and didn't really fit in with the culture. Part of her assignment was to achieve that cultural fit. However about halfway into the coaching, the executive was fired. This made Lucy feel like she and the coachee had been set up, so she became very protective of her coachee.

In *The organization as the primary client*, we look at Caroline who, after having a successful career in communication, has been a coach and a business image consultant for over ten years. Caroline is hired by an international train construction company in the US to coach Tom, a recently promoted director, to dress more appropriately for his new role. This coaching objective is not shared with Tom, and Caroline has to help him achieve this goal without clearly communicating it to him.

Case 3.1. The coach wears Zorro's cape

Lucy has been a coach for over 18 years, and one thing she has learned is to be very careful before she takes any assignment, making sure that all the stakeholders are aligned. This means that the organization hiring her has the same intention as the coachee. And most of the time "in her long career," as she said, she has not had any major problems or misalignments. However, she recently experienced a situation that had never happened to her before. She was hired to coach an executive who was fairly new to the organization and didn't really fit into the culture. Part of her assignment was to achieve that cultural fit. The designated coachee was the only woman among a team of men, and she was very nervous about her position at the company. And sure enough, about halfway into the coaching sessions, she was fired.

This left Lucy feeling like she'd been set up. She believed the organization hired her to "help" the executive, while in reality it was a way for them to ease the employee out. Lucy felt used because she trusted the integrity of the process. And then she started questioning herself. Had she not judged the situation properly? Looking back at it, she didn't think she had any reasons to suspect anything.

Reflexive questions

- If you were in Lucy's shoes, how would you have felt? In particular, would you have felt set up or used by the organization?
- What would you do if your coachee was fired mid-process?
- How do you handle misogyny or other signs of bias within a client organization?

Before the employee was fired, Lucy had a meeting with the boss and found him to be very impatient. He said that they were not seeing instant change and that the process was taking too long. This was a side of the boss she hadn't seen before. She explained to him very clearly that, in coaching, it takes time for an individual to learn and practice new behaviors. She also told the boss where they were in the coaching process without breaking confidentiality. Lucy further offered a full refund if he was dissatisfied with her coaching. It was important to her integrity as an executive coach to do good work and to satisfy the customer. However, he reassured her that this was not the case and that he trusted her.

About two weeks later, the coachee was scheduled to have her mid-year review, but instead of being reviewed, she was fired. Lucy then received an email from the boss saying that he would like her to continue working with the coachee during this transition. Lucy was very upset and felt protective of her coachee. Even after the contract ended, she continued working with her. Today, she is quite fond of her former coachee and intends to remain available to her indefinitely.

Reflexive questions

- Have you ever offered a full refund? Under what circumstances would you consider doing this?
- What do you think of Lucy's reaction to the news her coachee was fired? Is her protectiveness understandable? Would you continue to work with a coachee in a similar situation, even after the coaching assignment had ended?

Commentary 3.1.a

Clara Mandowsky Gun

When hired for an intervention in an organization, coaches are usually expected to develop the competencies or change the attitudes of their coachees. In Lucy's case, both motives seem present; however, despite the coaching request, the organization appears to have already made the decision to fire the coachee, but they need to justify it by hiring a coach as a last resort. Lucy might have been blind to this hidden agenda as coaches usually begin an assignment by trusting the "good" intentions of the organization. However, if, as a coach, you do not trust the client company, you should probably not work for them. Therefore, Lucy shouldn't feel guilty for not identifying the hidden agenda.

In this case, when the coachee is fired in the middle of the process, and the sponsor asks the coach to continue the intervention, I believe that the coach should do so. Indeed, from a coach's perspective, the priority is the coachee and the coaching process. If the coachee feels the process is working for her, the coach should follow through with the assignment.

As a coach, I have experienced being caught in the middle of the coachee and other stakeholders. A distinction in this case is that the stakeholders have decided to fire the coachee, and the coach does not agree with the decision. Lucy feels that the decision is not fair, arguing that the process is not over and that she needs more time. She tries to explain that the coachee is moving toward the goal while the sponsor is saying something else. As a result, Lucy feels she needs to cross a boundary, picking a side and defending the coachee, as well as the good work she has done thus far on this assignment. However, even if we as coaches do not agree with the stakeholders' decision, it is not our place to argue about it. In this scenario, it is very easy to move toward the coachee's side, to feel that she is being treated unfairly. As coaches, sometimes we are moved by our beliefs to cross a boundary and take the side of the coachee. This could create an ethical dilemma, where the coach may become involved in the relationship between the coachee and her sponsor. In my experience as a coach, when I'm feeling the need to cross a boundary, I continue my coaching sessions with heightened awareness of my feelings toward what is happening to the coachee and to me. Trying to protect the coachee is also crossing a boundary, which presents an ethical dilemma. The coach is getting involved in matters outside of her role.

One thing Lucy might not have detected is the misogyny within the organization. This prejudice, which is usually not shown openly, could be a reason to resign as a coach – especially when the coachee *and* coach are women. If this prejudice is present in an organization, no matter what the coach does, whether or not the coachee changes, the decision will likely be to fire her. If misogyny or any other bias is present in an organization, and the coach discovers it, she should point it out to the sponsor. However, when pointing out this matter, the coach has to show real proof of this conclusion. The ethical dilemma comes when the coach points out misogyny to the sponsors without having proof of it. I have not experienced this situation or anything similar, and none of my colleagues have talked to me about it; this is just my point of view on this matter, given my coaching experience.

On the question of refunding money, from my perspective, the coach should offer a full refund if the coachee or the sponsor is not satisfied with the outcome of the process. Both are very important. The coach must make clear from the beginning the scope and expectations of the coaching process. If this is clear, and either the coachee or sponsor is unsatisfied with the outcome, then the coach should refund the money.

Commentary 3.1.b

Konstantin Korotov

This case is an example of a coach's struggle with boundaries. This type of boundary-related issue often escapes the attention of academics and practitioners. In Lucy's situation we are talking about the borders of identity in a helping profession. Identity is the way we answer the question "Who am I?" And to answer this question we must consider how we see ourselves in exercising our professional activities. When we feel challenged, questioned, or devalued, the core of who we are professionally (and sometimes beyond) is often vulnerable to potential reassessment in the light of the external signals received. As the questioning is connected to the assessment of our worth, we might experience an identity threat – a feeling that our perceived identity is under attack. Further, when we observe the signals that could be connected to the quality of our work, and particularly to the perceived failure of our coaching (in this case, the dismissal of the coachee), we naturally look for explanations and develop a hypothesis regarding the problem that has caused the coach to fail to do the job properly.

Coaching, like many other helping professions, involves various challenges ranging from epistemological foundations of our knowledge to mundane economic questions of earning one's living as a supporter of others (for a review of challenges in the helping profession see, for example, Egan, 2010). As the profession still struggles with defining what coaching is and what it is not, the boundaries of what it takes to be a good coach continue to puzzle even those of us who have been doing coaching work for many years. The perceived quality of coaching interventions and the coach's role in achieving the desired outcome inform a coach's self-efficacy and internal view. A perceived failure in a coaching intervention may represent a significant identity threat. However, an important part of identity development for coaches is understanding the boundaries of their role, including contributions to the outcome of the coaching process. I haven't yet seen anyone argue against the premise that transformational outcomes are the result of the coachee's work supported by the processes that the coach puts in place.

Lucy, the coach in this case, faces a situation in which her coachee is struggling to make her way in what appears to be a difficult and non-inclusive environment. When the coachee gets fired in the middle of the coaching process, the coach has a feeling of having been set up to facilitate the coachee's exit process. The search for an explanation of the failure demonstrates that Lucy takes the dismissal of her coachee as something that she has contributed to by doing something wrong or failing to do the right things. The coach's suspicion of having been used for organizational political purposes should not be dismissed immediately (see, for example, a very good case by Reynolds, 2012, exploring this type of challenge).

Indeed, the organization might have used the coaching intervention as a social defense mechanism: avoiding taking serious action that might implicate the behavior of other executives and some of the potentially dysfunctional aspects of the corporate culture. Rather than asking themselves if the culture of the organization required analysis and possible change, the company's executives pass the issue onto an external coach with the ultimate goal of reassuring themselves that they have done the right thing and allowing them to maintain the status quo. Every now and then a coach might find themselves in a similar scenario.

What is puzzling, however, is Lucy's feeling of being set up in what seems to be an environment familiar to her. By taking an assignment with an explicit goal of supporting the executive in achieving a cultural fit with the organization, Lucy must have acknowledged her understanding of the company's culture. She might have even capitalized on her familiarity with the organization in securing her assignment. Assuming that she didn't have any ethical issues with the way things were done in the company, and that in fact the coaching was done well, the feeling of being set up in this case should, at minimum, be questioned. From the boundary perspective, the question of whether Lucy has set herself up might be worth considering. Could it be that Lucy's loyalty to the company or financial dependence on the assignment has impacted her ability to judge the feasibility of this assignment?

Lucy's willingness to satisfy the customer, which is reflected in her offer to refund the fees, on the one hand, and her need to be protective of the coachee, on the other, suggests she has a high internal feeling of professional responsibility towards the stakeholders of her work. It is here that the topic of boundaries kicks in again. How far should a coach go on behalf of the client (in this case, the organization) or the coachee? With Lucy's desire to satisfy the client and the coachee at all costs, the working hypothesis that comes to mind is that Lucy may be suffering from the "rescuer syndrome." Considering herself primarily responsible for the ultimate outcomes of the coaching engagement, she feels that she failed the expectations of her coachee, the organization, and herself. The hero has missed a shot or even fallen off the horse. For a discussion of the implications of the rescuer syndrome please see Korotov, Florent-Treacy, Kets de Vries, & Bernhardt (2012).

Lucy's conversation with the coachee's boss who complains about lack of instant results is a powerful moment when she could engage further with the organization on the topic of their culture and the support available to the coachee. While it is a scary moment for many coaches when the representative of the client shows irritation or impatience with the interim or final results, such a situation may be a good opportunity to exercise a real impact on the organizational system within which the coachee operates. Lucy could have asked the boss about what he had observed in terms of the coachee's efforts so far, what he and his colleagues have done to support the expected changes, and what obstacles might exist to hinder the coachee's fit into the culture. I would even go further and suggest that there be a meeting involving the coachee, the boss, and Lucy in order to evaluate progress and explore additional resources available to the coachee. Lucy's inability to do so and subsequent suspicion of having been set up suggest an opportunity to discuss possible collaboration between Lucy and the organization employing her as a coach.

An offer of a refund on Lucy's part is a good topic for a discussion with a coaching supervisor, or at least a good moment for self-reflection on the part of the coach. If Lucy is correct about her understanding of where the coachee and she are in the coaching process, she shouldn't feel pressed to justify the perceived lack of progress as seen by the boss. While at times it is possible to imagine offering the client an opportunity to pay based on the outcomes of a coaching session (for example, when the coachee is not familiar with coaching or is an independent coach), a refund offer might signify that Lucy is not doing her job properly process-wise, or that she wants to keep the client at all costs. And that can again be considered as lack of clarity on Lucy's part in terms of what constitutes her identity as a coach and as a helping professional.

Finally, getting close to and feeling protective of the coachee is another boundary issue. While I can imagine the coach and coachee developing a friendly relationship after the coaching intervention is completed, Lucy's intent to remain indefinitely available to her coachee might indicate her growing dependency on the relationship. In this case, Lucy may want to consider which aspects of her identity are getting activated, and to what extent the coaching side of her self-definition is playing out in the best interests of the coachee.

Case 3.2. The organization as the primary client

Caroline was hired to coach Tom, a director in an international train building organization in the US, with head offices in Europe. Tom was an engineer who worked his way up the company. He was strong technically and well respected across the organization. As an engineer, he was passionate about technical work and problem solving. The challenge for him was that, as he climbed the corporate ladder and became a director, he had to attend different types of meetings with a focus on management issues. And in these meetings, he had to exercise some influence in order to get the budget he needed for his team, to explain why projects were running late, or to win more business, etc.

Since he became a director, the feedback on Tom's performance from the Head Office was that he had no influence within meetings and didn't take part as much as he should. Even when he contributed, nobody took him seriously, because they didn't know him, and they weren't aware of his strong technical background. From their perspective, he came across as shy or simply not interested.

This went on for quite some time before Caroline was called in by the Head of Training in the US office who knew her from previous collaborations. The company had put Tom through several training courses but nothing had helped, so they turned to coaching, with a focus on changing Tom's attitude in meetings. They wanted him to speak with more confidence and to lead rather than to be reactive, so other people trusted that he knew what he was talking about. In addition, they wanted him to change the way he looked. They felt that he dressed "like an engineer," which didn't suit his new role. Of course, this was a sensitive issue, and they wanted someone from outside the organization to persuade him of the need to change. They worried that if they addressed this issue directly, he would reply by saying that he dressed the way "that was like him" and that he didn't want to change who he was.

The Head of Training had a brief discussion with Tom about the coaching, but didn't discuss the details. They wanted Caroline "to do the dirty work."

Reflexive questions

- What do you think of the organization not wanting to face the coachee and asking the coach to do it for them instead?
- If you were Caroline, would you accept this request?
- How do you deal with a sensitive or personal issue such as a coachee's way of dressing?

Caroline accepted the request because she appreciated the trust being given to her, and she wanted to make sure the company got the results they were seeking.

In the first session with Tom, she asked him why he thought he was there, and he had no clue. He said that it was probably part of his development. He was a bit reluctant at first; he didn't see any need to change because the company knew who he was before offering him the directorship. In the next few sessions, Caroline tried to get him to see how others might perceive him, without mentioning the changes the organization had requested. She worked with him on differentiating between who he was as a person and how he behaved in the workplace. Rather than seeing it as changing himself, he should view it as "playing the game." She helped him reach this place on his own, so he showed less resistance and became quite open to change.

Reflexive questions

- What do you think of Caroline's approach?
- Who do you think is the main client in coaching? The paying client or the coachee?
- How do you feel about hiding the actual coaching agenda from the coachee?

Commentary 3.2.a

Theo L. M. Groot

The case described is very common and recognizable: a good illustration of a situation where the coach is brought in by the organization to fix a problem. Tom is a seasoned and respected engineer who gradually climbed the corporate ladder, but the new role of director is quite different from his former role as lead engineer. The Head Office is disappointed by the way Tom carries out his new responsibilities: not assertive, not convincing in meetings, and last but not least, not "dressed appropriately." Their solution was to put him through several trainings but these didn't yield the expected results. Head of Training is therefore asked to bring in someone to do the dirty work and "fix the problem." Caroline is known by the Head of Training from previous collaborations and accepts the assignment, probably because she doesn't want to disappoint the Head of Training and likely because she doesn't want to jeopardize future work. This is a situation every coach struggles with at times.

All ingredients are in place for a soap opera or perhaps a personal drama with Caroline in the role of producer and stage manager. In the opening scene, Caroline and Tom meet for their first coaching session. Coaching is commonly seen as an exercise whereby the coachee with the support of a coach works on perceived challenges in either the private or professional sphere through self-understanding and self-changing (de Haan, 2008). The opening scene therefore surprises when Tom declares that he has actually no clue why they are meeting, perhaps something to do with his development? As the drama unfolds we see how Tom gradually with the help of the producer learns to "play the game." We are left in suspense regarding the final outcome, but indications are that Caroline fixed the problem with Tom, a down-to-earth engineer now playing the game of director to the satisfaction of the Head Office and the Head of Training, a happy ending all together.

We could be tempted to say "all's well that ends well" but a quite different, not so positive ending could equally have occurred. The case offers some interesting learning points that are relevant in complex situations in coaching. I will first raise awareness for the inner place the coach operates from and the proposed approaches to work and then discuss the different blind spots a coach has to be aware of in triangular contracts.

The inner space

What strikes in our case is that the intended coachee, Tom, is completely left out of all of the contracting; he is the "object" of the intervention. If coaching means that the coachee is in the driver's seat and determines the agenda, then strictly speaking there is no coaching relationship between Caroline and Tom. Second, Caroline signs a contract with a client who not only pays the bill but also determines the expected coaching outcome and sets the agenda. This is a rather bizarre situation bordering on unethical behavior, and it raises the question of the inner place from where Caroline operates. Who is the real client: Tom or the sponsor, in this case the Head of Training?

Otto Scharmer (2009), in his book *Theory U*, speaks of that inner place we operate from and the blind spots that exist in our interactions; his insights are readily applicable in a coaching context. We are often blind to the source dimension from which coaching comes into being. We know a great deal about what coaches do and how they do it, but we know little about the inner place, the source from which they operate.

O'Neill (2000) introduces the Rescue model and the Client Responsibility model. Edgar Schein called it the Doctor-Patient and Process Consultation model respectively (Schein, 1999). In other words, the coach could take the burden from the client's shoulders and bring about a solution for him using a variety of skills like facilitation and advising (Rescue and Doctor-Patient model). Or working from the other place of Client Responsibility or Process Consultation, the coach could use her position to get information on the table, change the conversation in the organization, and encourage the client(s), in this case both Tom and the Head of Training, to regain responsibility.

The inner space Caroline has clearly opted to work from is the Rescue model and although this may solve a specific problem, it leaves a high probability of similar problems in the client system reoccurring.

Furthermore, she uses coaching as her main approach while facilitation or mediation would have been more appropriate. When working from the space of Client Responsibility, the coach is secondary to the situation, not a primary player.

Blind spots

Triangular contracts are frequent phenomena when you engage in the coaching profession. In this particular case, the three parties are the Head of Training who represents the organization (sponsor) and signs off the contract with the coach, Tom as the person to be coached (coachee), and of course Caroline as the coach. The most plausible situation is one in which the sponsor and the coachee have all agreed that it would be good for the coachee to seek the support of a coach and that the organization will facilitate this coaching process (financially and in terms of time). There are, however, a number of possible blind spots that could jeopardize the coaching process, and the case at hand clearly illustrates where things can go wrong. Some questions and concepts to consider are:

- Who chooses the coach?
- Who sets the agenda?
- Transparency and hidden agendas
- Confidentiality and reporting to the sponsor.

Contracting

There seems to be an unspoken rule in organizations that whoever pays the piper calls the tune. A sponsor hires the coach, a contract is negotiated, and only then does the coach meet the coachee. We all know that however professional a coach may be, if the inter-relational chemistry between coach and coachee does not work, the coaching process will simply not yield the expected results. Contracting for that matter is not simply administrative; it is foremost psychological. Jones (2015) studied the matching of coaches and coachees and found that besides the initial criteria of knowledge, experience, and gender, less objective principles such as Trust (about boundaries and confidentiality), Touch (having a "click," feeling comfortable, and a whole person approach), and Relationship were considered much more important for a successful coaching engagement. De Haan and Duckworth (2012) therefore suggests "trial" sessions or "chemistry meetings," as they are often referred to in coaching circles.

Setting the agenda

In our case, Caroline got a clear assignment from the sponsor: fix the problem, get Tom to change his attitude, help him to speak with more confidence, and above all make him dress like a director. Caroline not only accepted this coaching agenda, she even decided to hide it from Tom. In my opinion, a line has been crossed here. I consider coaching an emerging process whereby the agenda is owned by the coachee and adjusted as the relationship unfolds. There simply is no coaching taking place when the agenda is not owned by the coachee. Often the sponsor and coachee have commonly decided that coaching would be a valuable support for the coachee, and they roughly agree on the outline of the coaching agenda. But frequently what was thought to be the initial topic to be worked on, shifts and changes once the coaching process gets underway. This process should be driven by the coachee himself.

I think there are two transparent ways of dealing with this, which Caroline should share with the sponsor. Although Tom is not the one who solicits coaching, Caroline could convey the concerns of the Head Office and check to see if he recognizes these issues. If he agrees that he indeed does not get sufficient budget, is unable to make his point in meetings, does not acquire more business, and does not know how to address these issues, Tom then could take ownership of the situation and agree to work with Caroline, exploring the issues during their coaching conversations. However, taking Tom as her real client and working from the place of Client Responsibility, the coaching could have different outcomes for the organization, not fixing the problem as they view it.

In the case, if Caroline opts to work from the place of the Rescue model, she could make it clear to the contracting client that she is not a "fixer" to whom they can outsource tricky problems and that coaching Tom is not the answer. Further, she could make it clear that she is in a position to help, but her role would be more of a facilitator and mediator. She could bring the different parties together and facilitate the conversation. Alternatively, she could decide that it would be better to have one-on-one conversations with all parties first, acting as an in-between.

Hidden agendas

A third blind spot is that of transparency or the lack thereof. In this case there are three binary relationships but each of them takes place in the absence of the other. Caroline as a coach is not aware of the conversations that have or have not taken place between Tom and the Head of Training; Tom in turn is not aware of what has been agreed upon between Caroline and the Head of Training; and finally the Head of Training remains uninformed about the coaching process between Caroline and Tom. It is important that Caroline is aware of what has been said or not said between the sponsor and the coachee; she needs to hear both versions. While discussing the contract, the sponsor will undoubtedly give his side of the story. Before signing a contract Caroline could insist on having a (paid) chemistry meeting with Tom; besides getting an idea of the relational probability, she would also get to know Tom's story about how the coaching sessions were proposed. If Tom feels comfortable with Caroline as a coach, she could then finalize the negotiations with the sponsor and share the contract with Tom.

Confidentiality

A final blind spot is the confidentiality issue in triangular contracts. Given the psychological contract between Tom and Caroline, the coachee needs to be absolutely sure that what is said in the coaching conversations remains between him and his coach. The coach will never report to the sponsor on content; for the purpose of invoicing the coachee could simply sign off an attendance sheet or something similar. It is important that the level of confidentiality is made absolutely clear in the contract. Sometimes sponsors insist on being kept informed about the progress. If this is the case, there are two options: either the coachee himself keeps his direct line manager informed and shares what he wants to share, or alternatively the coach writes short briefs as a reminder for Tom who can choose to share these with his line manager.

Conclusion

When being asked to enter a triangular contract the coach has to be clear from which place she wants to operate (Rescue or Client Responsibility model), propose the appropriate approach (Coaching, Facilitation, Mediation), and be aware of the different blind spots in the process.

Commentary 3.2.b

Scarlett Salman

Coaching prescribed in large organizations is often officially intended to develop or improve coachees' "soft skills" and their "emotional" and "social intelligence" (Goleman, 1995, 2006). Since the 1990s, large organizations have been expecting their managerial staff to acquire what is presented as new relational and communicational skills. This case study is about a European multinational in the industrial sector that is dissatisfied with the management approach of one of its directors, Tom, an engineer. The company sends him to management training courses and, as that doesn't work, calls in a coach, Caroline. This is a classic case of coaching prescribed for the purposes of acquiring managerial "interpersonal skills." The company seems to think that Tom is not doing his job properly because he does not sufficiently embody the role of a manager, right down to the way he dresses.

This case illustrates two major issues concerning both coaching itself and the organizations that use it. The first pertains to the externalization of the "problem" through coaching and the related issue of shifting onto the individual (the manager) the responsibility for the management's dissatisfaction. The second concerns the question of interpersonal skills and organizational expectations with regard to employees' – and particularly managers' – relational skills. What can the coach's role be in this configuration?

The term externalization denotes the fact of transferring to a third party, outside the firm – or in-house but outside of any hierarchical relationship – and considered to be an expert in the field. Here, the organization, that is, the Head Office and Head of Training, delegate to the coach the resolution of what they perceive to be managerial insufficiency, and entrust her with the task of making the coachee fit the role implicitly expected of him. The definition of the situation individualizes the interpretation: it is Tom who has to be changed. Externalization seems to be an appropriate solution from the organization's point of view for various reasons. First, it presents coaching as an appropriate solution because it is an expert one, suited to the problem of an individual, and because it's supposed to provide help to the coachee, which makes the organization seem caring and supportive of its managers in their career path. Second, because it is indirect, it precludes any rebellion by Tom, by avoiding an injunction that may seem too direct or top-down. One could say it euphemizes the power relations, and is thus believed to be more tolerable and effective in getting managers to change their attitude. While externalization is sometimes necessary, it can also reinforce the individualization of problems, and shift responsibility for them onto the individual, thus relieving the organization of responsibility.

In the present case, individualization of the problem that leads to the use of coaching – and that is symmetrically validated by that same use – consists in shifting onto Tom the responsibility of management's dissatisfaction with his way of managing. Yet, has the organization critically examined its own recruitment policy for managers? Why are engineers often chosen for these positions in large organizations (Guillaume & Pochic, 2007)? Why are managerial positions considered a promotion and given to engineers known to be technically strong, yet whose management skills and interest in the job are not considered – as in the case of Tom? In his case, he is criticized for dressing "like an engineer," when in fact he was promoted precisely because he is an engineer. There is, therefore, a first organizational contradiction that is not considered. Moreover, has the very concept of management itself been opened up to reflection? The underlying interpretation of the managerial role that is expected of Tom seems to be very much that of a chief who asserts himself and wields influence and authority (Cohen, 2013). The injunction, albeit euphemized by the externalization, sounds like a call to order to Tom: Keep to your ranks! Watch yourself! The company, which wants to appear to be fluid and to have a matrix organization, is then in contradiction with a classical hierarchical conception that is particularly insidious because it's not made explicit. Rather than critically examining the company's policy of "organizational making of managers" (Guillaume & Pochic, 2007) or the contradictions in its conception of management, the Head Office prefers to hide behind a diagnosis of insufficient professionalization of management, and to resort to coaching as a means to acquire these famous managerial skills. This is what I call the "palliative function" of coaching (Salman, 2008): to compensate for the organizational dysfunctioning (here: the choice of entrusting engineers with managerial responsibilities as a form of promotion; the contradictory injunctions between matrix organizations and hierarchical functioning), or to avoid opening the black box of the organization altogether. The problem (here: management considered to be unsatisfactory) is individualized, personalized, and externalized through coaching.

The second issue concerns that which is expected of Tom and constitutes the main mandate for companies resorting to coaching: interpersonal skills. According to Bellier (2004), this fuzzy concept e+ncompasses widely diverse aspects, ranging from personality (Tom is deemed to be too shy) to behavior (Tom is expected to assert himself in meetings), through cognitive aspects (spirit of synthesis, creativity, etc.) and even moral ones (loyalty, etc.) that are less present in Tom's case. He is criticized primarily for his way of interpreting his managerial role, down to the way he dresses. The case description draws attention to the question of respect for Tom's integrity, as a person, by indicating his possible reaction if the organization asked him directly to dress differently. This organization's expectation raises the question of the boundary between the personal and the professional, from a point of view that is both moral and political. Moral, in the name of respect for the person's privacy: the criticism is then Foucauldian, attacking an organization that seeks to control subjects, to shape them, and to limit their freedom, especially their freedom to dress as they wish. It may also be political, in line with the denunciation of "managerial over-humanization" (Linhart, 2015), the new form of alienation that exploits not only bodies but also subjectivity – a criticism that has been leveled at coaching. But apart from these moral and political considerations, what about the organization's expectations with regard to the managerial role itself? Are the company directors and human resource managers really trying to manipulate minds? What do they actually want? Changes in work – growing abstraction and tertiarization – require greater communication within organizations to be able to offset contradictory injunctions and the incessant updating that are now part of everyday life at work, especially for managerial staff. Relational skills are not just a managerial whim; they also correspond to transformations in work. Here we need to have more details on Tom's actual job and his department to know what types of problems have arisen, causing the Head Office to worry about his performance as a manager. The organization would need to keep its real productive needs clear of considerations of power, both hierarchical and statutory, that muddle the message, as for instance when it is mentioned that Tom was not taken seriously because he was shy.

The answer to these challenges, provided by coaching, is complex. In a sense, coaching corresponds to the accusation of "soft domination" (Courpasson, 2000), since it's taking charge of the company's non-explicit demand to make the manager change. And in this case the coach does that very well, since she herself uses a roundabout way to get Tom to change – which makes the injunction doubly invisible (first, by not making it explicit and second, by causing Tom to internalize it, through the way in which others might perceive him) and effective, since it facilitates Tom's change. From an ethical point of view, the coach – and this is probably how she would explain her position – is trying to preserve Tom's integrity, by dissociating him as a "person" from his behavior in the workplace. She has no difficulty performing this distinction because she is from the communication world, which takes image as a business object and therefore autonomizes it. Not only does this dissociation make coaching more effective, it also seems to be able to preserve the coach's integrity better. If we agree on the principle of coaching prescribed for the purposes of interpersonal skills, it is better to distinguish the "person" from the role played in the business. Yet this action seems questionable, for it constitutes soft domination that is made invisible and that clashes with a democratic conception of transparency. Moreover, to what point can this differentiation between the private and the professional person be justified, when coaching argues for a holistic conception of the individual? The coach – independent consultant? – is probably dependent on her client, the prescriber, due to the necessity to fulfill the prescriber/recruiter's demand in a portfolio market, and the importance of reputation in a "network-market" (Karpik, 2007). But ultimately, there is the risk for her (the coach in this case) of disappointing the prescriber, if the expectations are not explicit enough.

An alternative way of solving the problem, without individualizing it, would be to analyze the actual needs of the team that Tom manages, as well as those of people he has to deal with inside the company. What type of management would be appropriate in this configuration? Is the organization really expecting a hierarchical, statutory conception of a director's role? It would then be possible to envisage different ways of solving the problems encountered, by examining equally the recruitment and training practices, as well as the organization of work itself. It would be necessary to make the organization's expectations explicit in order to be able to talk about them. The coach could ask for this opening up to possibilities, if she were able to be more independent of the prescriber. But do coaches have the means to do so? And are they the only ones to decide? If the coach in this case does not feel independent enough to ask for a three-party interview where the organization's expectations are set out and discussed, perhaps she could at least join forces with other consultants to get the prescriber to pose the questions in terms that are not individualizing.

Conclusion

The cases and commentaries above have examined the issue of boundaries in coaching particularly when it comes to the coach's identity, the coach's role, and the coach's responsibility in achieving objectives.

First, let us start with the identity of the coach. Complex situations are pervasive to the point that they challenge the coach's perceived self-identity or the identity as projected to other stakeholders. Identities are not only questioned; they can even be "attacked," as noted by one of our experts. Through self-reflection, the coach will then re-assess her identity. In fact, this reminds us that the coach's professional identity is "locally displayed, negotiated and co-constructed" (Rettinger, 2011, p. 442) on a moment-by-moment basis, between the coach and the client (whether the coachee or the paying client). It is therefore important for the coach to reflect on those key moments and how they impact her identity.

As we have seen above, the coach might sometimes play the role of rescuer. As noted by Korotov et al. (2012), this could be linked to a dysfunctional compulsive helping behavior, but with greater awareness from the coach, it could be turned into a "constructive rescuer" role by creating reciprocity within the relationship, acting as a catalyst in the process of helping, and explaining to the client that they own the problem and the transformation. This is closely linked to the last point, which is the responsibility of the coach in achieving the coaching objective.

In fact, and as highlighted in the commentaries above, the coach needs to keep reminding herself that the responsibility is a shared one between coach, coachee, and organization. Each needs to accept this responsibility: the coachee taking ownership of the agenda and being fully engaged in the coaching process, and the organization accepting its share of responsibility in the problem – rather than individualizing it – and in the solution – rather than externalizing it onto the coach.

To conclude, as the profession is still developing, it is important for coaches to hone their awareness and understanding of the different boundaries in their profession, whether they be boundaries of their position, their role, or their contribution to the outcome of the coaching intervention. This will then allow for a discussion with the different stakeholders and the creation of sound conditions to achieve sustainable change.

References

Bellier, S. 2004. Le savoir-être dans L'entreprise. Utilité en gestion des ressources humaines (2nd edition). Paris: Vuibert.

Cohen, Y. (2013). *Le siècle des chefs: Une histoire transnationale du commandement et de l'autorité.* Paris: Amsterdam Ed.

Courpasson, D. (2000). *L'action contrainte: Organisations libérales et domination.* Paris: PUF.

de Haan, E. (2008). *Coaching: Journeys towards mastering one-to-one learning.* Padstow, UK: John Wiley & Sons.

de Haan, E., & Duckworth, A. (2012). The coaching relationship and other "common factors" in executive coaching outcome. In E. de Haan & C. Sills (Eds.), *Coaching Relationships: The relational coaching field book,* pp. 185–196. Oxfordshire: Libri.

Egan, G. (2010). *The skilled helper* (9th ed.). Belmont, CA: Brooks/Cole, Cengage Learning.

Fatien Diochon, P., & Louis, D. (2015). De Zorro à Polichinelle: Quand le coach est mis à l'épreuve dans son rôle de tiers. *Revue Interdisciplinaire Management, Homme(s) & Entreprise* 1(15), 85–103.

Goleman, D. (1995). *Emotional intelligence: Why it can matter more than IQ.* New York, NY: Bantam Books.

Goleman, D. (2006). *Social intelligence: The new science of human relationship.* New York, NY: Random House Large Print.

Guillaume, C., & Pochic, S. (2007). La fabrication organisationnelle des dirigeants: Un regard sur le plafond de verre. *Travail, genre et sociétés, 17*(1), 79–103.

Jones, C.W. (2015). *Choosing your coach: What matters and when: An interpretative phenomenological exploration of the voice of the coachee* (PhD thesis), Oxford Brookes University. Retrieved from https://radar.brookes.ac.uk/radar/file/5f4a52f7-efc5-4530-9134-ac62660bd0e7/1/jones2015choosing.pdf

Karpik, L. (2007). *L'économie des singularités.* Paris: Gallimard.

Kilburg, R. R. (1996). Executive coaching as an emerging competency in the practice of consultation. *Consulting Psychology Journal: Practice and Research, 48,* 59–60.

Korotov, K., Florent-Treacy, E., Kets de Vries, M. F. R., & Bernhardt A. (2012). The Rescuer Syndrome. In K. Korotov, E. Florent-Treacy, M. F. R. Kets de Vries, & A. Bernhardt (Eds.), *Tricky coaching: Difficult cases in leadership coaching* (pp. 25–40). London: Palgrave MacMillan.

Linhart, D. (2015). *La comédie humaine du travail: De la déshumanisation taylorienne à la sur-humanisation managériale.* Paris: Erès.

Louis, D., & Fatien Diochon, P. (2018). The coaching space: A production of power relationships in organizational settings. *Organization* (Paper conditionally accepted).

O'Neill, M. B. (2000). *Executive coaching with backbone and heart.* San Francisco, CA: Jossey-Bass Publishing.

Rettinger, S. (2011). Construction and display of competence and (professional) identity in coaching interactions. *Journal of Business Communication, 48*(4), 426–445.

Reynolds, M. (2012). Can you coach around a dead end? In K. Korotov, E. Florent-Treacy, M. Kets de Vries, & A. Bernhardt (Eds.), *Tricky coaching: Difficult cases in leadership coaching* (pp. 139–145). New York, NY: Palgrave MacMillan.

Salman, S. (2008). La fonction palliative du coaching en entreprise. *Sociologies pratiques, 17*(2), 43–54.

Scharmer, O. (2009). *Theory U: Leading from the future as it emerges.* San Francisco, CA: Berret-Koehler Publishers.

Schein, E. H. (1999). *Process consultation revisited: Building the helping relationship.* Reading, MA: Addison-Wesley Publishing.

4 Values in coaching

Introduction

Values represent basic convictions about what is desirable – the "right," the "good," the "wrong," and the "bad." Grouped into a system, they form frames of reference or worldviews that structure information and help make sense of the world (Mitchell, 1993). On a daily basis, value systems function as coping devices by providing answers to questions we have often stopped asking ourselves. But what happens when value systems are put to the test, for example, when the values of coaching stakeholders clash?

Typical "clashing" situations in helping professions often arise around political views, religious beliefs, or sexual orientation. For example, should a coach who is also a green activist accept an intervention in a nuclear plant? Should a pro-life coach continue working with a client who discloses that she intends to have an abortion? Should a liberal coach work for a communist mayor? What about the constitution of coaching groups according to religious beliefs (see the large number of Christian-based coaching associations in the United States) and sexual orientation (see Gay Coaching Alliances)?

Neutrality is a theme often discussed in coaching. How neutral and value-free should coaches be? Some coaches claim they can work with any client in any setting. Despite this claim, when the power of values is too rapidly dismissed, there is a risk of *value imposition*, i.e., the passive or active attempt to direct the client's values, attitudes, beliefs, and behaviors (Corey, Corey, Corey, & Callanan, 2015).

Working for the big bad wolf tackles the issue of values in coaching when choosing to work in a particular industry whose values collide with those of the coach's: being a strong environmental advocate, Martine must decide whether to work for a gold mining company. In *A big moral conflict*, Ellen, an internal coach, does not know how to respond to her employer who asks her to provide information regarding the skill gaps of one of her coachees in order to justify a layoff.

Case 4.1. Working for the big bad wolf

Martin was called by a gold mining company to do some team coaching in order to enhance the performance of some of their senior executives. But Martin was uneasy with this assignment because the company had faced many environmental scandals, their practices often causing damage to local ecosystems, rivers, and fish populations. This was against Martin's values. He found their practices to be unethical as he felt they were damaging the environment and doing nothing about it. Taking the assignment raised many questions for Martin such as: As a coach, did he want to work with a company like this? What criteria would he use to make his decision?

Reflexive questions

- Would a situation like this raise an ethical dilemma for you?
- As a coach, do you consider your clients' line of work and the way they do business before accepting a coaching contract?

On one hand, he didn't want to be associated with such a company. But on the other hand, he thought to himself, if he started judging companies in such a manner, he wouldn't be able to work with soda companies, junk food companies, pharmaceutical or chemical companies, petroleum companies, or even banks. Should he only work with people whose personal ethics and politics align with his own?

He also worried that by deciding not to work with certain clients based on some ethical judgment, he would be excluding the coachees themselves, taking away the possibility for them to evolve. Perhaps this was an opportunity for him to make a difference, even if it was minuscule. He had a reputation as a coach who challenged his clients, so he figured he had nothing to lose by accepting this assignment. Why should he avoid doing a job where it is most needed? He viewed it as an opportunity to challenge the senior executives and raise questions regarding river pollution and fish die-offs. With him as a coach, part of their development would be to get them to think about these issues.

Still unable to reach a decision, Martin sought the input of his supervisor. In the end, he decided to accept the assignment.

Reflexive questions

- What do you think of Martin's decision-making process?
- Would you seek external help if you faced a similar dilemma?
- How do you feel about Martin's intention to use the coaching assignment as an opportunity to address the environmental issues he cares about? Would this be considered as advancing his own agenda, and not that of the client?

Commentary 4.1.a

Kenneth Mølbjerg Jørgensen

Martin's situation raises an important ethical problem in coaching, one I chose to approach with the distinction that Hannah Arendt once made between ethics and politics in mind. She argued that the center of ethics is the self while the center of politics is the world. In this respect she confined the center of moral considerations to the dialogue the individual has with the self in solitude. Morality thus concerns the individual in his singularity, and the criterion of right and wrong depends on what the individual decides with respect to herself (Arendt, 2003, p. 97). These considerations are processed through what she refers to as a two-in-one dialogue with oneself, which constitutes thinking (Arendt, 2003).

This thinking space is important. Thinking refers to moments in which people are alone with themselves and therefore "free" and untouched by others. The ultimate standard of moral conduct here is the concern with the self, and the dictum is that it is better to be at odds with the whole world than to be at odds with oneself. It is, in other words, better to suffer consequences than to go against one's values. Thinking and remembering is the human way of striking roots, the processes through which people become persons instead of nobodies (Arendt, 2003, p. 100). We take an ethical stance and clarify our values through thinking. It follows that for Martin the argument would be it is better for him to lose the client than to accept the coaching contract – this would mean losing the money as a minor consequence, or losing one's job as a more serious consequence. This ethical solution can be seen as legitimate in the sense that the only person Martin can be sure he has to live with for the rest of his life is himself. The problem is, however, that with such an ethical stance, Martin decides to withdraw from the world. Hence, he loses the capability to act and transform. As noted above, these were part of Martin's considerations whether to accept the coaching contract or not. By accepting the contract he recognized the coachees' possibilities of evolving but also implicitly his position as an actor in the world.

This aspect is the key to understanding the distinction between ethics and politics mentioned above. It is also the reason why Arendt only granted moral reflections done in solitude a marginal role in relation to change and transformation. Change and transformation happen through action and in interaction with people. In Arendt's terms, a necessary move from ethics to politics has to be made because the self-purification process involved in thinking in solitude is not an effective guide for action. Action, which for Arendt is transformative, involves political choices whereby pure ethical principles and values will be violated. This does not mean that thinking in solitude is unimportant. It is important to clarify one's values. But if this clarification process leads to a withdrawal, thinking loses its meaning and purpose. It is through action that people can transform the world. Withdrawing from the world is only an ethical stance in extreme situations and is only legitimate whenever there is no reasonable space for taking action. The Holocaust, which provided much of the material for Arendt's ethical considerations (Arendt, 2006), was an obviously extreme situation. Non-participation was the result of an ethical stance not to kill or to partake in any system that kills. The ethical stance "it is better to be at odds with the world than oneself" was perfectly applicable because many citizens were not in a position to do anything about it. This dictum has also been designated as the moral responsibility to resist socialization (Arendt, 2006, p. 292). The moral dictum that follows from such extreme situations is one of non-participation because participation – even in the ranks of the functionaries – is an act of support (Arendt, 2003, p. 48). Transferred to Martin's case, he should accordingly not accept the coaching contract with the company because coaching them would be an act of support. However, as mentioned above, this response is only viable in extreme situations in which people have no possibility of doing something about it. If Martin, on the other hand, believes that he can influence company values through the coaching contract, the case is different.

Martin, in other words, believes that there is some space of freedom to act and transform the executives. Freedom is the key here, the reason why we can even speak of ethics, as Foucault (1997) has argued. This approach can to some extent clarify the ethical dilemma Martin finds himself in. Non-participation is only viable if he has no freedom to act and hence no freedom to shift the company to a more ethical stance towards the environment. If he, on the other hand, has some degree of freedom, it would actually violate another ethical demand, which can be derived from Arendt's writings, namely, to participate and try to change the direction of the company through action. This means that the move from ethics to politics is twisted into a singular demand to try to influence the senior executives to work towards new and more sustainable practices.

The degree to which this is possible is manifested in the coaching contract. What is actually meant by enhancing the performance of the company? Does the coaching only involve being more effective at what the company is already doing or does it involve more substantial personal, social, and professional considerations on the part of the senior executives? This touches on the issue of the kind of coaching that has been requested. Coaching is an umbrella discourse embedded with several different approaches. One is called leadership-based coaching in which the coaching space is governed and controlled by company strategies and values and in which coaching can be regarded as a technology of power – a particular disciplinary technology of the self (Foucault, 1988; Townley, 1995). Here the coaching space can be compared to a confessional space (Edwards, 2008). A demand for such coaching would be difficult for Martin to accept. He would then act as a representative of strategies and practices, which are non-ethical according to his own values. Even if he is the coach, he is also confined to a particular role within the coaching space, and this role would severely limit his freedom.

But other types of coaching exist that are more open to moral considerations and hence have a focus on the self-directed change and transformation that Martin wants. These forms of coaching include *narrative coaching* (Hede, 2010), where participants reflect on the power relations they are part of in order to perhaps change the narratives that accompany such power relations. Narrative coaching can involve the deconstruction of dominant narratives (Boje, 2008; Jørgensen & Boje, 2010) in order to problematize and question them. A third approach, protrepsis (Kirkeby, 2008), is inspired by a Socratic dialogic tradition and is directed explicitly towards the dialogue and reflection concerning deep moral values in the form of what is beautiful, just, true, right, and so forth. While leadership-based coaching and narrative coaching operate with an idea of self-awareness as the source of performance improvement through diagnostic analysis of the self, protrepsis is often used in executive coaching and works from an ideal of the individual's self-formation through an engaged and open dialogue concerning deep moral values.

The important point is that ethical considerations are ingrained parts of narrative coaching where individuals reflect on the power relations they engage in and enact. Ethical considerations are also embedded in the ideas concerning the dialogues of deep moral values. The narrative approach and protrepsis operate with a freedom to act through reflexivity and dialogue. Martin, however, cannot impose his values on the participants. He has to respect the coachees' freedom to reflect and evolve on their own. The three approaches to coaching are illustrated in the following table 4.1 drawn out from the work of Tobias Dam Hede (Hede, 2010, pp. 23–33). The table can be used for more systematic considerations concerning what kind of coaching contract one should accept, if one is in a difficult moral dilemma.

Table 4.1 Three approaches to coaching

Leadership-based coaching	Narrative coaching	Protrepsis
The coach represents leadership power. Coaching is a leadership and communication technique, where the leader/coach through coaching uses her/his power with a triple purpose. 1 To establish a reliable frame for using coaching to make a clear connection between visions, missions, goals, and employees' contributions. 2 To develop clear goals and action plans. 3 To create a continuous learning process through coaching where follow-up coaching helps the employees to reach agreed-upon goals and develop appropriate competencies. A governed and controlled coaching space in terms of the effects of coaching with a limited space of freedom.	Coaching as reflections on power relations. The purpose of coaching is not that organizations solve their problems and reach their targets. The purpose is to give people the possibility of reflecting on their own narratives and stories, without reaching any predetermined destination. Narratives and stories are at the center of this practice, countering and redistributing normalizing discourses. The coaching space must allow alternative language games that break with established discourses. An open coaching space in the sense that there is no given direction and no required result.	Protrepo: To turn people towards good actions by gaining knowledge of what is good. Protrepsis: To think and philosophize with a normative perspective. What is the good? What is the just? What are deeds? What are obligations? Individual emancipation on a personal level, which is subjected to an ethical perspective where the obligations towards community and society are maintained. An open coaching space centered around dialogues about the good, the right, and the just without preconceived destinations or expected results. The intention is the growth of the individual.

Commentary 4.1.b

Linda J. Page

We speak of values as "things," but they are abstractions related to our subjective choice of goals, purpose, and morals, in effect what we consider important, right, worthwhile, and meaningful. That is, values are not facts that are open to objective verification; rather, we choose them. We can infer values from behavior, but values are not the same as the actions we take. And the actions we take don't necessarily correspond to the values we claim to adhere to. We label behavior as "ethical" when it expresses preferred values. Ethical standards such as those required by various coaching organizations are attempts to regulate behavior in service of values characteristic of the profession of coaching.

The dilemma of being offered coaching work with an organization that does not share the coach's values is not uncommon. Martin's situation is an opportunity for all of us to examine our own values and to think about coaching values in general.

The title *Working for the big bad wolf* utilizes a metaphor from the Little Red Riding Hood fairy tale in which a wolf attempts to lure and eat the young heroine of the story by impersonating her grandmother. Both Little Riding Hood and the grandmother are saved by a woodcutter who kills the wolf with his axe. Let's apply this metaphor to Martin's situation. He was offered a coaching job "in order to enhance the performance" of a team of senior executives at a gold mining company, one which had faced "many environmental scandals." Comparing this corporation to a wolf pack that is both "big" and "bad" suggests that the purpose of hiring Martin to coach pack leaders is to help them and the whole wolf pack become "bigger" and "badder." That is, to accomplish the opposite of the environmental protection Martin claims to value.

Martin rationalizes his acceptance of the work with the hope that his confrontational style will stimulate his coachee's wolves to ameliorate their "bad" behavior. However, if the pack has been successful enough to get big, it is safe to assume that the leaders see their previous behavior as contributing to the pack's success and thus be unwilling to change it. The underlying values leading to this behavior may be couched in marketing terms such as "protein to howl for" and "more grandmother taste, no added woodcutters," and they may be hidden behind an idealistic mission statement such as "global leadership for canine health and well-being," but these are merely espoused values that differ from what is enacted in practice. Martin may hope to leverage the ideals of the pack's mission statement by challenging his coachees to find protein sources that do not deplete the supply of grandmothers. But success requires corporate packs, whatever their public pronouncements, to operate on the basis of exploiting every advantage to accumulate more profit in the short term – ANY advantage, even if it means irreversible consequences that threaten the ultimate survival of wolves themselves.

We can imagine that wolf-pack coach Martin will challenge the team members to come up with ways to ameliorate the pack's bad behavior – or at least the public's perception of it – while protecting or even increasing its profits. It might, for example, make a large (though tiny percentage of its profits) and well-publicized contribution to an environmental protection advocacy group. Or fund a think-tank that questions the science behind claims that the pack's behavior has a negative effect on the environment. Or pay an economist to write a book on how culling the overpopulation of grandmothers would lessen the burden of caring for the elderly. Or have the alpha wolf go on social media to take full responsibility and make a sincere apology for the latest scandal. Good coaching that challenges senior wolf pack members in this way would likely stimulate their creativity and make Martin feel that he had, indeed, made "a difference, even if it was minuscule." But would grandmothers be any safer?

Martin's dilemma pits his espoused value of advocating for environmental protection against the material reward and boost to his reputation of a coaching assignment with a multinational pack. Material reward wins. This comes as no surprise. Karl Marx observed that, ultimately, material interests prevail. After all, we are material creatures in a material world. As Martin points out, if he excluded potential coachees whose ethical or political views differ from his own, his only client would be the person in his mirror, and this does not result in putting meat on his table. As professionals, coaches are required to set aside our own chosen values, or agenda, in order to aid the enactment of the values of those who pay us – in this case to become a sheep in wolf's clothing.

We don't know the outcome of Martin's coaching engagement. Perhaps he will engage with a coachee who decides to be a whistleblower, playing the part of a woodcutter with his axe in order to reveal the inside truth about the pack. However, as many reformers have discovered, Martin is more likely to find that it is difficult to change a wolf's nature. Our profit-driven system has shown itself to be immune to "minuscule" efforts to influence its fundamental structure. This is true even for major global events such as the 2008 Recession. The likelihood that limited activities such as individual coaching engagements will result in the wholesale change of the prevailing economic system is not born out by recent history. Most likely, Martin's efforts would help the company espouse values more convincingly while in no way changing the underlying business model that guides its behavior. If Martin succeeds in eliciting ways for the corporation to appear more ethical while successfully continuing or increasing its damaging ways, he is betraying his own values; if the team does not enhance its performance, and profits fall, he is failing in his coaching assignment. This is a dilemma indeed.

Metaphors themselves are not true in any objectively verifiable sense. Gold company executives are not in fact wolves. Still, metaphors invite us to carry meaning from one often-imagined situation to another often-real one. This emphasis on meaning puts metaphors in the realm of values. The usefulness of metaphors is measured not by how "true" they are but by how well the imagined situation fits with the actual situation at hand. *The big bad wolf* metaphor is useful in helping us understand the difference between espoused and enacted values. However, it falls short of a perfect fit with Martin's dilemma in that corporate executives are not wolves even if their behavior appears predatory.

Rather, we are all, coaches and corporate executives and employees and customers around the world, one species with a thousand times more similarities than differences. We are each born into circumstances not of our choosing. Some of us who were born into privilege choose to think that this makes us more deserving than others. This creates a conflict between the belief that everyone, whatever their differences, is equally worthy and the belief that only "my kind" is worthy and the rest are dispensable. With its emphasis on respecting the client's perspective, listening to their story, encouraging them to explore their own meaning, acknowledging their strengths, believing in their capacity to change, and supporting their actions, coaching in general enacts the value of appreciating each and every person's uniqueness.

It is unfair to condemn Martin for what applies to coaching as well as to any other endeavor. We cannot act other than in the here and now. We cannot merely wish to create circumstances other than the ones we are facing at the time we decide to act. We can, however, avoid glossing over the difference between values that we espouse in the abstract and values that we enact every time we engage with a client. When these are in conflict, we can ask, "Which side am I on?"

Indigenous and ancient cultures tell stories similar to this: We each have a hungry wolf on one side that relies on violent predation to get what it wants. We also each have a loyal companion canine on the other side that relies on collaboration to meet its needs. These two struggle for dominance. Which one wins? The one we feed every day, with every interaction, every time we choose a side we value enough to actually stand on.

Case 4.2. A big moral conflict

Ellen was an internal trainer and talent management specialist, employed by an insurance company for over five years. As part of her responsibilities, she acted as an internal coach and worked with several junior people from a talent development program, preparing them to take on senior roles in the coming years. However, when the 2008 financial crisis hit, the organization began to lay off some of its employees. It was then that Ellen's manager, who also happened to be the HR Director, approached her with a request: he asked Ellen to write a report providing evidence of certain skill gaps or insufficiencies in one coachee in particular, in order to justify his layoff. This represented a major moral conflict for Ellen.

Ellen told her manager that she didn't believe the evidence was strong enough to let the person go. And she proposed a targeted and intensive development plan for the coachee for a specific period of time, to give him the opportunity to demonstrate that he was fit to work in the organization. Finally, she asked her manager to make his decision afterwards. Though he agreed, she worried that he had already made up his mind, and the report she would write would be used to fire her coachee.

Although Ellen understood that the main reason for the layoff was financial, and that the individual would likely be let go no matter what, she still didn't feel comfortable with the request.

Reflexive questions

- Would a situation similar to this present a moral conflict for you?
- What would you have done if you were in Ellen's position?
- How would such a situation make you feel?
- Do you think that the situation would have been different had Ellen been an external coach?

Ellen didn't feel comfortable with this request, but ultimately, she let her arm get twisted. She reasoned that by providing the report, she was not breaking any confidentiality, and she wasn't going to include anything that hadn't been previously discussed with the coachee. She also felt a sense of responsibility toward the organization, her employer, and believed it was their right to ask for the report, regardless of how they were going to use it. In addition to that, she didn't want to compromise her position at the organization, especially during a difficult financial crisis.

Despite her reasoning, Ellen still felt angry and powerless. She felt used. And she kept wondering whether there was anything she could have done to influence the situation.

Reflexive questions

- Do you agree with Ellen's decision to provide the report?
- Do you think there was anything else she could have done in this situation?

Commentary 4.2.a

Bob Garvey

Sadly, in my experience, this case is a common occurrence in larger organizations across all sectors. In my view, it raises many ethical questions.

Ellen's boss is the HR Director. With this role comes power, but also the responsibility to act in a way that demonstrates the values of the organization. Sadly, the HR Director fails at the first step. Lay-offs are an HR tactic to try to save costs. There may be alternatives to this, and little is said here about any consideration of the appropriateness of this tactic or any alternative. It seems to be an accepted corporate tactic, a norm. As long ago as 1998, Pfeffer, in his book *The human equation: Building profits by putting people first*, argued and demonstrated with case examples that there are many alternatives to this default response to financial concerns. However, let's be generous and assume the HR Director considered these. The fact that he asked Ellen to produce a report, using her close knowledge of a co-worker with the express purpose of providing evidence of "certain skill gaps or insufficiencies" is frankly outrageous and inhumane. Under EU law, the HR Director would be held accountable for this grossly unfair practice with the possible outcome of an unlimited fine charged to the company. The HR Director ought to know this. While I am not saying that legality is the same as morality, the law has the potential at least to address such injustices. Ellen is quite right to be concerned.

In suggesting that there was "insufficient evidence" and that an "intensive" development plan should be put in place, Ellen was attempting to behave responsibly. This can often be a softer approach and offer the possibility of a fair result. However, the use of the word "intensive" is worrisome as it suggests that the plan may be "setting the co-worker up to fail." By making it "intense" there could be the assumption that there are indeed some developmental or skills problems with the coachee that might be fixed with intensity! Further, it is quite possible that the HR Director took this form of words as a "green light" in support of the objective of getting rid of the co-worker. In this sense, Ellen could be seen as complying with an unreasonable request. On the other hand, Ellen, it could be argued, is the victim of the inappropriate use of power by the HR Director, and her position has been compromised.

Believing herself to have "a sense of responsibility toward the organization, her employer, and believed[ing] it was their right to ask for the report, regardless of how they were going to use it" is, in my view, an act of compliance gone too far. Arguably, the report is simply a vehicle to provide "evidence" of incompetence and could be viewed as a delaying tactic or a "nod" towards fairness. Her act, therefore, could be seen as moral cowardice. If I were Ellen, I'd be looking for another job because the context of this organization appears to be toxic. It is possible to behave ethically towards people despite financial pressures – honesty and integrity can and must still flourish. This organization chooses not to.

I lay responsibility mainly at the door of the HR Director. This act brings into question the whole basis upon which the coaching was introduced, and it is a case of coaching being used against people. Much coaching literature emphasizes the autonomous and emancipatory nature of coaching in an organizational context, and this case demonstrates the frailty of such laudable concepts. In this organization, it has simply become an instrument of surveillance (as many HR practices tend to be) and yet another example of management talking with a forked tongue.

Commentary 4.2.b

Paul Stokes

Ellen's situation in this case raises a number of issues about the ethics of coaching within organizations. These issues include tensions between professional boundaries as well as personal versus professional loyalty. I find it helpful to consider the "big moral conflict" through an ethical scheme, which can support a more in-depth analysis of the issues and possibly suggest alternative courses of action for the coach.

Carroll and Shaw (2013) put forward a framework through which we might examine the case and draw some tentative conclusions.

1   Ethical sensitivity – this refers to an awareness of the self, the harm of consequences, and the impact of behavior. Clearly, at this first level, Ellen has quite a strong awareness of potential harm to the coachee in terms of her own actions. What is less explicit is the consideration of her own actions and feelings. She is referred to as being "uncomfortable," but the precise source of this discomfort is not spelled out. What does not seem fully present is Ellen's own personal and financial self-interest.

2   Ethical discernment – this is concerned with the processes of reflection, emotional awareness, problem-solving, and ethical decision-making. It is interesting to note that Ellen's first instinct, in response to her manager's request is – rather than objecting to the request or voicing her ethical dilemma – to choose to engage with him by colluding with his managerial discourse (Western, 2012). As Western (2012, p. 179) argues, this managerial perspective "takes the focus away from the coachee's personal identity and focuses instead on the person-in-role." The HR Director invites Ellen to collude with him by seeming to take what Watson (2006) refers to as a systems-control framing of the organization, emphasizing the use of rational processes, rules, and systems as its form of governance. However, it is clear from the HR Director's request that the decision to fire the employee has already been made. The report that Ellen has been asked to write is not intended to explore the coachee's skill gaps or insufficiencies in order to inform a decision to lay him off. Rather, it is clear that there is another agenda informing the decision, given the context of the 2008 financial crisis. If Ellen, as is suggested, understands that the individual is to be let go, (a) why does she propose a "targeted and intensive development plan," asking her manager

to make the decision after its implementation, but more importantly, (b) why does the HR Director agree to it? My view is that both Ellen and the HR Director feel quite disempowered in this context. The HR Director appears to need the report to justify a decision that he is likely to make anyway for other reasons, and Ellen, for the reasons suggested above, feels similarly constrained. A problem throughout this case is that neither Ellen nor the HR Director appears to have a framework that they can use to address these ethical issues.

3 Ethical implementation – this refers to "what blocks me/what supports me," in effect how to implement decisions. It is my view that, in allowing her "arm to be twisted," Ellen is enacting what Argyris and Schon (1996) refer to as a defensive routine. Defensive routines are mechanisms/processes that we use in organizational life to protect us from embarrassment or threat. They work by seeking to divert responsibility to another agency, i.e., another person/group of people or something inanimate like an IT system or HR process. However, the critical aspect of enacting this sort of defensive routine is also that we do not acknowledge/deny that we are doing this. Instead, as Ellen does here, we seek to justify our actions by referring to rules/rationality about our responsibility to the organization. The problem with such routines, in the coaching world in particular, is that they militate against learning by remaining silent on mistakes/tensions that might embarrass or threaten us. In this case, it prevents Ellen from fully acknowledging her own processes in terms of how she arrives at the decision to write the report. While she does acknowledge her own sense of self-preservation, not wanting to jeopardize her position within the organization, this feels like it has been pushed to one side with the rational arguments for writing the report taking center stage.

4 Ethical conversation – this refers to how individuals go about defending their decisions, going public, connecting to principles. Ellen reports feelings of being used and of powerlessness. She seems to be struggling with herself in terms of justifying this decision. This is probably because she has no ownership of the issue and the decision to lay people off. In addition, her role as a trainer and talent management specialist suggests that she has some personal investment in these coachees and the development of their careers. Although this is not completely explicit, it seems likely that she was instrumental in developing the psychological contract between the coachee and the organization. In addition, the coaching space is

likely to have encouraged a sense of intimacy and disclosure on the part of the coachee. While Ellen rationalizes that she would include nothing in her report that had not been discussed with the coachee, would he have discussed such things with her had he known they would be used as part of an organizational downsizing initiative? I suspect not. In terms of her contracting with the coachee and with the HR Director, this sort of conversation does not seem to have occurred in sufficient depth to help Ellen.

5 Ethical peace – this refers to living with ethical decisions, use of support networks, and crises of limits, as well as learning from the process and letting go. It is clear from the case and from the preceding analysis that Ellen is definitely not at peace with the decision she has made. She is asking herself what she might have done differently and is uncomfortable with the process. However, it is not clear whether Ellen has access to coaching supervision as part of her work within the organization. Given that Ellen is a part-time internal coach within an insurance company and is doing this work as part of her HR role, it seems unlikely that she does have access to a supervisor. Discussing this issue with a supervisor may have helped her (a) make the decision to write the report and (b) live with the decision once made. I think it is particularly important that part-time internal coaches have access to some sort of support in order to avoid feeling isolated in the face of a difficult ethical decision. The other important thing to say, however, is now that she has made the decision, it is important that she is able to use her support networks to live with it. I do not agree with Ellen's decision to write the report in the way she did. However, it is nevertheless understandable. Being reflexive about her own processes and recognizing all motivations behind her decision are likely to lead to ethical growth and her development as a coach, discussed further below.

6 Ethical growth and development of character – is about utilizing learning to enrich moral self-knowledge, to extend ethical understanding and become more ethically attuned and competent. By being fully in contact with all the issues in the case, Ellen might now be able to reflect on these and recognize the source of the discomfort. This raises the possibility of doing something different in the future. For example, were a similar request to be made of her in the future, she might elect to share the ethical challenge with the client, in this case the HR manager. She could point to the importance of trust in the

coaching relationship and how, by writing the report, she might put that trust in jeopardy for all employees of the company she worked with as a coach. She could also share her dilemma with the HR Director in terms of wanting to do the appropriate thing for the good of the organization in the longer term.

Concluding remarks

As a coach, being asked to use knowledge gained in coaching relation-ships "for the good of the organization" is a common enough dilemma. It is not one that is unique to internal coaches – I have experienced this directly myself and supervised others in their coaching practice.

The challenge for internal coaches is that they often have a manage-rial/leadership role, which can pull them in a different direction from that of their coaching role. In Ellen's case, her talent management role was fairly consistent with her coaching role, until the HR Director asked her to write the report. Understandably, Ellen chose to make a decision to do what "the organization" was asking of her but sought to mitigate its impact by (a) seeking to intervene with the HR Director in terms of how he might use the report and (b) seeking to rationalize/justify her decision in terms of what she saw as her own ethical values.

Unfortunately, this created some dissonance between what she thought she should do and what she saw the impact of her chosen actions as being. Had she been in possession of a framework like that of Carroll and Shaw's (2013), I suspect she may well have approached the whole exercise differently and perhaps would not have experienced the dilemma at all. This might have involved better contracting with the various stakeholders, including the coachee, from the outset in terms of boundaries around confidentiality and role. Ellen may have also used support services such as independent coaching supervision to help her identify potential moral traps when engaging in such discussions. Supervision may have helped her develop a vocabulary to discuss this issue with the HR Director, even influence his actions. It would have also helped her to define a clearer path in terms of how she would deal with the outcome of such a conversation. This might have included, for example, asking another independent colleague to do a genuine review of the coachee's skills and attributes while Ellen maintained her coach-ing relationship with the individual in order to support him in achieving any organizational requirements that needed to be met. Even in the event that the coachee still needed to exit the organization, Ellen might have maintained her ethical integrity by helping to support the coachee in managing his exit from the organization positively and looking for new opportunities.

In my opinion, the most valuable lesson from this case is that of the importance of critical reflexivity – the ability to reflect fully on what is happening and, on the basis of that reflection, to identify a way forward that is consistent with the coach's values in the face of a challenging context.

Conclusion

If coaching were delivered through a computer-based program, would there be any value-related issues on the part of the computer-coach? It is probably because coaching as practiced today is fundamentally a human-based intervention that value-based challenges emerge. Therefore, in a way, we might be happy about the unsettling that occurs in these value-based challenges; "I doubt, therefore, I am [a good coach]" we could say.

Thus, while neutrality is often portrayed as important in coaching, the role of values in the practice is underestimated. In the first place, values might guide coaches who probably do not end up practicing it "by chance." Then, over the course of their activity, coaches seem far from "blind or dumb." During the intervention, they make value-laden choices (Fatien Diochon & Nizet, 2012): coaches do not hesitate to take a stance, practicing surveillance, serving profits only, neglecting the environment, or even serving military ends. This has been discussed thoroughly by our experts. We would like to emphasize two issues as well as two resources they pointed out.

First, through their commentaries, our experts emphasized that value conflicts emerge at and in-between different levels: the individual, team, organization, industry, or society level. Coaches' individual values can conflict with organizational values, coachees' values with their teams' values, and so on.

Second, while values are often portrayed positively as support mechanisms (what we refer to as "coping mechanisms" in the introduction), they can also act as barriers and filters that narrow views. Further, under the apparent veil of goodness, value systems can act as controlling devices, just as an externally imposed value system can.

Therefore, our experts recommend external moral consultation, such as the support of a code, a moral framework, and/or a supervisor. They also emphasize the importance of self-reflexivity and critical reflexivity, beyond reflectivity. While reflectivity basically designates a mirror activity, i.e., look back at what was accomplished and how, reflexivity relates to the challenge of one's assumptions: it is about "questioning what we, and others, might be taking for granted – what is being said and not said – and examining the impact this has or might have" (Cunliffe, 2016, p. 741). And while self-reflexivity is targeted towards self-examination (engaging in a dialogue with the self about one's beliefs and values, and the nature of one's relationships with others), critical reflexivity focuses on organizational practices, policies, social structures, and knowledge bases (Cunliffe, 2016). Self-reflexivity in coaching, for example, entails examining one's relationship with an issue and identifying any resonance in-between stories that might influence or interfere with one's interpretations. Critical reflexivity means examining the discourses that sustain the use of coaching in organizations, the ideologies and theoretical assumptions that inform coaching, and the role of coaching in forming new practices of control and discipline (Nielsen & Nørreklit, 2009), as emphasized in the commentaries. With such increased awareness, coaches can decide whether or not to take action – a key dimension of freedom as informed by Arendt, according to our expert.

References

Arendt, H. (2003). *Responsibility and judgment*. New York, NY: Schocken Books.
Arendt, H. (2006). *Eichmann in Jerusalem*. New York, NY: Penguin Books.
Argyris, C., & Schon, D. (1996). *Organisational learning II: Theory, method and practice*. New York, NY: Addison-Wesley.
Boje, D. M. (2008). Story Ethics. In D. M. Boje (Ed.), *Critical theory ethics for business and public administration* (pp. 97–117). London: Sage Publications.
Carroll, M., & Shaw, E. (2013). *Ethical maturity in the helping professions: Making difficult life and work decisions*. London: Jessica Kingsley.
Cunliffe, A. L. (2016). On becoming a critically reflexive practitioner redux: What does it mean to be reflexive? *Journal of Management Education, 406*, 740–746.
Corey, G., Corey, M., Corey, C., & Callanan, P. (2015). *Issues and ethics in the helping professions* (9th ed.). Belmont, CA: Brooks/Cole, Cengage Learning.
Edwards, R. (2008). Actively seeking subjects. In A. Fejes & K. Nicoll (Eds.), *Foucault and lifelong learning: Governing the subject* (pp. 21–33). London: Routledge.
Fatien Diochon, P., & Nizet, J. (2012). Les coachs, ni muets ni inactifs face à la dimension critique de leur travail! *Management & Avenir, 53*(3), 162–182.
Foucault, M. (1988). Technologies of the self. In R. Martin, H. Gutman, & P. H. Hutton (Eds.), *Technologies of the self: A seminar with Michel Foucault* (pp. 16–49). Amherst, MA: University of Massachusetts Press.
Foucault, M. (1997). The ethics of the concern of the self as a practice of freedom. In P. Rabinow (Ed.), *Ethics: Subjectivity and truth*. London: Allen Lane.
Hede, T. A. (2010). *Coaching: Samtalekunst eller ledelsesdisciplin (Coaching: An art of conversation or a discipline of leadership)*. København: Samfundslitteratur.
Jørgensen, K. M., & Boje, D. M. (2010). Resituating narrative and story in business ethics. *Business Ethics: A European Review, 19*(3), 251–262.
Kirkeby, O. F. (2008). *Protreptik: Filosofisk coaching i ledelse (Protrepsis: Philosophical coaching in leadership)*. København: Samfundslitteratur.
Mitchell, D. (1993). When the values of clients and counsellors clash: Some conceptual and ethical propositions. *Canadian Journal of Counselling, 27*(3), 203–211.
Nielsen, A. E., & Nørreklit, H. (2009). A discourse analysis of the disciplinary power of management coaching. *Society and Business Review, 4*(3), 202–214.

Pfeffer, J. (1998). *The human equation: Building profits by putting people first*. Boston, MA: Harvard Business School Press.

Townley, B. (1995). Know thyself': Self-awareness, self-formation and managing. *Organization*, 2(2), 271–289.

Watson, T. (2006). *Organising and managing work* (2nd ed.). London: Pearson.

Western, S. (2012). *Coaching & mentoring: A critical text*. London: Sage Publications.

5   Cultural issues in coaching

Introduction

Given our increasingly global environment, cultural issues play a major role in management practices and business relationships. In the specific context of coaching, culture-related issues include, but are not limited to, communication difficulties, complicated coach-client relationships, differing expectations when it comes to the coaching setting, and misunderstandings regarding the coach's role (Milner, Ostmeier, & Franke, 2013).

Moreover, if you consider that executive coaching is predominately a Western concept, rooted in Western thinking, business practices, and cultural characteristics (Lam, 2016), this adds another interesting set of challenges. As an example, Western coaching approaches often celebrate "the resourceful, self-directive individual" (Shoukry, 2016), which seems less relevant in non-Western cultures. As coaching is gaining popularity and presence across the world, we cannot help but wonder whether Western-inspired coaching concepts and practices are universally applicable (Nangalia & Nangalia, 2010), and if not, the considerations that might be required at the level of the industry as a whole, as well as at the level of the individual coaches in their practices.

Consequently, Chapter 5 addresses some of the cultural issues in coaching by examining two cases. In *Kalimera!*, the CFO of a Greece-based company directly contracts with Greg, a British coach. Greg was chosen by the CFO because of his Greek origins. But despite his origins, Greg has never lived in Greece and knows very little about Greek culture. As he starts coaching, he finds himself facing some cultural differences that he wasn't prepared for and that he needs to learn to deal with.

In *Breaking the cultural barriers*, Laura is hired by a nonprofit organization to coach low-wage earners, most of whom are immigrants, to adjust and overcome cultural barriers. One of Laura's coachees is Angela, a woman from the Philippines working at the kitchen of a local hospital. She needs Laura's support to overcome cultural and language barriers in order to get a better, more stable job in the US.

Case 5.1. Kalimera!

Greg was very excited about his new coaching assignment. He was going to coach Ioannis, the Chief Financial Officer of a multinational organization based in Greece. The CFO contacted Greg directly, expressing his interest in being coached as part of his own professional development, and he chose Greg because he was part of a well-reputed coaching company. His Greek family name didn't hurt, either. However, Greg was born in the UK and had lived there all his life. He didn't speak any Greek, and he knew very little about the Greek culture, having only vacationed there on a couple occasions. He explained this to Ioannis who still wanted to work with him as they had established a good rapport.

This was Greg's first overseas assignment. He didn't expect it to be all that different from any other coaching assignment he took in the UK. He always tried to adjust his style to fit his clients, and he assumed the same would be true of cultural differences, if ever they came up. Despite this attitude, Greg still wasn't prepared for the issues he was about to face.

Reflexive questions

- Do you think it helps when the coach and the coachee are from the same country or have the same culture? Why, or why not?
- Would you modify your coaching approach and practices to adapt to a client from a different culture, or would you try to make the person understand why and how you do things, adjusting to your approach?

The first issue came up regarding face-to-face sessions. Greg expected to conduct all coaching sessions via videoconferencing; however, Ioannis made it clear that he expected at least the first session to be conducted face-to-face. In the UK, he often coached clients he had never met in person, and this method worked well for him. But this wouldn't work with Ioannis.

Another thing Greg found challenging was that Ioannis was asking lots of questions about Greg's personal life. He wasn't meddling or being unprofessional; he simply needed to understand who Greg was as a person, a parent, and so on, not just as a coach. To Ioannis, building a personal relationship was essential. Greg struggled with this as it compromised the coach-coachee relationship as he perceived it. In the UK,

Greg's clients weren't interested in who he was. Nothing mattered outside the coaching goals.

Greg faced another barrier when he asked for access to other people in the organization in order to help Ioannis with his development. Even when hired directly by the coachee, Greg normally conducted a 360-degree appraisal, to get more insights into the person. But Ioannis refused. Greg later understood that Ioannis didn't want to lose face in the organization, a common concern in Greek culture.

For the same reason, Ioannis declined to give Greg a reference letter after completing the coaching. Ioannis was afraid that a head hunter or executive search specialist would see that he had been coached. In Greece, working with a coach still comes with some stigma.

Reflexive questions

- What other challenges do you think a coach might face when working with someone from a different culture?
- How might a coach prepare to deal with cultural differences?

Commentary 5.1.a

Sybille Persson

This case about a British coach is exemplary to develop reflexive and critical thinking about the cultural issue in coaching by overcoming the mainstream of cultural differences. I assume that Greg has never read French philosopher François Jullien, who is also a sinologist and philologist (expert in the study of literary texts). Jullien, who can read French, German, but also classic Chinese and Greek, is used to examining texts in their original language instead of their translations, which do not always respect the original meaning. On a fundamental level, the thought analysis begins with language (Wenzel, 2010): it is impossible to think without language. So let us first examine this issue of language to assess Greg's dilemma.

Beyond language, Greg's dilemma

The uncomfortable feelings of the British coach are real and need to be taken into account. But how? Does Greg have to run and visit his supervisor who probably also comes from the same Anglo-Saxon cradle of coaching? And if Greg lived in Greece, wouldn't things be simpler? The account of the *Kalimera!* case ("kalimera" means day of god or good morning in Greek) does not specify what language is used in the coaching interaction, but I can undoubtedly guess that the coached CFO speaks English. In the coaching session, Greg can use his own language (English), but he experiences the distance, the gap between two behavioral and cultural sets of habits.

In her cross-cultural approach, Wierzbicka (2014) explains how millions of people can become "prisoners of English." Academics, lawyers, diplomats, writers, scholars, but also coaches working in an international context are affected. Even in cross-cultural studies, people are imprisoned in English, especially in culture-specific concepts. Concepts and ways of thinking matter more than the practice of language because they are often ignored and *un-thought.* Wierzbicka (2014, p. 64) warns:

> In a globalized world in which English has become, effectively, the first ever global lingua franca, it is increasingly easy to forget that the whole world doesn't think in English. If humankind does share some deep moral intuitions on which a global ethic could build, then these intuitions must relate to particular speakers' conceptual worlds.

Today many executives are able to communicate in another language than their own. That is less true for native English speakers. How many coaches are able to speak another language than their own when they are British or American?

In fact, beyond language, the coach seems to be facing an ethical dilemma: does he have to escape the usual reserve of the coach shaped in the Anglo-Saxon mold and cease to follow the normative code of the good coach in the neutral shadow? After fully accepting this unusual situation, can he adapt and even take advantage of it without feeling either uncomfortable or guilty? After examining these questions on a practical level, I suggest that we go further into Jullien's approach.

On the practical level

Fatien Diochon and Nizet (2015) have outlined major limitations from the codes of conduct in the specific context of coaching. "One size does not fit all!" they argue. A code of conduct cannot think even if it has been thought out and built by good contributors. This is even truer in an intercultural context. Greg is able to feel the distance with Ioannis. He now has to think of it and accept that the code cannot think in his place.

When it works in an intercultural context, the coaching dialogue needs to be even more pragmatic, looking for intelligibility between actors, without being severed from sensitivity and compassion (Boyatzis, Smith, & Blaize, 2006). The coach is especially in charge of understanding his client; he is not expected to promote an incantatory quest for truth, justice, or absolute meaning only built from an ethnocentric perspective.

If I were Greg's supervisor, after carefully listening to him, I would share the above reflection based on reflexivity and compassion in order to:

1   Get Greg to feel legitimate in his discomfort and accept it;
2   Help him to take advantage of this situation to develop more reflexivity about his own culture and welcome the culture of the coached CFO;
3   Give Greg 1) protection to feel free to behave as he wishes in front of the coached CFO and 2) permission to emancipate from the code of conduct he usually follows;
4   Ask Greg to prepare adapted explanations for the coached executive to initiate a real intercultural dialogue able to nurture the coaching exchange.

From an ethical perspective, Greg's feeling of discomfort is the first sign indicating an awareness of the cultural distance with his coachee. For that, Jullien's practical concept of cultural resources can help.

Cultural resources with François Jullien

Jullien wrote about 40 books, the majority of which have been translated into 30 languages. He has especially used the roots of traditional Chinese thought in order to de- and re-construct a philosophy of living, which appears as one of the most original and powerful thoughts of the day. In an interdisciplinary approach, his work is a real opportunity to provide original and fresh views for Organizational and Management Studies. In regards to managerial topics related to coaching, I can highlight some issues such as HRD (Persson & Wasieleski, 2015; Persson & Shrivastava, 2016; Persson, Agostini, & Kléber, 2017), efficacy and strategy (Chia, 2013; Shrivastava & Persson, 2014), and transition and change (Chia, 2014; Ivanova & Persson, 2017).

Jullien (2016) deeply mistrusts the notion of cultural identity. His approach is embedded in his refusal to compare cultures in order to better take advantage of each of them through the notion of cultural resources. By focusing on resources instead of identities, Jullien creates the conditions for a real and deep dialogue between constantly evolving cultures. In his view it is impossible to compare cultures without favoring (often implicitly) an a priori system of norms. Thus, Hofstede in his famous work on cultural differences adopted a system of norms (measurement and values) built from the West. He certainly did not intend to be ethnocentric, yet he unfortunately was. Even if he has been criticized by some (for example McSweeney, 2002; Fang, 2012), most of the intercultural studies (in teaching or in research) use this comparative approach. It should not be the case in the process of coaching.

Uniform versus universal

To become aware of the hazards of ethnocentrism in cross-cultural studies, I outline Jullien's explanations about two concepts, *universal* and *uniform*, in order to avoid their tricky confusion in a time of globalization (Jullien, 2014). This is of special interest for coaches working in cross-cultural contexts.

"Universal" refers to philosophy and to what could be unquestionable hypernorms for all human beings (Jullien, 2014). In the West, prevailing hypernorms are the heritage of ideal platonic values and the European development of moral philosophy. Because hypernorms are "fundamental conceptions of the right and the good" (Donaldson & Dunfee, 1999, p. 52), they are embedded in "principles so fundamental to human existence that . . . we would expect them to be reflected in a convergence of religious, philosophical, and cultural beliefs" (Donaldson & Dunfee, 1994, p. 265).

"Uniform" is related to an economics-oriented standardization; it echoes globalization in organizational behavior for management (and coaching). If the scale of value is increasingly "uniform" as a value of production, it is not a "universal" value in a moral sense (Jullien, 2014). Universal does not mean uniform.

The uniformity that can be found in Western ways of life for economic purposes has now spread through the entire world. Economic purposes do not directly embody superior values. In the same way, management practices do not need to become globally uniform (Li, Leung, Chen, & Luo, 2012). Especially, one should consider a common array of fundamentally rooted issues (Persson & Shrivastava, 2016). These include the best conditions and processes for supporting human resources in the context of their unique environments (profession, climate, weather, culture, sector, industry, etc.). That is also true for coaching practices.

As a conclusion

For Jullien, "the primary ethical exigency" is based on an intelligent dialogue between cultures (2014, p. 143): "A subject constitutes himself only in so far as he has known how (dared) to take a step back in his mind, to reconsider the buried and sedimented prejudice from which he thinks and, hence, to rediscover an initiative in his thinking." That is the price of real reflexivity, a core topic in the field of coaching especially in an intercultural context as in the *Kalimera!* case.

Following Callon and Rabeharisoa (2004) in their sociological study, reflexivity strengthens the sensitivity of "being affected" as an aspect of "being in phase" (Jullien, 2007). "Being affected" is related to the other; "being in phase" is related to the environment and the propensity of things (Jullien, 1999), especially with one's professional environment in a coaching process. The success of being in phase cannot be measured "by conformity to some aim but rather by capacity to induce forgetfulness" as "a shoe is adequate when it makes us forget the foot" (Jullien, 2007, p. 109). The embodied dimension of organizational culture has to be taken into account (Flores-Pereira, Davel, & Cavedon, 2008).

Commentary 5.1.b

Irina Todorova

Background of cross-cultural coaching

The topic of cross-cultural coaching has been discussed extensively during the last two decades and has become more prominent recently. This is related to the fact that coaching as scholarship and professional practice has matured and many of its variations are being explored in greater detail. Additionally, coaching has been expanding to and within many geographical areas, as has the international mobility of both coaches and potential clients. Coaches in all areas, including organizational, executive, and health coaching, are developing coaching relationships, which are characterized by diversity, including diversity of cultural backgrounds. The increased interest of organizations and individuals in engaging with coaches goes hand in hand with increasing diversity of approaches, places in which coaching is practiced, and expectations for effectiveness.

Thus, the questions that the *Kalimera!* case presents will be more and more relevant – they can come up at the stage of setting the agenda, agreeing on the logistics of the sessions, in the understanding of the nature of the relationship, and throughout the coaching dialogue. Since groups can be of varying size and location, including across and within countries, and people can self-identify as belonging to different groups, cross-cultural coaching can cover a wide range of situations. While *Kalimera!* illustrates an international coaching engagement, its relevance is broader – conversations across different cultural backgrounds also happen within countries, as they are themselves diverse.

When discussing intercultural sensitivity in coaching, Nieuwerburgh (2017) proposes a working formulation of "culture" as "generally accepted beliefs, conventions, customs, social norms, and behaviors associated with people who self-identify as members of a particular group" (p. 441). Much of the work in cross-cultural relations has been based on categorizations of cultural types according to increasingly nuanced dimensions (such as power-distance and individualism-collectivism) (Hofstede, 2011). These dimensions open important understandings and can broadly inform coaching; however, they can also create expectations about cultural backgrounds depending on their location within these categories/continuums.

From a narrative perspective, culture can be seen as "the stories we live by" (Howard, 1991), and identities as constructed in and through historical and social contexts, including the cultural meanings in which one is immersed (Drake, 2015, p. 56). People's narrative identities are dialogical, and their stories are both uniquely personal and at the same time interwoven with broader (cultural) narratives. These broad narratives can be contradictory – they empower as well as silence groups and individuals and sustain hierarchies (McDonald, 2014). People live and work immersed in several dominant narratives, which they internalize and position themselves within (Drake, 2009). Cultural narratives also embody intersections of gender, race, class dimensions of privileged and inequalities which play out in coaching (Greenstein, 2016). In this sense, cultural sensitivity in coaching would mean being open to ongoing listening and exploring the complexity of multiple narrative threads.

Kalimera!

Coaching cross-culturally entails knowledge and sensitivity about the shared meanings of groups to which the coachee identifies as belonging, but the coach might not identify with. It would also mean shifting between a knowledge of general cultural characteristics and an exploration of how they play out for the person in particular, how they are internalized and/ or resisted. Additionally, it would entail self-reflective awareness of what cultural meanings and expectations the coach brings to the relationship and to coaching itself.

We can discuss the specific examples brought out in *Kalimera!* through our working understanding of culture as meanings shared by a group, as well as uniquely intertwined within people's narratives. At some level, cultural similarity between coach and coachee could be of benefit to establishing a mutually trusting and respectful relationship. Since many meanings would be shared and understood by the two people participating in this process, such a relationship can be established and flow relatively smoothly. Some of the issues brought up by the case are understanding norms of communication, expectations of behavior in organizational hierarchies, and the acceptability of reciprocal exchanges within a coaching relationship, as well as how coaching is viewed in the culture. Another example that would certainly come up would relate to what is considered humorous – cultural differences clearly emerge in what people laugh about. In a situation of shared cultural backgrounds, many exchanges might not need to be explained or explored, as commonality of meanings is assumed.

However, when coach and coachee are from the same country, group or sub-group, this can lead to making quick assumptions. Such assumptions about the meanings of what the coachee is saying can impact listening or shift the direction of the questions and conversation. Taking for granted that the coach understands what the coachee means because of shared culture could be a limitation in communication. A position of "not-knowing" and participation in the interaction with openness and non-assuming attitudes would be appropriate especially when it seems that the two people share a common culture.

Assumptions can also be made when a coach has achieved an in-depth understanding of the cultural background of the coachee. As Nieuwerburgh (2017, p. 447) states, "An in-depth understanding of a personal cultural context may be unnecessary and in some cases unhelpful. Any relevant information needed about a coachee's cultural identity can come from conversations with the coachee." Thus it is recommended that the coach engages in an ongoing reflection on their own cultural assumptions and how they play into the interactions (Abbot & Salomaa, 2017).

In the case of Greg and Ioannis, even though there is a shared Greek heritage, they have grown up in different countries; Greg goes into the coaching knowing that he is not that familiar with Greek culture. However, he does make assumptions about characteristics of Greek culture, which he invokes to understand some of the issues that come up in the initial stages of the relationship. Broad generalizations (or stereotypes) of whole nations might be helpful for orientation in confusing moments, but they might be irrelevant to smaller groups and individuals. Even when working in one's own country or local culture such stereotypes can shape the expectations of the coach, yet be minimally relevant to the coachee.

For example, Ioannis is asking Greg many questions about him and his personal life. Greg assumes that these expectations on the part of Ioannis stem from Greek culture. This is a reasonable conclusion since according to the dimensions of individualism-collectivism, Greek culture is considered more collectivistic. A similar example is also presented by Chatwani (2015) from an Indian context, also a collectivist culture, where people assume that the coaching relationship has characteristics of friendship and reciprocity. Nevertheless, Greg could explore what else might be playing into Ioannis' call for an equally open conversation between them, which might open other avenues for the conversation – perhaps his personality, his position in the organization, or his understanding of coaching in general, which in the literature is usually described as an egalitarian relationship. From some of the other information we have about Ioannis, it seems that he is hesitant to share much with his colleagues in the organization; might he feel isolated in his role? Greg and Ioannis can explore these possibilities to deepen their understandings of each other.

Greg can share his understanding of his role as coach and his boundaries for self-disclosure, and perhaps find some flexibility within those. In any case, respecting local culture does not mean that Greg needs to adjust to a type of communication, which is incompatible with how he sees his role and presence in the relationship. Cultural understanding and a non-judgmental attitude are crucially important to a successful engagement – imposing the coach's own cultural values is one of the behaviors to be avoided in cross-cultural coaching (Nieuwerburgh, 2017). At the same time, it does not mean compromising personal or professional codes of ethics, or practicing in ways that are incompatible with how one sees their role as a coach. Taken further, openness and a non-judgmental attitude do not need to mean accepting cultural traditions that the coach sees as unethical, unsafe, or discriminatory.

The meaning and acceptability of practices such as coaching and more broadly consulting, mentoring, and counseling in local contexts are also of importance. Chatwani (2015) draws attention to the "cultural assumptions inherent in the coaching process itself." Coaching is a practice, which is diverse in theoretical frameworks and practical approaches, yet comes mainly from a Western perspective and might not equally resonate everywhere. The flourishing of the individual is valued broadly, but in some contexts is seen as much more closely intertwined with community (Chatwani, 2015). Research in coaching predominantly follows individual outcomes such as well-being, job engagement, self-efficacy, and goal achievement. More recently there has been a call to address context in coaching and its impact on processes and outcomes (Athanasopoulou & Dopson, 2017).

Thus, it is important to understand and respect the local meanings of coaching itself. The practice could be seen as a remedial intervention (and thus embarrassing as it is for Ioannis), as a service available only to the elite, or as a benefit that should be available to all. In some contexts, the aim of coaching is associated with goal achievement, increasing productivity, and return on investment. In other contexts, reflection and contemplation might be what is valued (Chatwani, 2015). What are considered best practices in coaching can also vary between countries – Gentry, Manning, Wolf, Hernez-Broome, & Allen (2013) found both similarities and differences between what coaches in Europe and Asia see as best practices – for example, one of the differences found was that coaches in Asia focused on the results, objectives, and goals of the sessions while one definition of best practices in Europe was the coach's own development (Gentry et al., 2013).

Sensitivity to the meaning of coaching in local contexts is important to avoid ethnocentric imposition of what it "is" or "should be." Greg could explore the history and practice of coaching in Greece either in preparation for his engagement or along with Ioannis. They can figure out where they are both comfortable and decide together whether the 360-degree assessment is of crucial importance considering the context. While the 360-degree assessment would add to the contextual understanding of the organization and Ioannis' role in it, an insistence from Greg to go ahead with it could be incongruent with the organizational culture and jeopardize the relationship. Further discussion of behaviors on the part

of the coach that demonstrate cultural sensitivity or insensitivity are summarized by Nieuwerburgh (2017).

Conclusions

Cross-cultural coaching is a dance between old and new meanings,
between personal narratives and the ways in which they are situated
within and shaped by broader cultural ones. Ultimately, it is about a relationship based on listening, openness, and curiosity, creating trust and
mutual respect between partners, as well as respect for each other's
culture and convictions. As Abbot and Salomaa (2017) point out, "Para-
doxically . . . all coaching is cross-cultural – and none" (p. 342). Cross-
cultural coaching is a process deeply embedded in cultural, political, and
historical "local worlds" situated in a global community.

Case 5.2. Breaking the cultural barriers

Laura was born and raised in Singapore, where she started her professional career as a trainer. At that time, she was working for a company
in Singapore that had expanded worldwide. Laura was in charge of training employees on HR-related topics, traveling to different countries such as
Germany, the Netherlands, Spain, China, and Hong Kong. Training people
from different countries and cultures required tremendous cultural awareness and flexibility, as she needed to adopt a different approach for each of
the countries where she worked. This increased cultural awareness helped
her relate to her trainees and adapt to the various cultures she encountered.

Later in her career, she became a coach, based in the United States.
She worked for a nonprofit organization that supported low-wage, nonnative workers, helping them adapt to the US culture and deal with the
different professional challenges they faced. These workers originated
from Mexico, the Philippines, China, Vietnam, Russia, and so on.

Laura regularly worked at a local hospital. Typically, for such assignments, Laura would get a room on the fifth floor – the maternity ward –
and she'd spend the day there. Employees who needed coaching could
stop by without an appointment, and they could come back for as many
sessions as they needed.

One day, a woman named Angela walked in, asking to be coached.
She was from the Philippines, where she had completed three years
of college before marrying a Japanese man. She then lived in Japan

for years where she learned the language. Later, she got divorced and moved to the US with her two kids because she had family there. She was working part-time in the hospital's kitchen and had a second job at a Japanese market. She had no insurance, working hard to sustain her family as a single mother. She felt that she had the skills to achieve more, but she was lacking confidence in her ability to fit in culturally.

Reflexive questions

- What differences, if any, exist between coaching a senior executive or a CEO versus a low-wage worker?
- How might having a specific coaching agenda based on the organization's needs differ from an open agenda, such as in this case?
- How efficient do you think coaching is when there is no commitment to a specific goal, timeframe, number of sessions, etc.?

Laura ended up working for weeks with Angela whose goal was to get a full-time office job. During the coaching sessions, the main issue that Laura focused on was to raise Angela's self-confidence and help her break down the barriers she had created for herself when it came to cultural differences and language challenges. As a result of the coaching, Angela went out and took evening classes. She then applied for an opening at the hospital, and she landed the job.

Laura ran into Angela at the hospital almost a year later, and her transformation was visible, her self-confidence palpable. This was an extremely rewarding experience for Laura.

Reflexive questions

- What kinds of challenges do nonnative employees typically face as a result of cultural and/or language differences?
- Would coaching be a good way to support them? How?
- How important do you think it is to have an international background when coaching clients from different countries and cultures? What skills and experiences do coaches need for such situations?

Commentary 5.2.a

Maroussia Chanut

Cross-cultural coaching is a quite recent specialization within the field of coaching. Until recently, cross-cultural coaches have essentially relied on common sense, communication techniques, and psychological perspectives such as behavioral psychology and emotional intelligence. Given the increasing challenges of a global and turbulent environment, more training and strategies in this subfield seem necessary. According to Rosinski (2003), "traditional" coaching has assumed a worldview (i.e., American, and to some extent Western European) that doesn't hold true universally. Different cultures have to be considered for global coaching to be effective. This professional growth has been accompanied by increased research interest, which can be traced back to 1999 (Hicks & Peterson, 1999).

In the specific case of Laura, we understand that the coachee, a Filipino woman named Angela of unknown age and social upbringing, shows up at the coach's office in a hospital to address personal difficulties regarding her professional expectations and achievements. Specifically, Angela would like to shift from working two part-time jobs to one full-time position with benefits. She also consults the coach on the issue of self-confidence regarding her adaptation to American culture. It is a common assumption among many international and/or expatriate spouses and immigrant female coachees that expatriation means shifting goals for professional success to lower paying and less interesting professional opportunities (Expat communication, 2011). Also, I have noticed that women often tend to express a lack of confidence or some sort of complex towards the language barrier and their accent, even when they have reached a professional proficiency sufficient enough to land a job. Over the course of my practice, I have worked with many expatriated clients who have at first experienced a rather harsh position as foreigners, not being understood by locals. This difficult start often leaves them with a mental barrier, which seems to remain even when they have improved their ability to express themselves in the local language.

I have also noticed that the language barrier as raised in this case frequently hides a larger issue of cultural adaptation, which prevents these individuals from adapting to the new culture. It can be difficult to accept that the life they once had is over, to grieve in order to build a completely new experience that they can appropriate as their own. I would also comment that this phenomenon frequently increases in the specific case of spouses who follow their husbands/wives and find themselves still being defined as "followers" as time goes by. Once they realize the barrier is only a smokescreen, they tend to feel more fulfilled and energized to go out there, try out new relationships, and achieve new professional goals. My hypothesis, within the limits of my observations and past experience encountering this kind of phenomenon, is that as a result of traditional unconscious machismo, women tend to discriminate against themselves and build lower self-confidence as they pressure themselves to fit in more.

In order to illustrate the feeling of cultural differences during expatriation, and from a specific situation, Lysgaard (1955) stressed a four-stage process of cultural adaptation, the U-curve of cultural adjustment, starting with a Honeymoon phase, described as a starting point when the expatriate discovers (with delight) his new surroundings through his own frame of reference, just like a tourist would. Then a quite difficult phase of Culture Shock occurs, made of disillusionment and frustrations. What is observed is that people suffer from their own inability to adapt to the new cultural frame of reference and tend to hold on to what they already know, which is comforting and makes them feel secure. This potentially dangerous phase can be so disconcerting and destabilizing that some people might remain stuck, on a psychological level, in its vividly negative effects, even when they have supposedly moved up to the next phase. At this point, they are not always able to seize the positive elements in their lives. The next phase is Adjustment, or gradual cultural integration, which occurs whenever the expatriate is ready to adopt the new frame of reference without letting go of his own. The last phase, called Mastery, is characterized by the progress of the individual to operate in the new culture and to integrate the local rules as his own.

In the case of Angela, building on the information provided, we can assume that she is seeking coaching because she is leaving the Culture Shock phase and moving to the Adjustment phase. This is an excellent opportunity for Laura to seize because it means that Angela is ready for change, bearing in mind the challenges that this type of coaching, as part of a nonprofit organization, presents in terms of unspecific goals, timeframe, and number of sessions, as well as an unstructured relationship with the coachee.

One thing that Laura might consider is how coaching could be a good way to support Angela, a nonnative employee. Laura could base her thinking on the prevailing coaching style from the perspectives of the coach and the coachee's native cultures. In the United States, coaching is rather non-directive. The coach does not control the client focus or objectives (Frank Bresser Consulting, 2009). Rather, the relationship is co-created as a collaborative partnership with the client directing the focus of the coaching (Sherpa Coaching, 2015). In effect, there is no prevailing coaching style as such – the whole range from directive to non-directive coaching can be found in North America. Further, there is a significant amount of virtual coaching (usually by telephone) as opposed to face-to-face coaching, which is the predominant method found in other regions of the world. Another aspect to note is that the client-coach relationship is co-created as a collaborative partnership, with the client directing the focus of the coaching. The coach does not control what the client focus or objectives are.

In contrast, there is no prevailing coaching style in Asia. However, there is a slant towards directive coaching when compared with other continents: in the 2009 Frank Bresser Consulting Survey, 13 countries were identified as predominantly directive (Philippines included), whereas six countries claimed non-directive coaching as the predominant style (Japan, Malaysia, Singapore, Tajikistan, Thailand, Vietnam). Within countries and even regions, local characteristics and preferences in the way coaching is understood and delivered vary. So, diversity prevails.

A number of local coaching initiatives (APAC, ICF chapters) have already emerged in Asia and have started to define and develop coaching. So coaching is clearly on the rise and in the process of becoming more mature in Asia in terms of quality and infrastructure. However, coaching remains mainly driven and determined by multinational clients. As a result, you rarely find specific Asian coaching forms and approaches. Hence, while local initiatives increasingly take place in Asia, these still remain rather limited.

From an academic perspective, we might therefore ask ourselves whether a non-directive approach might be suitable for a coachee whose native culture prevails a directive approach. In my experience, I have noticed that there is a limit to coaching using the frames and cross-cultural tools designed to ease the uncertainty of communication from one culture to another. I also do not share the opinion that there is a need to master the many subtleties of the coachee's culture in order to gain a positive outcome in a coaching intervention; general knowledge, Jungian archetypes, and insights might suffice, coachees being well aware that their international coaches do not share their cultural backgrounds. Also, usually the coach will be chosen by the coachee for specific reasons that do not need to be related to their own culture. In such a case, adopting a pragmatic, open-minded way of evaluating success is key: did the coaching work? Were the outcomes rewarding on both parts? With time and practice I have come to believe that the success of a coaching intervention also depends significantly on the coach's open mindedness to the client's frame of mind.

To address the client's frame of mind, an ethno-psychiatric approach can be helpful, as can an inner sensitivity to the coach's feeling of being different in a so-called nonnative culture, which fails to bring him a feeling of cultural wholeness. The entry point is that of the coachee, whatever that might be, however he might feel, and the journey to his soul might be as ravishing and stunning as those we make across the globe. In my opinion, embracing whatever the coachee thinks or expresses as a deep truth is essential, and therefore, the coach has to be ready to let go of his own truth to do so. This is a key step in establishing trust in order for the coachee to be able to broaden his thinking to a full range of options from which he can later choose.

I personally doubt that coming from an international background might automatically help, particularly if this environment has always been the norm and there has been no need or space for reflexive questioning or doubts, no experienced feelings of rejection whatsoever.

As a matter of fact, one can walk through life, crossing or intertwining paths with others, without understanding the least bit of what it feels like to be estranged. My hypothesis is that there is a need to have felt unfit in an unfamiliar environment in order to understand and help people progress with cultural change.

Another analogy I might draw, re-using the Lysgaard U-curve, is that of the coaching process as a journey, being experienced both by the coach and the coachee, which is not without taking some risks. In the first stage it is indeed an exciting delight for the coach to go and discover a new human being, all seems great and interesting in his client, if not harmonious. The coachee too is full of energy and motivation despite his problems, he senses that there might be good things for him happening. Then at the culture shock point (a value clash might occur for instance) there might be disenchantment for the coach (at this point a supervisor can be of a great help so the coach can work on his issue towards the coachee). The coachee might disagree with something the coach said, or some line he drew, and is showing it if not expressing it. This phase can potentially be dangerous, and the coach needs to be extremely careful.

He also needs to clear whatever might stand in the way for the coaching process to continue. When the storm is dealt with, the coach will help the coachee Adjust his new frame of reference without letting go of his old one. Mutual growth really start from this phase. At the end of the coaching both are at the acme of their art, in a Mastery phase that will leave them more mature. The coachee feels powerful and autonomous, he can progress now all by himself and is proud to share his achievements with the coach. The coach is filled with satisfaction and joy, like a parent bird who just fed and taught his offspring everything he knew and is watching them proudly as they fly away. They can then prepare themselves to say goodbye, and of course wish each other a nice trip!

Commentary 5.2.b

Christian van Nieuwerburgh

In my reflections below, I will focus on the "cross-cultural" or "intercultural" aspect of this case study. Cross-cultural coaching is a response to the assumption that it can be problematic for people from different cultures to communicate effectively. Before I discuss this case study, it should be acknowledged that I am reflecting on this piece as a Belgian citizen who was raised in Lebanon by a Japanese mother and now resides in the UK. Further, when offered the opportunity to provide comments on one of the case studies in this book, I chose to comment on this one because I have an interest and particular perspective. In other words, I have a bias toward celebrating diversity and encouraging practices that treat people with respect regardless of their self-identified cultural groups. It may also be the case that some readers of this case study share a similar interest or bias.

In this case study, both the coach and the coachee have culturally diverse experiences. It may be significant that the coaching is taking place in the US (a third country) and that both have chosen to live and work in the US. In many ways, this seems to be a relatively typical coaching topic. Often coaches support people to develop the confidence needed to achieve their potential. According to Rosinski (2010), a leading expert in the field, intercultural coaching requires a high level of flexibility and cultural awareness. And it seems that the coach in this case, Laura, has significant experience delivering training in different countries as an HR executive. This experience will undoubtedly have informed Laura's coaching practice. Perhaps even more importantly, it seems to have positively impacted Laura's own confidence in having coaching conversations where cultural issues may be raised. This case study is a good example of Rosinski's definition of intercultural coaching: "to enable more effective work across cultures (internationally and also when working with people from various organizations and backgrounds)" and "to offer in essence a more creative form of coaching" (Rosinski, 2010, p. 121). From the description of the coaching assignment, it seems that Laura was able to support the client (Angela) by allowing her to become more self-confident. To achieve her goals, it was necessary for Angela to overcome perceived cultural barriers or differences (including language). This outcome became possible when Angela was able to think more creatively about the challenges that she faced.

Citing the increasingly interconnected world we live in, Abbot and Salomaa (2017) argue that cross-cultural coaching is a necessary and emerging practice. According to these authors, "coaching across cultures is a highly contextual and emergent field that requires practitioners to be across multiple disciplines and practices. Coaches need to be experts in adapting their approaches to the individual and unique challenges of their coaching clients" (pp. 465–466). There is little doubt that Laura has been able to do this with Angela, resulting in the client overcoming self-imposed barriers and taking a proactive role in working toward important professional goals.

So far, this seems like a strong endorsement for cross-cultural coaching. But perhaps it is helpful to ask a few questions at this point. First, how significant was it that the coach had a high level of cultural awareness? Second, to what extent was the issue "cultural"?

How significant was it that the coach had a high l evel of cultural awareness?

While I do not have an answer to this question, I wonder whether the coach's high level of cultural awareness and relevant life experiences were the primary reasons for a successful coaching conversation. Wouldn't an excellent coach (without the life experiences of Laura) have been able to support Angela successfully?

To what extent was the issue "cultural"?

Having read the case study, I feel that the main hurdle for the client was a lack of confidence rather than a specific cultural issue. Based on the short synopsis of her life, it is clear that Angela is both proactive and resilient. What she lacked temporarily was the confidence to pursue her aspirations. For this reason, we should be cautious addressing "cultural issues" when it may be the case that they are simply contextual factors.

One thing that can be agreed upon is that the case study is an example of good coaching practice. We should hope that an effective coach (less culturally experienced than Laura) would have been able to support this client. It is essential for us, as coaches, to ensure that we do not inadvertently "problematize" cultural differences. Much of the writing about intercultural coaching continues to highlight *difference.* The risk is that coaches assume that "being different" is the problem. For example, *Diversity in Coaching* (Passmore, 2013) has a section on "coaching difference" with chapters entitled "coaching with men: alpha males," "coaching with women," "coaching disabled people," and "coaching gay and lesbian clients." While the intention is positive, my concern is that highlighting such "differences" is ultimately part of the challenge that we face today.

I have argued elsewhere (van Nieuwerburgh, 2017) that it is helpful for coaches to develop "intercultural sensitivity" (a term introduced by Bennett, 1993). Intercultural sensitivity refers to the ability to meet clients as respected equals. It does not require an in-depth understanding of the client's cultural background, but it does necessitate "accepting the coachee's cultural views and social norms without judgement" (van Nieuwerburgh, 2017, p. 175). In practice, this means ensuring that a coaching client does not feel judged during the coaching conversation.

So that the sense of "difference" does not impact our clients, it may be helpful to think of creating a new "culture" in every coaching relationship. In other words, during the initial contracting phase, the coach and the coachee can outline the "culture" (agreed-upon rules, ways of behaving, etc.) of the coaching relationship. Because this "culture" is neither the culture of the coachee nor of the coach, both are of equal status, and both "belong" to this culture. Each can then be respectful of the other's self-identified cultural group while operating within a culture that has been created for the purposes of the coaching conversation. Ultimately, it is the quality of the relationship between coach and coachee that matters most. In this relationship, neither party should feel like a "foreigner," an "outsider," or an "other." It is a relationship in which both people are of equal value as human beings. All coaching should support coachees to develop pragmatic solutions (workable in the coachee's particular context) that are aligned with their deeply held values and principles.

Conclusion

Numerous tools and frameworks are available for coaches to use in cross-cultural settings, such as the Cultural Orientation Framework (Gilbert & Rosinski, 2008), the Cross-Cultural Kaleidoscope (Plaister-Ten, 2013), or the Framework for Cultural Adaptation of Coaching for Asian Clients (Nangalia & Nangalia, 2010). Despite their definite usefulness, they do not suffice. The above commentaries point out that for coaching to be effective when practiced across cultures, coaches need to develop an intercultural mindset, and they need to reflect on how their own culture influences them and their interactions with their coachees (Milner, Ostmeier, & Franke, 2013). From there, they can develop the knowledge and skills to support coachees across cultures.

When it comes to coaching expatriates in particular, coaching plays an important role and has a significant impact on career capital development, in particular to the "knowing-how," "knowing-why," and "knowing-whom" capabilities (Salomaa & Mäkelä, 2017).

According to our experts, cross-cultural coaching doesn't require the coach be an expert in other cultures, or even have international experience or cross-cultural communication skills and awareness. Certainly, when the coach or the coachee is using a nonnative language, it can be a barrier, and communication becomes much trickier. Careful listening and avoiding making assumptions appear of further importance and should ensure that the real issues don't get "lost in translation."

In addition to language and communication, an extra effort is needed from the coach to situate things in the local context of the coachee and to avoid resorting to personal preferences.

Finally, and as highlighted above, beyond national cultures, the skills that can be used in cross-cultural coaching can also apply to different types of cultures, such as the organizational culture, where we also have shared meanings, values, and beliefs among a group of people. They can be relevant to address any differences that could exist between coach and coachee, where assumptions and expectations can be made by the coach or by the coachee based on their previous experiences and backgrounds, which could impact the current coaching relationship.

References

Abbot, G. N., & Salomaa, R. (2017). Cross-cultural coaching: An emerging practice. In T. Bachkirova, G. Spence, & D. Drake (Eds.), *The sage handbook of coaching* (pp. 453–469). London: Sage Publications.

Athanasopoulou, A., & Dopson, S. (2017). A systematic review of executive coaching outcomes: Is it the journey or the destination that matters the most? *The Leadership Quarterly, 29*(1), 70–88.

Bennett, M. J. (1993). Towards ethnorelativism: A developmental model of intercultural sensitivity. In R. M. Paige (Ed.), *Education for the intercultural experience* (2nd ed., pp. 21–71). Yarmouth, ME: Intercultural Press.

Boyatzis, R. E., Smith, M. L., & Blaize, N. (2006). Developing sustainable leaders through coaching and compassion. *Academy of Management Learning & Education*, 5(1), 8–24.

Callon, M., & Rabeharisoa, V. (2004). Gino's lesson on humanity: Genetics, mutual entanglements and the sociologist's role. *Economy and Society*, 33(1), 1–27.

Chatwani, N. (2015). A cross-cultural approach in coaching as viewed through the Guru-Sisya Parampara. In V. Pereira, & A. Malik (Eds.), *Investigating cultural aspects in Indian organizations* (pp. 69–78). New York, NY: Springer International Publishing.

Chia, R. (2013). In praise of strategic indirection: An essay on the efficacy of oblique ways of responding. *M@n@gement*, 16(5), 667–679.

Chia, R. (2014). Reflection: In praise of silent transformation – allowing change through letting happen. *Journal of Change Management*, 14(1), 8–27.

Donaldson, T., & Dunfee, T. W. (1994). Toward a unified conception of business ethics: Integrative social contracts theory. *Academy of Management Review*, 19(2), 252–284.

Donaldson, T., & Dunfee, T. W. (1999). *Ties that bind: A social contracts approach to business ethics*. Cambridge, MA: Harvard Business School Press.

Drake, D. (2009). Identity, liminality and development through coaching: An intrapersonal view of intercultural sensitivity. In M. Moral, & G. Abbott (Eds.), *The Routledge companion to international business coaching* (pp. 61–74). London: Routledge.

Drake, D. (2015). *Narrative coaching: Bringing our stories to life*. Petaluma, CA: CNC Press.

Expat Communication (2011). *Panorama de l'expatriation au féminin*. Retrieved from www.expatcommunication.com

Fang, T. (2012). Yin Yang: A new perspective on culture. *Management and Organization Review*, 8(1), 25–50.

Fatien Diochon, P., & Nizet, J. (2015). Ethical codes and executive coaches: One size does not fit all. *The Journal of Applied Behavioral Science*, 51(2), 1–25.

Flores-Pereira, M. T., Davel, E., & Cavedon, N. R. (2008). Drinking beer and understanding organizational culture embodiment. *Human Relations*, 61(7), 1007–1026.

Frank Bresser Consulting (2009). *Consulting report: Global coaching survey*. Retrieved from www.frank-bresser-consulting.com

Gentry, W. A., Manning, L., Wolf, A. K., Hernez-Broome, G., & Allen, L. W. (2013). What coaches believe are best practices for coaching: A qualitative study of interviews from coaches residing in Asia and Europe. *Journal of Leadership Studies*, 7(2), 18–31.

Gilbert, K., & Rosinski, P. (2008). Accessing cultural orientations: The online cultural orientations framework assessment as a tool for coaching. *Coaching: An International Journal of Theory, Research, and Practice*, 1(1), 81–92.

Greenstein, G. (2016). *Intersectionality and executive coaching: Transforming perspectives*. (PhD thesis). Columbia University, Teachers College.

Hicks, M., & Peterson, D. (1999). Leaders coaching across borders. In W. H. Mobley, M. J. Gessner, & V. H. Arnold (Eds.), *Advances in global leadership* (Vol. 1). Stamford, CT: Jai Press.

Hofstede, G. (2011). Dimensionalizing cultures: The Hofstede model in context. *Online Readings in Psychology and Culture*, 2(1).

Howard, G. S. (1991). Culture tales: A narrative approach to thinking, cross-cultural psychology, and psychotherapy. *American Psychologist*, 46(3), 187–197.

Ivanova, O., & Persson, S. (2017). Transition as a ubiquitous and a continuous process: Overcoming the Western view. *Journal of Change Management*, 17(1), 31–46.

Jullien, F. (1999). *The propensity of things. Toward a story of efficacy in China*. New York, NY: Zone Books.

Jullien, F. (2007). *Vital nourishment departing from happiness*. New York, NY: Zone Books.

Jullien, F. (2014). *On the universal, the uniform, the common and dialogue between cultures*. Cambridge: Polity Press.

Jullien, F. (2016). *Il n'y a pas d'identité culturelle.* Paris: Editions de l'Herne.

Lam, P. (2016). Chinese culture and coaching in Hong Kong. *International Journal of Evidence Based Coaching and Mentoring, 14*(1), 57–73.

Li, P. P., Leung, K., Chen, C. C., & Luo, J. D. (2012). Indigenous research on Chinese management: What and how. *Management and Organization Review, 8*(1), 7–24.

Lysgaard, S. (1955). Adjustment in a foreign society: Norwegian fulbright grantees visiting the United States. *International Social Science Bulletin, 7*, 45–51.

McDonald, B. (2014). Coaching whiteness: Stories of 'Pacifica exotica' in Australia high school rugby. *Sport, Education and Society, 21*(3), 465–482.

McSweeney, B. (2002). Hofstede's model of national cultural differences and their consequences: A triumph of faith a failure of analysis. *Human Relations, 55*(1), 89–118.

Milner, J., Ostmeier, E., & Franke, R. (2013). Critical incidents in cross-cultural coaching: The view from German coaches. *International Journal of Evidence Based Coaching and Mentoring, 11*(2), 19–32.

Nangalia, L., & Nangalia, A. (2010). The coaching in Asian society: Impact of social hierarchy on the coaching relationship. *International Journal of Evidence Based Coaching and Mentoring, 8*(1), 51–66.

Passmore, J. (Ed.). (2013). *Diversity in coaching: Working with gender, culture, race and age* (2nd ed.). London: Kogan Page.

Persson, S., Agostini, B., & Kléber, A. (2017). In Praise of a Flexible and Sustainable HR Support, *Journal of Management Development, 36*(3), 298–308.

Persson, S., & Shrivastava, P. (2016). Sustainable development of human resources inspired by Chinese philosophies: A repositioning based on François Jullien's works. *Management and Organization Review, 12*(3), 503–524.

Persson, S., & Wasieleski, D. (2015). The seasons of the psychological contract: Overcoming the silent transformations of the employer-employee relationship. *Human Resource Management Review, 25*(4), 368–383.

Plaister-Ten, J. (2013). Raising culturally-derived awareness and building culturally-appropriate responsibility: The development of the cross-cultural kaleidoscope. *International Journal of Evidence Based Coaching and Mentoring, 11*(2), 53–69.

Rosinski, P. (2003). *Coaching across cultures.* Boston, MA: Nicholas Brealey.

Rosinski, P. (2010). *Global coaching: An integrated approach for long-lasting results.* London: Nicholas Brealey.

Salomaa, R., & Mäkelä, L. (2017). Coaching for career capital development: A study of expatriates' narratives. *International Journal of Evidence Based Coaching and Mentoring, 15*(1), 114–132.

Sherpa Coaching (2015). *Executive global coaching survey.* Retrieved from www.sherpacoaching.com

Shoukry, H. (2016). Coaching for emancipation: A framework for coaching in oppressive environments. *International Journal of Evidence Based Coaching and Mentoring, 14*(2), 15–30.

Shrivastava, P., & Persson, S. (2014). A theory of strategy: Learning from China: From walking to sailing. *M@n@gement, 17*(1), 621–644.

van Nieuwerburgh, C. (2017). Interculturally sensitive coaching. In T. Bachkirova, G. Spence, & D. Drake (Eds.), *The sage handbook of coaching* (pp. 439–452). London: Sage Publications.

Wenzel, C. H. (2010). Isolation and involvement: Wilhem von Humbold, François Jullien and more. *Philosophy East and West, 60*(4), 458–475.

Wierzbicka, A. (2014). *Imprisoned in English.* New York, NY: Oxford University Press.

6   Contracts in coaching

Introduction

Contracts in coaching are often portrayed as building blocks of successful interventions. However, their complexity should not be underestimated.

First, it is important to acknowledge the existence of a *multiplicity* of contracts (Fielder & Starr, 2008). These include the *learning contract* – mainly covering the purpose and objectives to be achieved, as well as timelines and potential types of assessment; the *legal contract* – i.e., service standards, guidelines for relevant business practices, confidentiality statements, cost and payment details; and the *relational contract* – guidelines on honesty, openness, and reliability between the coachee and the coach as well as details relating to giving and receiving feedback, availability of the coach, follow-up, and documentation, etc. These contracts aim to ensure positive outcomes for all stakeholders by clarifying roles, establishing clear objectives, defining business and interpersonal practices, and avoiding misunderstandings (Ennis, Goodman, Otto, & Stern, 2012).

Second, these contracts can be both *explicit* and *implicit* (Fatien, 2012). While the legal contract is most of the time formalized and explicit, the learning and relational contracts are more often informally covered, which can potentially result in challenges.

Indeed, due diligence in defining and establishing the terms of the contract(s) might not suffice to ensure alignment between the expectations of the different stakeholders. This is precisely what this chapter will explore. We will highlight two situations in particular; the first one is related to subcontracting, and the second to confidentiality agreements.

The first case, *Coaching for a coachee or his manager?*, presents the situation of Carol, who coaches a client in the context of a subcontract. Subcontracting corresponds to a situation when a consultancy firm hires a coach or a coaching organization to provide coaching in the consultancy firm's client organization. This adds complexity as it involves additional stakeholders and different types of relationships, accountabilities, and deliverables. Especially, as we see in Carol's case, the acting coach may not be part of the initial conversation with the client organization. This initial absence does not allow control over agenda setting or the contractual arrangement, which can cause troubles later as the intervention unfolds. In Carol's case, she is surprised by a request from her colleague who wants her to influence certain behaviors of her coachee based on his manager's request and is unsure of how to respond.

In the second case, *To tell or not to tell*, we see that while confidentiality agreements are an integral part of any coaching contract, coaches' views might vary on how to approach them. We look at the case of Anna who, early in her career, always used confidentiality agreements as part of contracting, but later decided to drop them completely as they were an impediment to her way of practicing.

Case 6.1. Coaching for a coachee or his manager?

Carol was an executive coach at a coaching firm, which was hired by a consulting firm to work with several executives from one of their client organizations. Being subcontracted to another consulting firm has its share of complexities; for example, Carol's coaching firm only met the client organization after the coaching agenda had been established with the consulting firm. In effect, Carol and her colleagues were supposed to deliver what was agreed upon without their input or consent.

More specifically, Carol was coaching Ben, one of the executives in the client company, and Carol's colleague, Michael, another executive coach, was working with Ben's manager. Usually Carol made sure to meet with her coachee's manager at the start of the assignment in order to ensure that the expectations were clear and the goals aligned. But in this case, this wasn't possible, given that the subcontracting consulting firm had already had these conversations with the client organization.

A few weeks after the coaching began, Ben's manager told his coach, Michael: "I really want to see some changes in Ben's behavior. Can you make sure he gets that out of coaching?" But this request was not part of the initially agreed-upon coaching goals. Michael came to Carol and said: "You need to make this happen with Ben." That request created some tension between the two coaches because Carol felt that her colleague was asking her to depart from the originally agreed-upon contract. She didn't think it was within the scope of her job, and she thought to herself, "Am I supposed to be doing that?" As a result, she felt some tension, resistance, and confusion around her role.

Reflexive questions

- What do you do when a manager or other stakeholder wants to change the coaching agenda midstream?
- How might subcontracting alter the relationships and power dynamics in a coaching assignment?

Working with the intermediary of the consulting firm was definitely different from her usual coaching assignments. When she contracted directly with clients, she had more control over the process, e.g., the relationships, communication, and possibility to clarify expectations. This situation presented several complexities for her. First, she needed to look after Ben's best interest, making sure he was benefitting directly, and she wanted to be honest with him. Second, she needed to handle the relationship with her colleague, Michael, who felt that the request from Ben's manager was reasonable. From her perspective, Ben's manager was the one who really needed to make some changes, and she didn't want to see her coachee become a scapegoat. Finally, she had to take into account the subcontracting firm and the contract signed with her coaching firm. In the end, she wondered whether she could use this situation and the new information acquired through Michael to help her client. But she had to be careful not to disclose her source in order to ensure complete confidentiality. Carol finally decided to go back to her colleague and explain her thoughts and feelings about the situation. She said that she wouldn't modify the original agenda unless clearly discussed between Ben and his manager. She also encouraged Michael to seize this opportunity to coach Ben's manager on how to step up and perform his role as a manager.

Reflexive questions

- Would Carol's situation raise an ethical issue for you? Why?
- What would you have done in Carol's position? How would you have handled your colleague?
- What do you think the role of the consulting firm should be in such a situation?

Commentary 6.1.a

Charline S. Russo

Contracting in coaching is key to "facilitate more productive outcomes and . . . reduce the likelihood of misunderstandings and failed expectations in the future" (Bluckert, 2006, p. 38). This is achieved by "establishing both the personal and organizational objectives for the coaching and by clarifying everyone's roles and responsibilities in the process" (p. 39). In this case, a lack of clarity on the objectives and roles of the different stakeholders results in Carol's tension, resistance, and overall confusion, as well as potential missed opportunities or even damages for her client, Ben. Moreover, we see how hidden agendas coexist with explicit agendas. Additional complexity is created by the role the subcontracting firm plays in this situation, multiplying the number of stakeholders and related contracts.

In fact, a coaching engagement typically includes different interrelated contracts; Berne (1974) identified three: *Administrative, Professional,* and *Psychological.*

The *Administrative Contract* is the business contract, including the terms of the contract (i.e., frequency and length of meetings, start and end dates, fees, services provided, legal limitations, etc.) (Hay, 1995). The *Professional Contract* includes achievable objectives, methodology, observable results, as well as clarification of the stakeholders' roles in realizing agreed-upon results (Krausz, 2005). This contract is often referred to as the Three Cornered Contract (English, 1975), as it is usually between the direct manager, the coachee, and the coach. Occasionally a fourth corner, Human Resources, is included.

The *Psychological Contract* tends to relate more to the personal unspoken needs of those directly involved in the coaching engagement (Berne, 1966) and to the "beliefs" that each stakeholder has regarding the terms and conditions of their relationships (Rousseau, 1989). In other words, the psychological contract includes both a "promissory" contract that coaches make with their clients regarding the coaching relationship and the clients' expectations (Salicru, 2009).

What are the different contracts in Carol's case? Who are the stakeholders, and how explicit are the various contracts to each stakeholder? What are the consequences?

The *Administrative Contract* is set between the consultancy firm (with Carol's coaching firm as a sub-contractor) and the organization client.

This case adds another layer of complexity because Carol's coaching firm is a sub-contractor to the consulting organization who contracted with the client organization. The *Administrative Contract* took place before Carol entered the picture, so she could not have any input on the agreed-upon contract. Additionally, she seems to have accepted the assignment without clear awareness of its components. Consequently, Carol, as the sub-contractor, is "supposed to deliver what was agreed upon without her input or consent." By accepting this, she is merely a "deliverer," not someone whose added value also lies in the establishment of the contract. This raises the question: When does a coaching contract really begin? Is administrative contracting not already part of the coaching process?

The *Professional Contract*, as English (1975) noted, is the Three Cornered Contract. However, in some cases, such as this one, there are potentially many more Corners, which include here the consulting organization, the client organization, the coaching organization where Carol works, Ben's Manager, Michael (Ben's manager's coach), Ben (Carol's coachee), and Carol. This challenge to the perimeters of the contract creates confusion for Carol. She is left unclear of what she is expected to deliver on when Ben's manager (through Michael) introduces new expectations, to change Ben's behaviors, violating the Professional Contract.

The *Psychological Contract* entails the unspoken expectations. While they can remain unspoken during a coaching engagement, they can surface, too, as in this case. As Lee (2012) noted, a psychological contract becomes evident primarily when it is violated. Ben's manager's unspoken expectations surface when he tries to use coaching to change Ben's behavior. While this request certainly raises ethical issues (that of behavioral conformation, but this is another topic!), we can see how ethical dilemmas arise when unspoken expectations are not made clear during the initial meetings. These dilemmas come from "wishful interpretations and unrealistic expectations by a client" (Lee, 2012, p. 52). In my experience, this lack of clarity and understanding with the client organization, with the manager, and with the coachee, leads to difficult conversations later in the process, usually around the achievement of results, or in this case, the lack of achievement since the request was not part of the original understanding or agreement.

Still, it is not unusual for coaches to work within subcontracted assignments: however, this should not prevent the coach from achieving an effective and potentially successful coaching engagement. Thus, when a coach inherits a subcontract, such as in Carol's situation, what are "healthy" ways of proceeding? For Carol, this will mean trying to follow her usual process as much as possible.

First, in regard to the *Administrative Contract*, Carol can ask for access to the consulting company-client organization contract for clarification even though she was not part of its establishment.

Second, Carol has an opportunity to correct the *Professional Contract* at this early stage of the engagement. She can review the agreement made by the consulting organization with the client organization and ensure clarity and alignment in expectations. She can then meet with the client organization and stakeholders – the other corners of this contract – and review the need for coaching (why?), the expectations (what?), its temporality (why now? For how long?), and the intervention process (how?). As Ben's coach, Carol can meet with him individually to discuss pending issues. She can talk also with Michael, Ben's coach, to review her process, the boundaries of confidentiality, and the zones of privacy that are necessary for the system to support the coaching process.

Third, regarding the *Psychological Contract*, given its implicit nature, it is paradoxical to want to have it made explicit. Still, coaches should be aware that these implicit expectations are always part of an engagement. And this case provides a good demonstration of how unspoken expectations create confusion and tension. In Carol's case, an added complexity lies in the fact that part of the psychological contract was made explicit not by Ben's manager himself, but by his coach, Michael. This creates an additional interference in the process. To me, Michael's discussion with Carol seems inappropriate. It violates client confidentiality and challenges ethical coaching behavior. Additionally, it sends the message to Ben's manager that Michael could influence or dictate his wishes to Ben's coach, Carol. Carol's decision to speak with her colleague, Michael, and explain her thoughts and feelings about the situation was the proper step to take. Reviewing the *Professional Contract* with Michael seems appropriate. However, Carol's encouragement of Michael "to seize this opportunity and coach Ben's manager on how to step up and perform his role" is now Carol "invading" the coaching space between Michael and his client, Ben's manager. Michael did this with Carol, and it was inappropriate. Carol now returns the "favor" by telling Michael what his client should do. Her request is inappropriate because of its partiality: she is basing this feedback on her interaction with Michael. What other data does she have? She doesn't even have feedback from her coachee, Ben, at this point. All she has is Michael's relayed information.

Overall, what stands out for me is that Carol's focus on Ben, her coachee, comes late (hardly at all) in this process. If Carol had focused on her client in the beginning of the process, she could have either avoided or at least mitigated many of these issues. This corner of the *Professional Contract* and the personal aspects of the *Psychological Contract* between Ben and Carol would not have been so overlooked. She also could have avoided the ethical challenges she is now facing, specifically client identification and client confidentiality in the coaching engagement.

Table 6.1 is a snapshot of the issues discussed in the contracting focus on Carol's coaching dilemma.

Table 6.1 Types of contracts as identified in Carol's case

Type of contract	Definition	Application to Carol's case	Recommendations
Administrative	Business contract, including frequency and length of meetings, contract start and end dates, fees, services provided, legal limitations, etc.	Agreed upon between client organization and consulting firm before Carol entered the picture and not shared with her.	Carol asks for access to this contract to understand the agreed-upon terms.
Professional	Objectives and roles, methodology, observable results.	The Five Corners were not aligned, no clear expectations of each corner in the coaching process.	Carol reviews the *Professional Contract* with the consulting firm and client organization, then sets two meetings: 1) with Ben and his manager and 2) with Michael.
Psychological	Personal unspoken needs of those directly involved usually including concealed or unknown wishes and concerns.	Not discussed with the "clients" in this process. By not discussing these, each client may be unaware of the needs they are expecting to be met in this coaching engagement.	Carol meets with each client to go over the intervention, attentive to alignment and misalignment. These surfaced needs, originally unknown, often derail a coaching engagement if they are not unearthed.

Addressing these multiple (implicit and explicit) contract-related issues in the beginning of the engagement seems essential for a positive coaching relationship. Yes, some of these discussions are difficult. But they do not really become less difficult as the engagement progresses. In fact, they can become more problematic and arduous, often taking the coaching relationship down a spiraling cone of failed relationships and disappointment. I have learned to attend to the three contracts – *Administrative*, *Professional*, and *Psychological* – as part of my process, in the beginning, and to revisit them with stakeholders during the engagement. These discussions allow for the re-establishment of confidentiality guidelines and zones of privacy with the coachee, their manager, and the client organization. They secure the trust relationship for all participants, including the coach.

Commentary 6.1.b

Felipe Paiva

Coaching interventions entail multiple types of configurations, from the simple, direct relationship between the coach and the paying coachee, to Carol's complex multi-layered relationships involving four stakeholders: the coachee, the client company, the consulting firm, and the coaching firm. Her role seems to be predetermined by the prior arrangements made between the consulting firm and the coaching firm, with little regard to her personal operational and ethical approaches.

It seems to me that the consulting firm prescribed coaching as an instrumental solution to facilitate a change process inside the client company, in accordance with management's expectations of the coach to inform and carry messages across the organization. In this case, these expectations were not aligned with Carol's. Further, the roles, responsibilities, and ethics were not aligned among the different stakeholders – Carol, the coaching firm, the coaching team, the consulting firm, and the client firm. In this complex web of relationships, the absence of aligned expectations left Carol in uncertainty, doubt, and discomfort.

One way of alleviating such uncertainty and discomfort could be for Carol to reach a stronger alignment with her contractor, the coaching firm, in terms of the procedures for the coaching job. This would entail clarifying roles, responsibilities, boundaries, and ethical standards. As a subcontracted coach, Carol could have clarified issues of confidentiality and supervision, communication between coaches, and communication with the client company and the consulting firm in order to reduce ambiguity. However, negotiating with larger organizations may represent a difficulty for individual coaches as coaching firms may have different approaches.

Another strategy for addressing this ambiguity is to clarify the coaching objectives with the coachee and his boss. Starting a coaching job without aligning the expectations, objectives, and procedures with the coachee and his boss may represent a risk to quality coaching. In Carol's case, as it was not allowed, she could have worked with her coachee to clarify the objectives directly with his boss. Also, Carol could have addressed the issue with her coaching partner, Michael, defining boundaries to their collaboration in this organizational context. Additionally, she could have challenged Michael to work with his coachee to address the objectives with Carol's coachee directly.

In the absence of the coaching firm's supervision, Carol should have talked to Michael to clarify boundaries and establish the limits of their information exchange and expectations regarding the work to be done.

As the case suggests, Carol is in a double bind situation. On one hand, she wants to maintain a good relationship with the coaching firm, and on the other, she aims to be true to her professional ethics, doing the best for her coaching client.

From a commercial perspective, the coaching firm is Carol's main client, capable of providing multiple opportunities in the long term, while the coaching client may represent a one-time job. From a coaching practitioner's perspective, the coaching client is the main client, as at the core, he is the object of the service.

As markets shift and companies move to relying upon one-stop shops and single contracts for many operations (businesses and regions), larger coaching firms are forming alliances with local coaching firms (nationally and internationally), or hiring local coaches directly, mixing different practices that could prove confusing for coaches, organizational clients, and coachees.

Coaching firms with large contracts have the strength of position to impose their terms, especially in a market saturated with coaches. This case illustrates the difficulties for independent coaches to negotiate terms with their contractors while maintaining their professional integrity.

In the absence of clear guidelines or in ambiguous contexts, the coach has the responsibility to clarify and set the basis for the coaching relationship, even if this means doing more than described in the contract and without pay (e.g., including an extra session to clarify objectives with the coachee's boss).

Case 6.2. To tell or not to tell

Early in her coaching career, Anna used to follow the code of conduct of her professional coaching association to the letter. This included maintaining confidentiality regarding the coaching assignment. With each new client, she explained that everything discussed in the coaching sessions would remain strictly confidential. While she would provide a final report at the end of the coaching intervention, it would focus solely on the progress made in relation to the initially agreed-upon agenda. In addition, she included confidentiality forms as part of the contract.

Reflexive questions

* What are your views on confidentiality when it comes to coaching?
* How do you feel about confidentiality agreements?
* What type of information do you think should remain confidential and what type of information can or should be shared with third parties?

Over the years, Anna began to feel that confidentiality agreements were a bit restrictive. And while she focused 100% on building relationships with both the coachee and the manager, her view was that, first and foremost, she worked for the organization. So, whenever she was asked to coach an executive because he or she was failing the organization in some way, either through performance or behavior, she believed that she needed to ensure the best interests of the organization. Further, she felt that if the organization was paying her, then she needed to deliver what they wanted.

As a result, today she probably often discloses to the manager more than other coaches would. For example, she would give an honest assessment of her coachee without sharing that with the individual himself. She considers it to be up to the organization to use this information the way they see fit. From her perspective, the information could be helpful for the future development of the coachee after the coaching contract has ended.

Of course, she wouldn't share any personal information, such as issues related to the coachee's private life or family. But she has no problem sharing anything that she feels is pertinent to the coachee's performance or could impact the organization. For her, this is totally impersonal, and there is no point in having lingering bad feelings about it.

Reflexive questions

- What do you think of Anna's attitude toward confidentiality issues?
- Do you agree with Anna's view on the organization as her main client?

Commentary 6.2.a

Julian P. Humphreys

What do we lose and what do we gain when we do away with privacy? This is the question at the heart of Case 6.2., *To tell or not to tell*, in particular when Anna, the coach in the case, matter-of-factly claims that the information she is sharing about her coachee with the sponsor organization "is totally impersonal, and there is no point in having lingering bad feelings about it." Indeed, according to Anna, "The information could be helpful for the future development of the coachee after the coaching contract has ended."

Well, yes, it could, but it could also *not* be helpful for the future development of the coachee. And to understand why this is so requires first taking a moment to consider the purpose and value of confidentiality agreements more broadly. In doing so, I will take a philosophical approach based on a performative perspective, one that sees words – written or spoken – as not just describing the world, but acting upon the world and hence producing worlds as we experience them (Austin, 1962). And, to avoid this discussion becoming overly abstract and theoretical, I will apply this approach to the two contrasting scenarios described in Case 6.2.

In scenario one, Anna follows the code of conduct of her professional coaching association to the letter. We don't know what professional coaching association she belongs to, but let's assume it's the International Coach Federation (ICF), currently the largest and most globally recognized. To act in accordance with the ICF's Code of Ethics, Anna is required to "have a clear agreement about how coaching information will be exchanged among coach, coachee and sponsor" (ICF, 2015), and she is also required to communicate the conditions under which confidentiality may not be maintained, with both coachee and sponsor agreeing, in writing, to that limit of confidentiality.

It is important to note that – in this scenario – there is nothing that precludes Anna from making an agreement with the coachee and sponsor organization that she will provide "an honest assessment of her coachee without sharing that with the individual himself" (Case 6.2). However, to do so without the explicit consent of the coachee would put her on the wrong side of her association's code of ethics.

In the second scenario, where she discloses to the manager "more than other coaches would," she presumably[1] does not negotiate a confidentiality agreement that includes the right to share information freely with the organization, instead choosing to empower the organization with information about the coachee that she a) does not share with the coachee himself, and b) has not been authorized by the coachee to share with the organization. She does this because she believes she has an obligation to do what's best for the organization that is paying her, which includes, from this perspective, providing the organization with "an honest assessment of her coachee," among other possible disclosures.

Viewing both scenarios from a performative perspective, what worlds are being created in each scenario?

In scenario one, coach, coachee, and sponsor exist in a world governed by rules set out in a code of ethics – a constitution if you will – drawn up by senior members of the coaching community under the aegis of the professional coaching association. This document, like any code of ethics, is the result of extensive negotiations, informed by best practices and legal considerations, themselves the result of negotiations, implicit and explicit, dating back millennia, with no clear origin. By agreeing to be governed by these rules, coach, coachee, and sponsor have a clear framework for building and maintaining trust, which they implicitly take to be necessary for the coaching relationship to produce the most effective outcomes for all concerned.

In scenario two, things are a lot less clear. Does Anna tell the coachee that "issues related to the coachee's private life and family" will be held in confidence, while "anything that [Anna] feels is pertinent to the coachee's performance or could impact the organization" is not? And is that even possible? Are the private and the organizational as easily distinguishable as Anna assumes? And are her feelings a reliable enough indicator of when to share and when not to share?

There is a lot of murkiness in scenario two, and it is tempting to retreat to scenario one to avoid this murkiness. But I want to at least consider the possibility that there may be some value in Anna's more casual approach to confidentiality. I do this with some reluctance as, when I first read the case, it seemed cut and dry that Anna's cavalier approach to confidentiality was inappropriate. But there may be reasons that differ from Anna's own for why a more casual approach to confidentiality might benefit both coachee and sponsor and, as a result, Anna.

The world being created in scenario two is a world of extreme uncertainty, where each party to the relationship needs to navigate and create for themselves the context within which they all can optimally succeed. And in addressing that significant challenge, all parties to the relationship may developmentally grow to a greater extent than when an "off the shelf" solution to the problem of building and maintaining trust is implemented.

In exploring this possibility, I am influenced by Solomon and Flores' (2001) text, *Building trust in business, politics, relationships and life*, in which the authors advance this thesis:

> Trusting is something that we individually *do*; it is something we make, we create, we build, we maintain, we sustain with our promises, our commitments, our emotions, and our sense of our own integrity. . . . Authentic trust does not necessitate the exclusion of distrust. To the contrary, it embraces the possibilities of distrust and betrayal as an essential part of trust.
>
> (pp. 5–6)

In other words, in the struggle to build trust freely, without the crutch of an externally imposed set of rules and obligations, parties to the relationship are called upon to act with conscientious integrity, to *make* trust rather than simply implement it. Thus, the trust that is built is potentially more real, substantial, and transformative.

Authentic trust, however, requires a great deal of pre-existing ethical maturity and commitment on the parts of all parties to the relationship, and whether you believe this is the case depends in part on your view of human nature. Are you, like Thomas Hobbes, a pessimist when it comes to human nature, believing that human beings are essentially selfish, that without the harsh imposition of externally imposed rules life will be "nasty, brutish and short"? Or are you an optimist like John Locke, believing that humans are essentially social creatures, capable of negotiating their own rules and governing themselves peaceably?

For my own part, I can relate *somewhat* to the shift Anna identifies in her own approach to confidentiality agreements. Early in my coaching career I, like Anna, was very much reliant on my coaching association's code of ethics for managing the coach-coachee-sponsor relationship. But I found myself often encountering situations where I felt compromised in one way or another. Either the sponsor would provide me with confidential information about the coachee that then made me feel I was keeping something from the coachee; or the sponsor would ask me for information about the coachee that put me in a seemingly no-win situation – I could either invoke the code of ethics and upset the sponsor, or compromise it and keep the sponsor happy.

These days, I still refer to the code of ethics in my first meeting with the coachee, but I do so in passing – more or less as a formality. I do this because I don't want the formal mechanism for building and maintaining trust to distract from the informal process of *actually* building and maintaining trust. Ironically, since becoming less dependent on the code of ethics I have found myself significantly less compromised ethically. If a sponsor provides me with confidential information on the coachee, I advocate strongly for the sponsor to provide that feedback directly to the coachee or, if that's not possible, I find out why, from the sponsor's perspective. Similarly, if the sponsor asks me for confidential information about the coachee, I don't simply invoke the code of ethics, but instead ask the sponsor for more information – what is it they are really wanting to know, and what's getting in the way of that information passing freely between coachee and sponsor? In other words, I coach my way out of potentially compromising situations, as opposed to simply invoking the code of ethics.

The relationship between sponsor and coachee is enhanced as a result of the coaching engagement, rather than diminished by it. Barriers to communication that could have gone up or stayed up as a result of invoking a formal confidentiality agreement are weakened or removed, and the coach-coachee-sponsor relationship goes from being mediated and structured to informally co-created and co-responsible.

There are many potential dangers in foregoing a rigid reliance on a code of ethics in favor of a more improvised, spontaneous, mutual ethics. But there are also substantial benefits. As Solomon and Flores (2001) note, "People who authentically trust one another live in a more vibrant and adventurous world than those who do not" (p. 91). Following the spirit of the code of ethics rather than the letter means that more authentically trusting relationships become possible. Just as a society where everyone feels compelled to obey the law at all times feels overly constrained (we all want to feel we *could* jaywalk, even if we ultimately choose not to), so does a triadic relationship that is rigidly bound by a code of ethics.

In conclusion, therefore, a) I disagree with Anna's reasons for lessening her reliance on the code of ethics, b) I have concerns that she is being irresponsible in her relationship with both sponsor and coachee, and c) I'm not convinced she has the ethical maturity to embrace the complexity of building authentically trusting relationships. Still, I cannot condemn outright the search for a better alternative.

Commentary 6.2.b

CB Bowman

What is underlining this case is the issue of confidentiality as related to the coaches' commitment to the field of executive coaching. However, what should be discussed is the coaches' relationship to the field AND THE LEGAL ASPECTS OF COACHING. Aside from Anna's belief system, which seems to favor her client, her beliefs may lead not only to built-in bias, but also to disclosure which directly conflicts with the *laws of confidentiality*.

Often confusing in the world of coaching is having confidentiality agreements as part of a code of conduct. Codes of conducts are professional association mandates and have nothing to do with the actual legalities of confidentiality although confidentiality clauses may be stated in the code of conduct.

While the executive coaching profession is not governed by the same legal system as older, more established and federally mandated professions, we would be wise to review the laws of these organizations and use them as a guide so that coaching matures as a profession with policies and regulations in place.

In its 2007 International Good Practice Guidance, "Defining and Developing an Effective Code of Conduct for Organizations," the International Federation of Accountants provides the following working definition: "Principles, values, standards, or rules of behavior that guide the decisions, procedures and systems of an organization in a way that (a) contributes to the welfare of its key stakeholders, and (b) respects the rights of all constituents affected by its operations" (International Federation of Accountants, 2007).

A code of conduct can be further defined as "a written set of guidelines issued by an organization to its workers and management to help them conduct their actions in accordance with its primary values and ethical standards" (Business Dictionary, n.d.).

Confidentiality is defined, as "a set of rules or a promise that limits access or places restrictions on certain types of information" (TechTarget, n.d.).

A **confidentiality agreement** is a legal document which is also known as a **non-disclosure agreement** or NDA; it is a contract that involves mutual confidentiality and a non-disclosure agreement between two or more parties in which the parties express their intention to disclose certain information for specified purposes and agree that such information will be used only for the intended purposes; furthermore, other access to the information will be restricted (Massachusetts Medical Society, 2014).

However, what most coaches and coachees do not realize is this agreement does not afford the same rights of protection, as do such agreements/contacts between a doctor and patient or between an attorney and client.

The concept of "doctor-patient confidentiality" derives from English **common law** and is codified in many states' statutes. It is based on ethics, not law, and goes at least as far back as the Roman Hippocratic Oath taken by physicians. It is different from "doctor-patient privilege,"[2] which is a legal concept. Both, however, are called upon in legal matters to establish the extent to which ethical duties of confidentiality apply to legal privilege. Legal privilege involves the right to withhold **evidence** from **discovery** and/or the right to refrain from disclosing or divulging information gained within the context of a "special relationship." Special relationships include those between doctors and patients, attorneys and clients, priests and confessors or confiders, guardians and their wards, etc.

The Oath of Hippocrates, traditionally sworn to by newly licensed physicians, includes the promise that "Whatever, in connection with my professional service, or not in connection with it, I see or hear, in the life of men, which ought not to be spoken of abroad, I will not divulge, as reckoning that all such should be kept secret." The laws of Hippocrates further states, "Those things which are sacred, are to be imparted only to sacred persons; and it is not lawful to impart them to the profane until they have been initiated into the mysteries of the science."

Doctor-patient confidentiality stems from the special relationship created when a prospective patient seeks the advice, care, and/or treatment of a physician. It is based upon the general principle that individuals seeking medical help or advice should not be hindered or inhibited by fear that their medical concerns or conditions will be disclosed to others. Patients entrust personal knowledge of themselves to their physicians, which creates an uneven relationship in that the vulnerability is one-sided. There is generally an expectation that physicians will hold that special knowledge in confidence and use it exclusively for the benefit of the patient.

The professional duty of confidentiality covers not only what patients may reveal to doctors, but also what doctors may independently conclude or form an opinion about, based on their **examination** or **assessment** of patients. Confidentiality covers all medical records (including X-rays, lab reports, etc.) as well as communications between patient and doctor, and it generally includes communications between the patient and other professional staff working with the doctor.

The duty of confidentiality continues even after patients stop seeing or being treated by their doctors. Once doctors are under a duty of confidentiality, they cannot divulge any medical information about their patients to third persons without patient consent. There are, however, exceptions to this rule (USLegal, n.d.a).

Attorney-client privilege is an evidentiary rule that protects communications between a client and his or her attorney and keeps those communications confidential. It protects both attorneys and their clients from being compelled to disclose confidential communications between them made for the purpose of furnishing or obtaining legal advice or assistance. The privilege is designed to foster frank, open, and uninhibited discourse between attorney and client so that the client's legal needs are competently addressed by a fully prepared attorney who is cognizant of all the relevant information the client can provide. The attorney-client privilege may be raised during any type of legal proceeding, civil, criminal, or administrative, and at any time during those proceedings, pre-trial, during trial, or post-trial.

However, even when all the requirements have been met, the courts can still compel disclosure of the information sought. The courts base exceptions to the privilege on rule 501 of the Federal Rules of Evidence, which states, "The recognition of a privilege based on a confidential relationship . . . should be determined on a case-by-case basis." In examining the privilege on a case-by-case basis, the courts weigh the benefits to be gained by upholding the privilege (preserving the confidence between attorney and client) against the harms that may be caused if they deny it (the loss of information valuable to the opposing party).

The attorney-client privilege is considered as one of the strongest privileges available under law (USLegal, n.d.b).

Given the above, the question of validity and use of confidentiality agreements comes into play. They tend to be "feel good" documents with only **superficial** privileges between the coach, coachee, and the hiring party.

Having said this, I believe that all information should be closely held between the coach and the coachee except if harm to self and/or others is on the table. Any other information might be released to specific parties with clarity around intended use and scope. Further, the party receiving the information should be held accountable to the same confidentiality agreement as between coach and coachee.

Further, the coach explained that she would provide a final report at the end of the coaching intervention. It would focus solely on the progress made in relation to the initially agreed-upon agenda. This statement in itself leaves the door wide open to opportunities to reveal confidentialities. It would be a challenge to sanitize such a report to present it without revealing communications that the coachee might deem confidential. For example:

> John Smith showed remarkable understanding and use of the 5 steps of leadership by demonstrating improved communication among his staff. This resulted in less staff re-work, reduced staff overtime, and increased sales in his division.

The confidential "reveal" is his lack of effective communication techniques and how it affected the organization's profit margin, employee enhancement, and quality of life. Statements like Anna's represent a slippery slope in relation to confidentiality and certainly offer no legal protection for any of the involved parties.

To manage the exposure of possible legal repercussions, it is best to determine upfront what specifically the paying/hiring party needs to know about the success of the relationship between the coach and the coachee. A possible solution for Anna to manage confidentiality (knowing that Anna has a stated propensity to lean towards protecting the hiring party over the coachee) might be to obtain permission from the coachee to allow the manager to observe behavior, followed by a group "lessons learned discussion." In the scenario I've presented, the hiring party might only need to *observe*; the result is less staff re-work, reduced staff overtime, and increased sales without receiving a report from the coach. Observable results can be a powerful tool when trying to avoid breaking confidences.

Conclusion

The complexity of having different stakeholders and multiple types of contracts combined in the relatively young and rapidly evolving profession of coaching requires flexibility and malleability on the part of the coach in handling contracting issues to maintain high standards and ethics at all times.

Our experts have adopted different perspectives (from a philosophical or a performative perspective to a strictly legal one) and put emphasis on different types of contracts in coaching (from administrative and legal to psychological and relational contracts) to dissect the issue of contracting in coaching.

A first key point across all commentaries is the importance of ensuring clarity in the expectations of the different stakeholders, the coaching process, and the ethical standards at all times and across the different phases of the coaching relationship.

That said, issues might emerge over the intervention. As shown in our cases, the interests of the different stakeholders might surface later in the relationship, or even change as a result of coaching. In fact, we suggest looking at coaching contract(s) as a living part of the coaching relationship: the contract(s) that can evolve and develop along with the unfolding of the coaching relationship. And it seems the coach's responsibility to ensure that such complexities and related changes are dealt with in a way that maintains the rights and best interests of the different stakeholders (Fielder & Starr, 2008). According to our experts, helpful and healthy practices to achieve that responsibility range from shedding light on and clarifying any ambiguous matters as they arise to maintaining open communication channels and trust with the different stakeholders, and revisiting the different contracts when needed by seeing beyond the written codes, guidelines, or contracts.

Notes

1 It is not clear from the case exactly what provisions have been made here.
2 Doctor–Patient Privilege is a legal privilege, arising from a doctor's obligation of confidentiality. It refers to the right to exclude from discovery and evidence in a legal proceeding any confidential communication that a patient makes to a physician for the purpose of diagnosis or treatment, unless the patient consents to the disclosure. This privilege belongs to the patient, not the doctor, and therefore, only a patient may waive the privilege. A patient can sue the physician for damages if the doctor breaches the confidence by testifying.

   In the US, the Federal Rules of Evidence do not recognize doctor-patient privilege. At the state level, the extent of the privilege varies depending on the law of the applicable jurisdiction. For example, in Texas there is only a limited physician–patient privilege in criminal proceedings and civil cases. https://definitions.uslegal.com/d/doctor-patient-privilege/

References

Austin, J. L. (1962). *How to do things with words*. Cambridge, MA: Harvard University Press.
Berne, E. (1966). *Principles of group treatment*. New York, NY: Grove Press.
Berne, E. (1974). *What do you say after you say hello?: The psychology of human destiny*. New York, NY: Bantam Books (original work published 1972).
Bluckert, P. (2006). *Psychological dimensions of executive coaching* (pp. 38–39). Buckingham, UK: Open University Press.

Business Dictionary (n.d.) Code of ethics definition. Retrieved from www.businessdiction ary.com/definition/code-of-ethics.html

English, F. (1975). The three-cornered contract. *Transactional Analysis Journal*, 5(19), 152–154.

Ennis, S., Goodman, R., Otto, J., & Stern, L. (Eds.). (2012). *The executive coaching handbook: principles and guidelines for a successful coaching partnership.* Wellesley, MA: The Executive Coaching Forum.

Fatien, P. (2012). Ethical issues in coaching. In M. Esposito, M. Smith, & P. O'Sullivan (Eds.), *Business ethics: A critical approach: Integrating ethics across the business world* (pp. 302–316). London: Routledge.

Fielder, J. H., & Starr, L. M. (2008). What's the big deal about coaching contracts? *The International Journal of Coaching in Organizations*, 4, 14–27.

Hay, J. (1995). *Transformational mentoring.* London, UK: Sherwood Publishing.

International Coaching Federation (2015). *Code of ethics.* Retrieved from www.coachfedera tion.org/about/ethics.aspx?ItemNumber=854

International Federation of Accountants (2007). *International good practice guidance.* Retrieved from www.ifac.org/publications-resources/defining-and-developing-effective-code-conduct-organizations

Krausz, R. K. (2005). Transactional executive coaching. *Transactional Analysis Journal*, 35(4), 368.

Lee, R. J. (2012). The role of contracting in coaching: Balancing individual client and organizational issues. In J. Passmore, D. B. Peterson, & T. Freire (Eds.), *The Wiley-Blackwell handbook of the psychology of coaching and mentoring* (pp. 40–57). Chichester, West Sussex, UK: John Wiley & Sons, Ltd.

Massachusetts Medical Society (2014). *Mutual confidentiality and non disclosure agreement.* Retrieved from www.massmed.org/Physicians/Practice-Management/Practice-Ownership-and-Operations/Mutual-Confidentiality-and-Non-Disclosure-Agreement/#.WgXFEoZrwyk

Rousseau, D. M. (1989). Psychological and implied contracts in organizations. *Employee Responsibilities and Rights Journal*, 2(2), 121–139.

Salicru, S. (2009). *The impact of the psychological contract in executive coaching.* Paper presented at the Australian and New Zealand Academy of Management (ANZAM) Conference, December, Melbourne (Australia).

Solomon, R. C., & Flores, F. (2001). *Building trust in business, politics, relationships, and life.* New York, NY: Oxford University Press.

TechTarget (n.d.). *Confidentiality definition.* Retrieved from http://whatis.techtarget.com/definition/confidentiality

USLegal (n.d.a). *Doctor patient confidentiality.* Retrieved from https://healthcare.uslegal.com/doctor-patient-confidentiality/

USLegal (n.d.b). *Attorney-client privilege law and legal definition.* Retrieved from https://defini tions.uslegal.com/a/attorney-client-privilege/

7   Money in coaching

Introduction

Money is "many-faceted," holding multiple roles in relation to all professions in general and to the coaching profession in particular. It feeds, it rewards and motivates, it overcomes barriers, and it opens doors, but it also distracts, vulgarizes, and distorts (May, 1999). Given that coaching is a paid profession, money is definitely an unavoidable – even if often avoided – issue.

First, from the paying client's perspective (often the organization), money plays an important role in the coaching relationship given that coaching can be a costly investment, with rates exceeding $500 per hour at the executive level (Conference Board, 2008 report). Accordingly, organizations are constantly seeking evidence for the value of the coaching they are investing in.

From the coach's perspective, this activity is certainly a source of income. That said, like in any helping profession, money issues may come second to the desire to help, and coaches' commitment to their clients often "transcends" the financial interest of the intervention (May, 1999). Here benefits are not appreciated only in monetary terms, but in more self-fulfilling terms (derived from the satisfaction that the coach gains from helping another person).

Chapter 7 first examines the situation of coaches trying to get established as independent professionals, whether it is a first career choice, or a career change as we see with most coaches (Louis, 2015). This in fact brings lots of financial challenges for the coach. With an unstable source of income, the coach struggles to get customers and to make a living coaching. This might cause coaches to feel pressure to take on any coaching assignment that comes their way even if they are not totally confident in that particular assignment. This is the case of Adam, a former HR management consultant trying to establish himself as a coach, explored in *I need that client!* When he is called by an automotive company to coach Chris, a totally disengaged coachee, on performance-related issues, Adam needs to decide whether to accept the coaching assignment as he is struggling financially, or to refuse it because he feels that it won't be a successful one for the client.

In the second case, *Better late than never*, we examine a challenge that is relevant even to well-established and experienced coaches. Coaches play different roles in their practice, and develop, in addition to coaching skills, secondary skills such as sales to get new customers, marketing to build their coaching brand, general management skills, contracting and financial skills, and so on. In this case, Pat struggles from the start of a team coaching assignment, having only agreed orally on the financial terms without signing a contract. Pat has to go back and deal with the financial aspect of the contract with a difficult client, without impacting the commitment to the coaching process and clients.

Case 7.1. I need that client!

After working for many years as an HR consultant, Adam recently made a career shift to executive coaching. He was excited about his new career, as he loved coaching and believed he could bring a lot to organizations. He also loved the freedom of working as an independent coach, as opposed to joining a consulting firm. He was eager to start building a client base and a reputation; however, it proved harder than he'd originally thought. While he relied heavily on the network of connections he'd built as an HR consultant, coaching contracts over the past six months had been scarce. Consequently, he grew worried about whether he would be able to maintain his coaching business financially. So, he was thrilled when he got a call from an organization he'd worked with before as a consultant.

The HR department asked Adam to coach Chris, one of their executives, on a performance-related issue. As they put it, Chris was "a little rough around the edges"; this had been an issue with some of his customers, who all happened to have big accounts with the organization. Adam asked to meet with Chris' manager to get further information about the issue, which seemed to be aligned with HR's request. Finally, Adam met with Chris, who seemed to be quite compliant, saying that he agreed with the coaching agenda and was willing to participate. However, deep inside, Adam had doubts about Chris' authenticity. He didn't believe that Chris really accepted the need to change, and it proved difficult to establish a trusting connection with him. Adam didn't feel comfortable with how the conversation went. He felt that while Chris agreed to being coached, he wasn't actively engaged with the process. In other words, Adam felt that this coaching assignment was doomed to fail. This put him in a difficult position. He wasn't sure whether he should accept the coaching contract, which he needed financially, or reject it, because he wasn't convinced it would be successful.

Reflexive questions

- Would you accept a coaching assignment if you had doubts about its potential success?
- Do you think that early career coaches are susceptible to accepting any coaching assignment that comes their way, either for financial reasons, or in order to build their client portfolio?
- What are the consequences of doing this?

At first, Adam considered taking the coaching assignment with the understanding that he would only be paid upon a positive outcome; however, he quickly dismissed this option, as he didn't want to invest a lot of time and energy into something he didn't believe in. Adam decided to go back to the HR department and clearly express his concerns about the success of the coaching intervention. He told them that he didn't believe that Chris was ready for the process, and he didn't want to waste their money or hurt his reputation as a coach by failing to deliver. In the end, he decided to turn down the coaching assignment.

Reflexive questions

- Do you agree with Adam's decision?
- What would you have done?
- Would you ever take on a coaching assignment with payment contingent upon the client's satisfaction with the outcome?

Commentary 7.1.a

Brenda Dooley

Every executive coach has experienced the dilemma of whether or not to accept an assignment, particularly early on in one's career. Aside from the obvious motivation of potential income, there are other factors involved in this acceptance, including the desire to build and maintain a reputation, develop credibility and to secure a client base from which to springboard to other opportunities. But I would argue that the deciding factor in accepting any assignment is whether or not the coach has the professional competence and confidence to develop a meaningful relationship that would facilitate attitudinal and behavioral change for a client.

In Adam's case, however, given his relative inexperience, I sense his decision may actually have been more about his professional naivety, rather than rejecting what he felt was a resistant client. The case study does not mention whether Adam has undertaken a formal coaching qualification and developed an appropriate suite of approaches, tools, and methodologies to help guide him through issues such as this.

In reviewing this case, I will examine issues around contingent fee coaching, professional competence development, the contracting phase, and the value of supervision, and I will suggest a methodology for developing trust and rapport that might assist Adam in future assignments.

One of the most interesting aspects of this case is that despite his reservations, Adam considered taking on the assignment with the understanding that he would only be paid upon a positive outcome. Personally I haven't come across **contingent fee coaching** and would never offer or accept a coaching assignment under such conditions. Perhaps this idea can be attributed to Adam's relative inexperience, or maybe he had some experience with this approach when he worked as an HR consultant. I know that the "no foal, no fee" principle tends to operate primarily in the legal community on personal injury cases, but I haven't heard it applied in the business field. The concept of coaching being contingent upon a specific outcome raises a number of fundamental issues. While we as coaches of course seek a positive outcome and a change in the client's behavior and attitude, we cannot guarantee that to either the client or their organization. As Downs (2002, p. 235) states, "It is up to the client, not the company or the coach to ensure that benefit is derived from coaching." The old English proverb comes to mind here, "You can bring a horse to water but you can't make it drink." Second, this approach raises an ethical dilemma, in that it would directly impact the authenticity of the coaching and the motivations of the coach. Of course we all want to be paid for our work, but if payment is contingent upon a certain outcome, then that becomes the primary motivation for the coach, not the client or the coaching process. I would argue that this then objectifies the client and makes the coaching a transaction rather than a process of growth.

While the coaching industry is still unregulated, coaches who are serious about their practice and **professional competence** are committed to their ongoing professional development and, at the very least, hold membership in one of the recognized coaching associations. The Association for Coaching/European Mentoring and Coaching Council have developed a combined Global Code of Ethics which refers specifically to the practice of excellence and the ability to perform. Paragraph 4.1 states, "Members will have the qualifications, skills and experience, appropriate to meet the needs of the client and operate within the limits of their competence. Members should refer the client to more experienced or suitably qualified coaches, mentors or professionals, if appropriate." I would question whether Adam is suitably qualified or accredited as a coach, and committed to his own professional development. It strikes me that Adam rashly decided that the assignment was "doomed to failure." Despite Chris' willingness to participate in the coaching, Adam wasn't comfortable with how the initial conversation went and didn't believe him. A more experienced coach would not have made that judgment without exploring this with Chris to establish the real reason for what was felt to be resistance.

If the assignment were outside the bounds of his professional competence, Adam was correct in his decision to turn down the opportunity. However, I would also question the reasons he gave to the organization for his refusal. I take particular issue with his statement that he didn't want to hurt his reputation as a coach (hardly established given his lack of work in the past six months) by failing to deliver. It clearly shows that his primary motivation for refusing the assignment was personal and less to do with his ability or inability to help Chris. Moreover, he seems to have given little thought to Chris' reputation within the organization or how HR or management would react to being told that he wasn't ready for the process when he already said he was willing to participate. Adam should have had the confidence and competence to have explored that with Chris, and if Chris wasn't ready for the process, then he could have concluded that himself and advised management.

I was recently asked to meet with a potential coaching client, and during our "chemistry" meeting she explained that she wasn't opposed to coaching but felt she was being sent to me. She didn't really know why in that she had always received excellent ratings, and her 360-degree feedback indicated that she was performing well as a manager. Confirming the confidential nature of our discussion, I asked a simple question about what had been going on generally, and she disclosed that the only negative event in the past year was that she had been the subject of a complaint by a departing staff member. The matter had been independently investigated, determined to be a vexatious complaint, and the manager had been cleared of any wrongdoing. However, the divisional director thought it would be a good idea if she had some coaching. The client was hurt by this, and after a discussion, we concluded that she needed to go back to her manager and director to establish the coaching needs from an organizational perspective. We have met since, and the coaching relationship is well established. We are working on a development plan that has been mutually agreed upon by all parties. I see a weakness in how Adam managed the contracting process in that the coaching needs were not agreed upon by all parties.

The problem Adam faced provides an ideal coaching scenario to bring to **supervision**. On one side is the issue of whether or not he accepts the assignment and what the motivations and drivers might be for his decision. More importantly, supervision would provide him with the opportunity to discuss strategies for establishing trust and handling a resistant client as he judged Chris to be.

Each of the coaching associations recommends that their members undertake supervision, not just for accreditation purposes but as good reflective practice and ongoing professional development. It provides a safe space to discuss experiences and dilemmas with a more seasoned coach. As a novice coach, Adam should prioritize the securing of a coaching supervisor who could help him build the competence and necessary awareness, as well as to assist him in developing an ethical framework for his practice.

A supervisor might also remind Adam that the first step in the coaching process is the establishment of a **relationship of trust**, during which time the client assesses the coach's relationship skills and professional credibility (Kampa-Kokesch & Anderson, 2001). Adam indicated that he found it hard to establish a rapport and trusting connection with Chris. Clearly, he is acutely aware that trust is the foundation on which a coaching relationship is developed and maintained, but perhaps he is as yet not experienced enough to find ways to establish this important connection with the client. Trust of course is mutual, so I would ask: What could Adam have done to ensure that Chris trusted him? The answer could lie in the fact that Adam had already worked with the organization in a consultancy capacity – so perhaps Chris felt he couldn't trust him to be totally impartial because of this? Did Adam outline that his role as a coach is bounded by strict client confidentiality? Moreover, had Adam any previous knowledge of Chris other than what he gleaned during the briefing from HR and his manager? Had he already formed a judgment on Chris based on the briefing and did Chris sense that from him? While it is important to understand the coaching need from the organization's perspective, the coach uses this information as a method of developing a working hypothesis as opposed to making a pre-judgment about the client.

When meeting a client for the first time, I like to adopt the person-centered approach originally developed by Carl Rogers. According to Joseph (2010), this approach is based on the philosophical assumption that clients are their own best experts, possessing an intrinsic motivation for development and growth. The core conditions of this approach facilitate the development of a trusting relationship and require the coach to both experience and demonstrate unconditional positive regard, empathy, and congruence. It ensures that the coach is present in the moment, is fully attuned to the needs of the client, and seeks to understand the client's perspective through reflective listening. I tend to ground myself with this approach particularly upon meeting a client for the first time. Table 7.1 summarizes the elements of this approach.

Had I been in Adam's position, I would not have accepted the assignment *only* if I felt it was outside of my level of professional competence. I would have had a three-party meeting with Chris and his manager to establish and mutually agree upon the coaching objectives. If I still sensed that Chris was resistant in my one-on-one conversation with him, I would share that with him and explore it further to identify and address the underlying reasons. If Chris decided he didn't want coaching, I would ensure that he went back to management and declined the coaching rather than refusing it myself on the basis of resistance. Finally, I believe if one acts honestly with credibility and integrity, there is no need to worry about one's reputation as a coach.

Table 7.1 Core conditions of the person-centered approach

Unconditional positive regard	The coach experiences a positive and non-judgmental accepting attitude toward the client.
Empathic understanding	The coach accurately senses the feelings the client is experiencing and communicates this understanding to the client.
Congruence	The coach is tuned into his/her own inner experience and feelings and can express them honestly and openly, if appropriate.

Commentary 7.1.b

David A. Lane

What is my sense of this case?

Reading this case brought a sense of recognition – been there – and concern for Adam – did he take any advice before starting a new business? Many years ago, when I considered moving from secure employment to self-employment I was given sage advice. Work out with your partner how small a house you are prepared to live in. The difference in value between what you have now and what you could accept is the sum of money you both need to be prepared to lose. If you are not prepared to lose, don't start a business. If you still want to start, then plan, take advice, understand the market, find out who can make decisions to spend in an organization, and work out your value in that market. What is it you bring that would induce a decision maker to pay you for your services?

My concern for Adam is that he does not seem to have done any of this, but rather he has started a business because he loved coaching and wanted to be his own boss. This is a crowded market with many more coaches than there are clients – unless you really understand your value to stakeholders, worries about money will drive your activities. Adam's love of coaching will be difficult to sustain if cash flow dominates his life. However, aside from this concern about Adam, I also worry about the HR department's conception of coaching as an individual remedial process. This approach to coaching seems ill conceived.

In reflecting on my concerns regarding this case, I will identify four areas that both Adam and the organization need to address. I really wish Adam's love of coaching had extended to him using a coach to explore the business, before jumping into the world of business creation.

Starting a business

There are any number of sources of support out there for those who wish to start a business. Books, courses, workshops, videos, incubators, even grants abound. If you want to start a coaching business, remember it is a professional service business – it will depend on working contacts, networking, and extensive cold calling to build a profile. Further, you have to understand what you can offer, which adds value. Adam even now needs to go back and do this work, seek advice before he runs out of funds, and ends up moving to the smaller house (George, 2003).

Prior reputation

No one comes to coaching from a nil base. We were all something else before we became coaches. Our reputation has been built on other successes. When approached by a company that knew you previously, it is what you were before that is driving their interest. Adam was a consultant – what type of advice did he give based on consultancy models? If he was seen as a fixer of problems, then HR will approach him with the notion that he can provide remedial action. In seeking to build a new reputation, moving away from the past or using the past to build the future has to be choreographed. Adam needs to address this by having a conversation with HR about how they see him and what it is they believe he can offer. He knows them – they have a positive view of him – so what are the implications of that prior perspective on what they are seeking now (Lane, Kahn, & Chapman, 2016)?

Initial scanning of the context

Coaching starts not when you meet the proposed client but in the first coaching meeting. In business, you have multiple clients (Kahn, 2014), and you need to understand all of them. A clear commission has to be established based on a real understanding of the context. The organization presented this as an individual problem with Chris to be fixed by remedial/performance coaching. This potentially indicates that they have a narrow view of performance and coaching. Adam needs to spend time exploring with them their understanding of what drives performance and what they see as the role of coaching. This is a coaching conversation to enable the HR Director to understand that organizational context is part of what drives value creation. The role that Chris is asked to play and the value he brings is part of a broader number of roles and value chains contributing to the outcome (Kahn, 2014). Once Adam has that understanding from the HR Director's perspective, he needs to explore which other stories need to be heard. Who might he talk with as well as Chris? With those perspectives framed, he can then explore with Chris how he sees his performance and role within the organization and his understanding of how the different value chains interrelate. Presumably, Chris has been successful in the past, reaching the executive level, so how does he understand his past successes, and what does he see as different now?

It could be that this initial scanning reveals a broader issue in the organization, a need for team coaching, or further sessions with Chris to scope the work. At present, it seems Adam has simply accepted this as an individual issue with Chris solely responsible for the situation. If he is the scapegoat for wider organizational problems, it could explain his compliance (or possibly impotence and resignation). There is perhaps even a sense that Adam is mirroring that failure in his own concerns that the assignment will fail and thereby damage his reputation. He needs to reflect on his own role in this. He seems to think he has a reputation to protect, but that is from the past as a consultant; he has not built a sense of himself as a coach in the initial conversations.

Reflecting on Adam's dilemma

According to Adam, the dilemma he faces is a problem of balancing financial needs with reputational damage by taking on work likely to fail. If I was supervising Adam, I think I would want to explore this. He perhaps is like Chris, "a little rough around the edges." What reputation does he want to build? Is he a coach who can explore difficult challenges, or one who only takes simple cases with a high degree of success? Why is this case likely to fail – is that to do with Chris or the organizational context in which he is expected to perform? Adam could potentially engage Chris with that dilemma in a coaching session.

Given his reputation as a consultant, he can take work as a consultant to pay the bills while he builds a separate coaching business or treat coaching as one of the offers within his consultancy. Most coaches do a number of different things (working a portfolio career); few earn enough from coaching in the early days to sustain themselves. Why does he want to conflate finance and coaching? I think I would want to explore this with him. He does need to begin to reflect on the brand he wants to build for his business. However, "I love coaching and want to be my own boss" is not a brand. The dilemma is presented as the contrast between the needs for money and success as a coach, but he has not really explored what it would be like to coach Chris in this organization now. What does he think is at risk for himself, Chris, and the other organizational stakeholders?

He rejects payment by result – very wise in these circumstances. Payment by result works when the coaching can be set up in such a way that each party has a real stake in success, which can be measured in simple behavioral terms. All stakeholders have to understand what behavior the coaching is intended to elicit, why it matters to them, and how it can be measured in a way that is meaningful. Payment by results is a linear process, which is fine for simple (or complicated) concerns but ill-fitted to complexity or chaos (Down, & Lane, 2015).

The main problem here is the premature decision to go back to the HR department to express concerns that are based on little more than a hunch. If challenged by the HR Director on what evidence he had to support that decision, what could Adam say? Without first having the necessary conversations with key stakeholders, he is not in a position to make this judgment.

What are the core themes that need to be explored?

1   Branding:

   a   What is Adam's brand as a coach?

      i   This needs some detailed reflection from Adam. How can he draw upon all his experience and understanding of how organizations work to consider what he can offer to enhance value for clients?

   b   What does "coaching as a brand" look like in the organization?

      i   How an organization views the place of coaching is an important part of the exploration in any assignment. Where that view is narrowly focused, as in this case, the initial coaching conversations should explore any potential movement from the different perspectives. Can Adam explore these before deciding to reject the contract?

2   Initial contracting:

   a   Who are the stakeholders?

      i   A contract in an organization is not between coach and coachee; all of those who have a stake in the outcome need to be considered. This is a coaching conversation, not simply a contract negotiation. Adam could try to identify these stakeholders.

   b   What stories need to be heard?

      i   In this case the HR Director presented a remedial story. What other stories might exist? Who needs to be heard? Adam could ask the question: Who do I need to hear from in order to understand this organization?

3   Structuring the value proposition:

a   What does the value chain look like within the organization?

i   Coaching operates within the value chain of the person, their role, and the contribution of that role to the business. It is nested in other value chains, the team, peers, and customers. If Adam can understand the value chain, he can better structure the proposition to the client to add value.

b   What is Adam's value as a coach?

i   Adam is bringing a range of experiences, not just coaching – how can he lever this to create a value proposition for himself in terms of how he can use coaching to enhance value for this client?

4   Culture and coaching in the organization:

a   How does the culture of the organization support success?

i   Coaching does not succeed because of the expertise of the coach in fixing a single poor performer. It succeeds through influencing how success is supported in the organization. Can Adam explore the way the culture operates to enable (or disable) performance? Coaching designed to fix the fallout from disabling organizational cultures provides a band-aid not a resolution.

b   How can a coach add value to that culture?

i   A coach can add value, in part, by helping the organization to modify its approach to supporting success. Can Adam enlist multiple stakeholders in the coaching assignment so that value can be added?

Conclusion – coaching the coach to define his value
proposition in the context of the organization

Adam is early in his coaching career and has embarked on the venture with enthusiasm, but little apparent preparation. He needs to find a coach to help him think through what he has to offer as a business. He also seems to think that being offered a piece of coaching work is about accepting without question the terms of the coaching assignment, then working with the individual referred. While coaching in organizations looked like that perhaps ten years ago, most now recognize that the value proposition in coaching in organizations means engagement with multiple stakeholders (Gray, Garvey, & Lane, 2016). This does mean that the initial meeting is not one of accepting the given assignment but helping the organization to explore the issues they confront and reflect upon how coaching fits within this. The value chain in organizations extends well beyond the person sitting in the room with the coach. Adam can perhaps be helped to reflect not on money, but value within such a chain.

Case 7.2. Better late than never?

Patrick was starting a new team coaching assignment. He was quite happy with the assignment in the beginning. As is his practice, he met different team members to get a better understanding of context before he finalized the contract. Thus, he orally discussed the terms of the contract with the team's manager, who was also part of the coaching process, including: the frequency of team meetings, the amount of the overall contract, the payment schedule, etc. The signed agreement was late to get back to him, but he wasn't worried; it was summertime, and the administrative services were probably on vacation. After the initial team coaching sessions, he sent his first invoice. Then, to Patrick's surprise, the team's manager raised issues with the first invoice. She said it didn't correspond to the contract. Immediately, Paul felt tense and uncomfortable.

Reflexive questions

- How would you have felt if you were in a similar situation?
- What are some challenges to starting a coaching assignment before ensuring the commercial contract is signed?
- How would you handle the team manager's reaction in this case?

Patrick felt that this unresolved issue prevented him from doing his job as a coach, which involved confronting clients. Because the commercial contract was not set, he, in effect, was prevented from providing honest feedback, especially to the manager. He wanted to challenge her on her unexpected behavior: Why was she suddenly questioning something they had orally agreed upon? Paul identified what he called "manipulative" behavior, and he worried that she might be exhibiting this behavior with her team, too. He thus felt that it was part of his job as team coach to confront her on this issue. But Paul further explained that it was in fact always touchy to wear both hats in coaching: the commercial and the coaching hat. Further, he felt like they contradicted one another. When he was wearing the commercial hat, he had to please the client. When he was wearing the coaching hat, he was both empathetic and confrontational. And being confrontational is not always what the client wants. Paul believed that while clients buy coaching because they say they want to implement change, they are in fact not always willing to do so. And they might hire the less confrontational coach to keep "more of the same." In brief, Paul feared he'd be rendered powerless by his client, i.e., unable to do a good job as the team's coach, by a client who kept power over him through unresolved financial issues.

Reflexive questions

- How do you understand Paul's unease in wearing both the coaching and commercial hat?
- Like Paul, do you think that they are often contradictory? Why, or why not?
- What other hats do coaches wear?
- More generally, what roles does money play in coaching? What other money-related challenges should coaches expect to face?
- If you were Paul, what would you do now that the coaching has begun and the contract still hasn't been signed?

Commentary 7.2.a

Geoff Abbott

I will focus on several related themes in this case. Most significantly, there is the way in which the various stakeholders manage the inherent and paradoxical tension between the commercial aspects of coaching and the "other" element related to identifying and achieving the objectives of the coaching. There is the question of Paul's identity, and how he views his role as a coach. Then, there is an issue around clarity of communication.

Paradoxical and polarized thinking

Paul talks about wearing two hats. We note that he has only one head. Wearing both at the same time is problematic, awkward, and unattractive. His guiding "hats" metaphor therefore may limit him from seeing the opportunity to leverage value from both perspectives. Money is in the room with the coach regardless of artificial boundaries that actors might construct. I've written about this before in the context of cross-cultural coaching where the point of difference is usually around cultural orientations or dimensions (Abbott, 2014). In this context, the "cultural" dimension seems to be about, on the one hand, the culture of "financial and contractual control," and on the other, a culture of "team and executive development." Paul has identified that the team manager's handling of the financial, contractual control dimension may be symptomatic of a wider issue. This could well impact the team and executive development dimension, yet his deeper position seems to be guided by the idea that they are not related – or that they "should not" be related. How might he look at this differently? In my narrative, I introduced the idea of two hands working together. The challenge is to find ways that the two dimensions can be held in positive and creative tension. This is adopting paradoxical thinking and can be aided by a polarity map.

A polarity map (Johnson, 1991) provides a landscape for people to identify and explore inherent sources of tension relating to achieving an intention, goal, or objective. This might be at the level of an individual, a team, a department, an organization – or even society. In this case, the source of tension seems to be between the kind of culture that is being constructed and nurtured – one that gives primacy to finance and control, the other to team development. With the help of a polarity map, the "actors" tease out the advantages and disadvantages of giving attention to each pathway, solution, or approach. The outcome is to accept that both are valid, and to establish a way of monitoring, navigating, and influencing the flow, tension, and energy between the two. Polarity mapping has been explored in coaching before by Glunk and Folini (2010).

Their model describes how coaches can guide their clients through a process of discovering polarized thinking, exploring poles, and softening boundaries to become more comfortable with interdependent opposites. The sense of play in the use of paradoxes is encouraged by the insights of the educationalist philosopher John Dewey, who wrote, "To be playful and serious at the same time is possible, and it defines the ideal mental condition." Coaches are actors in the paradoxical play as they explore with their clients what might be going on and encourage a mindset that can position tension as opportunity (Dewey, 1910, p. 218).

Identity

We talk about "coaches" as a homogenous group of people who turn up to assist individuals and organizations in achieving success (defined in different ways). Variations in training explain variations in practice. Scraping the surface, you have a collection of individuals with some common values and practices, but also some deeply engrained positions, beliefs, cultural frames, and assumptions that come out when triggers of various kinds are pulled. Money, power, and manipulation are all wonderful ways to trigger all sorts of things! Some coaches would not blink if put in the situation in this case study. I discussed the case with a CEO-turned-executive coach, and she didn't even see the issue. "Just lay it clearly on the table, establish a position, and move on with the coaching – or walk away if a position can't be agreed upon." In Paul's case, I noticed that he came from an internal coaching background (a decade ago) before moving to team coaching. Perhaps he has a lingering sensitivity to issues around confronting people in power? Maybe he is relatively inexperienced in the commercial realities of establishing coaching agreements, specifically where the coach is also negotiating the contract, and the other side of the negotiation is a participant in the program. Lastly, Paul may or may not have the financial resources to simply step away.

Paul appears to have had training from a psychological/psychodynamic perspective that most likely asked him to look at his values and assumptions. Under pressure, maybe this team manager interaction and the lingering uncertainty have shaken him away from his professional foundations? There are lots of possibilities. None of these elements would be "wrong" or a "problem" in and of themselves. There is always a challenge when one's triggers are being pulled. Flight, fight, and freeze responses tend to lead to a bypassing of high-level functioning. A principle is to come from a "know thy self" position and to be able to step back when feeling triggered. From this position, it is easier to call relevant knowledge of self-in-context into the moment, and hopefully make better decisions. (This approach comes from many related fields of research and practice including mindfulness, emotional intelligence, and subject-object shifts in the context of adult development.) Self-awareness is also helpful in noticing the circumstances under which the triggers are being pulled and who might "in reality" be pulling the triggers – if anyone. The questioning in this situation of what is a fact and what is a belief might be helpful. Is it true, for example, that the CEO is exhibiting manipulative behavior? There might be psychological transference going on where some previous nasty behavior by a CEO affected Paul, and he has interpreted this situation through that lens – or not.

Communication

Coaches get paid quite well and part of the reason is that they are expected to navigate in and around complex situational challenges – including their own client-sponsor-coach interactions. Highly effective coaches will relish the challenge and use their cognitive and emotional skills to probe around for clarity in the interests of a successful outcome (noting that success is a muddy construct. All organizational actors – including coaches – will differ to some degree in their views of what coaching success looks like). The importance of clarity in communication cannot be understated, provided that what is being communicated reflects a depth of understanding about what might be going on in the game. Coaching clients are not always great communicators. The team manager in this case seems to have some challenges. This is an opportunity for the coach to find ways of 1) establishing a shared understanding of the contract and 2) making a difference with the team manager and her team. Obstacles are opportunities in the world of paradox and play.

TEASING OUT THE CASE

A simple consideration of where and how to put the focus in the situation, keeping in mind the three elements above (paradoxical thinking, identity, and communication), could be enough to give Paul some clarity. He would need to accept the premise that coaching a team for development *and* working with issues of financial and contractual control might be of high value in getting a high impact outcome. Some thoughts, not knowing the details:

- Paul can notice his own discomfort and use it as motivation to develop as a coach: "OK, this is a tough one but I'm sure there will be more of these, particularly as I go to higher level assignments. This is the challenge I need if I'm going to grow as a coach." The worst that could happen if he forces the team manager's hand is that he is not paid, and he walks away. This might be the developmental step that Paul needs in his career – and a badge in the market. "What kind of coach am I if I don't practice what I preach and stick to my values?"
- The CEO is focused on the coaching, or she would not have questioned the bill. Paul could choose to reflect this back as a positive ingredient in engaging with the CEO in moving to a contract: "I find when the CEO takes a close interest in the way the team coaching works, it encourages other team members to engage. Let's sort this out."
- The incident might be an indication that the corporate culture includes "value-for-money." If so, Paul can leverage this into encouraging commitment to the team coaching to ensure that the opportunity is not wasted. "It's clear in this company that you like to get value from your meetings and interactions. I share that view. To do that, it's important I get clarity around the contract and the price."

Commentary 7.2.b

Daniel Doherty

A brand new coaching assignment

It all began so promisingly. After months of trying to land myself a team-coaching assignment – in part to recoup the costs of my weeklong team-coaching accreditation course – a chance encounter on a train put me on the trail of a prestigious commercial client. I was introduced by my contact to the CEO, who, after listening to my pitch, said that he would like me to work with his intact team, as he felt they were not aligned around his audacious marketing plan to blow financial services wide open. I felt flattered to be asked. In that first meeting, I experienced the frisson that comes from being taken into the confidence of a powerful person, of being offered a place at his confessional table. He exuded urgency, saying he wanted me to get started really soon, nodding impatiently when I interrupted his flow to outline my fees and modus operandi. He said simply, "Put your modus operandi MO down as heads of agreement. Then I will get my finance director to sign it off. Let's not get lost in the contractual weeds here." He continued, "The chemistry between us is good, so just get going in the best way you see fit. Then report back to me when you feel you have a doable action plan."

From that point on, things began to move quickly. I cleared my diary and enjoyed an exhilarating entry-gaining process with the team, swiftly building trust and rapport. I put together my early diagnosis of team dynamics to deliver to the executive. Contentious issues had emerged, but I felt confident that my analysis was robust. However, on the morning of the executive feedback meeting, the CEO stopped me in the corridor and said we needed to talk – "My office, right now." He said he had seen my preliminary invoice, and that it was way in excess of what he expected to pay. "Bluntly, I am not going to pay it." He snorted at my reminder of our heads of agreement, saying that he was prepared to pay a global sum at the end of the work, but that I had better make the quantum realistic. He reminded me that he had other options, including going to a reputable consultancy firm, or simply pulling the plug. He said he was worried that I had been talking up problems with some maverick team members, and he was having trouble seeing my value-add at this point.

I left his office in a state of shock, casting my eyes down in embarrassment as I walked past the glass-fronted offices of the other executives sharing the C-suite. My immediate feeling was to beat myself up for failing to have made the financial contract more robust. I sat in my car, beating the steering wheel in frustration. It felt like I had walked into a gigantic trap. Clearly, it was up to me to figure a way out of this mess, yet I could not see an easy way around it. What was I to say to my family, who had been cautionary about me investing time and money in this precarious business to team coaching? How could I face my coaching peer group at our regular meeting the following week, given that I had been bragging to them about this prestigious piece of work, while there I was, poised on the brink of humiliation?

As I sat in the car, trying to calm myself, I realized that this was not the first time I had experienced this sense of betrayal at an early stage of intervention, though never before on this scale. Taking some agency for this, I detected that much of this unwelcome circumstance was due to my pattern of simply wanting to get on with the work and to do it really well, to the point where the client would not challenge the commercial value of it. In my mind, I justified this "let's just get on with it" approach through David Megginson's provocative question posed to the Critical Coaching Research Group in 2010: "Does contracting make you smaller?" How can we possibly know what the client needs to work on until the conversation has progressed to the point where outer layers of resistance are peeled away, and emergent themes have begun to surface? Only at that point, once the psychological contract is established, can we begin to talk meaningfully about the deeper aspects of intervention strategy and fee structuring. While I still agreed with this wisdom, this advocacy of emergent strategy was clearly not working for me in this particular instance. Lost as to how to proceed, I remembered that I had a supervision booked for the following week. That seemed a good place to take my dilemma, as I could not yet share with my family the threats this disruption posed to our prosperity and to my self-esteem.

Taking my dilemma to supervision

My supervisor listened carefully as I talked her through this unfolding drama, nodding as I mentioned my pattern of charging in before the consulting "tent-pegs" were fully in place. When she asked as to my underlying emotional state, I expressed that I was torn between flight and fight. The flight instincts were saying that I was stupid even to think that I could pull off a team intervention in a highly politicized culture without gathering some protections around me, including secure financial contracting. "Cut your losses," said the voice of flight, return to your one-to-one coaching business where you charge by the hour, a simple arrangement that everyone understands. Flight said "walk away from this CEO and his games-playing, write this episode off as a lesson learned before deeper engagement starts to seriously undermine your sense of worth."

"And the voice of fight?" asked my supervisor. Taking a breath, I talked of wanting to hit out. To use all of the information gathered from my interviews regarding the bullying nature of the CEO's approach, to confront him as a "trickster," and to point out that his treatment of me was symptomatic of just such bullying. There was clear evidence of a "parallel process" in play here, though I really doubted whether the CEO would allow that conversation. Fight spoke of the option of whistleblowing to expose the CEO, of revealing to his team what had occurred, and urging them to proceed in common cause with me by way of dramatically catalyzing change. This was exhilarating to countenance, yet I knew in my heart that I did not have networks strong enough to support this challenge. Fight also spoke of taking legal action, but it was clear that there would only be one winner in that scenario, and I knew it would not be me, pitted against the company's deep pockets.

Somewhere between flight and fight was the option of soldiering on, dropping my price, seeing this one through to the end, then putting the whole thing down to experience and moving on. I knew though that in taking this submissive route, my hurt and resentments regarding this betrayal would surely leak out, and I would look more ineffectual than ever. I thought back to my team coach training and asked how the theories and practices learned there might help me through. I could see how all we had learned about Torbert's continuum of leadership behaviors would explain the trickster nature of the CEO. I could see how the corporate psychopath literature would inform this also. But otherwise that training course, which cost me so much, offered no ready answers to my commercial dilemma. The only helpful insight came from Ed Schein (1999) asking the question: "What does the interventionist do when the team leader is the problem? And most often the team leader is the problem."

In the end, our discussion of these reflexive impulses surfaced the more measured option of my compiling a short interim report of findings to date, with suggestions for my continuation, dependent on satisfactory renegotiation of the financials, without which I would walk away. I decided to commit to this option, holding onto the slim hope that the power of my diagnosis would hold sway. My supervisor then asked how this episode might cause me to contract differently in the future. Reflecting on this question, I mused that even if I had put in place tighter contracting processes and taken advantage of the comprehensive EMCC contracting template, I still doubted whether such a document would stop the CEO from sabotaging the intervention, if he were so inclined. I allowed myself some forgiveness at that thought.

I believe it was Dick Beckhard who said that the most powerful consultant is one who does not need the fee (1969). I was taken by this truism, but it did not help to move further along. In fact it accentuated my fear of impending destitution, should I continue to follow my integrity rather than collude and make nice with the client. Our conversation turned to the tensions created through fusing the roles of delivery and financial management into one role. Larger consultancies manage this tension by separating financial contracting from delivery, leaving it to their expert staffers to deal with their procurement and HR counterparts within the client organization. This realization prompted the option of signing up for such a consultancy, trading independence of thought and action for a degree of protection and security. Or else I could return to my previous incarnation as an in-company consultant, commissioning work from externals (such as I am now), often pressing them until their pipes squeaked. I realize now with some shame what it was I was putting those independents through financially, while they carried all the risk client-side.

My supervisor encouraged me to work my way through this particular piece of unpleasantness first, to allow the shock of this reality-check to subside, and only then consider my options. All very well for her to say, yet some of these dilemmas seemed irreconcilable. In fact her default of exuding Zen-like calm was beginning to annoy me. I could not repress a flash of anger welling up from deep inside:

> *I think coaches might do themselves a favor by being more realistic about the fact that coaching is not entirely a utopian mission to make the world a better place. Of course, I still believe that coaching is for the good, but it is subject to manipulation. There is also a commercial reality to it, and in this scenario, I do not find myself on the right side of that reality. I feel foolish, duped, naive, and humiliated. Not just by this client, but by the marketeers who sold me the training in this latest bright, shiny thing, assuring it would make me money many times over, by the professional bodies that promise to offer protection and standards when these are few, by the same bodies that continue to insist that I spend money I don't have on my CPD, and yes even on you, my supervisor, whom the body insists I retain as part of my license to operate.*

> I took a breath. *This client insists that I show evidence of return on investment, on ROI. I know I cannot give him any assurances on this, though I do know of consultancies that boast of clients making one-on-six returns from coaching. I worry that they just make this stuff up, but then they know that money talks, and they have to be confident, persuasive. Academics have researched ROI on coaching to the death, but, so far, robust evidence isn't there. I have invested all of my extra money in reinventing myself as a coach. I realize only now that I sit at the bottom of a giant Ponzi scheme, and I see no way that I am going to realize a personal ROI from*

> *this strange dance. The sunk cost has been great, but perhaps it is*
> *better late than never. My every instinct says get out now, while you*
> *can, before this sense of disillusionment and resentment consumes*
> *you. I have had enough of the lot of you, for now.* Rant over, I did not
> wait for my supervisor's reaction before I headed for the door.

Conclusion

As the above cases and commentaries show, it is difficult to address the issue of money in coaching in isolation. In addition to the question of income and making a living from coaching, money matters can be linked to and impacted by other issues such as contracting, the financial value of coaching, and reputational concerns.

Let us start with the issue of contracting, in particular the financial part of the contract. An important question related to money and payment is what was referred to in the commentaries as "contingent fee coaching" or "payment by result." This is when the coach will be paid only if an agreed-upon outcome is reached. Our experts raised some serious concerns regarding this approach as it compromises the coaching, which becomes focused on a particular outcome, as stated in the contract, rather than on what might turn out to be, through the coaching process, in the best interest of the coachee and the organization.

This takes us to another question related to money and coaching fees, which is the value of the work delivered by the coach, as perceived by the coach and the organization. As noted in one of the commentaries above, organizations paying for coaching expect to see a return on their investment (ROI). But how can success be measured in coaching? And what financial value can be linked to this success? Grant (2012) rejects this focus on ROI in coaching and calls for a more holistic approach, measuring the well-being and the engagement of the coachee.

ROI can also be important for the coach who must determine the value of the service they are providing and the fee related to their work. In fact, they often consider their previous experience, the training and education they have invested in, as well as their professional reputation. This is reflected in the differences we see in coaching fees. While coaches' previous experience is an important factor in determining the value of their offering, starting a new coaching business might mean building a new reputation and could come with a financial impact.

This chapter shows that though the motivation for starting a coaching career can be driven by the desire to help, to make a change in a coachee's life and in the organization, the coach must develop many skills and play different roles, one of which is managing the commercial and financial aspects of coaching, something that coaches are not always equipped to deal with. Coaches, therefore, should gain more awareness of the importance of financial issues and their ramifications, and seek supervision when needed, as suggested in the commentaries.

References

Abbott, G. N. (2014). Cross-cultural coaching: A paradoxical perspective. In E. Cox, T. Bachkirova, & D. Clutterbuck (2010). *The complete handbook of coaching* (2nd ed., pp. 342–360). London: Sage Publications.

Association for Coaching (AC) & European Mentoring & Coaching Council. (2016). *Global code of ethics for coaches and mentors*. Retrieved from https://c.ymcdn.com/sites/www.associationforcoaching.com/resource/resmgr/Legal/Global_Code_of_Ethics.pdf?hhSearchTerms=%22code+and+ethics%22

Beckhard, R. (1969). *Organization development: Strategies and models*. Boston, MA: Addison. Conference Board 2008 report. Retrieved from www.conference-board.org

Dewey, J. (1910). *How we think*. New York, NY: D. C. Heath & Publishers.

Down, M., & Lane, D. D. (2015). Leadership for resilient organisations: The changing context of organisational resilience and leadership. In P. Grant, U. Afridi, J. Sternemann, & E. Wilson (Eds.), *Business psychology in action: Creating flourishing organisations through evidence-based and emerging practices*. Kibworth Beauchamp: Matador.

Downs, A. (2002). *Secrets of an executive coach*. New York, NY: Amacom.

George, B. (2003). *Authentic leadership: Rediscovering the secrets to creating lasting value*. San Francisco, CA: Josey-Bass.

Glunk, U., & Folini, B. (2010). Polarities in executive coaching. *Journal of Management Development, 30*(2), 222–230.

Grant, A. M. (2012). ROI is a poor measure of coaching success: Towards a more holistic approach using a well-being and engagement framework. *Coaching: An International Journal of Theory, Research and Practice, 5*(2), 74–85.

Gray, D. E., Garvey, B., & Lane, D. A. (2016). *A critical introduction to coaching and mentoring*. London: Sage Publications.

Johnson, B. (1991). *Polarity management*. Amherst: Human Resource Development Press.

Joseph, S. (2010). The person-centred approach to coaching. In E. Cox, T. Bachkirova, & D. D. Clutterbuck (Eds.), *The complete handbook of coaching* (pp. 68–79). London: Sage Publications.

Kahn, M. S. (2014). *Coaching on the axis: Working with complexity in business and executive coaching*. London: Karnac.

Kampa-Kokesch, S., & Anderson, M. Z. (2001). Executive coaching: A comprehensive review of the literature. *Consulting Psychology Journal: Practice and Research, 53*(4), 205–228.

Lane, D. A., Kahn, M. S., & Chapman, L. (2016). Understanding adult learning as part of an approach to coaching. In S. Palmer & A. Whybrow (Eds.), *Handbook of coaching psychology: A guide for practitioners* (2nd ed.). Hove: Routledge.

Louis, D. (2015). *Complexity in executive coaching: Toward a theoretical framework to analyze the nature and management of multiple stakeholders and agendas* (Unpublished doctoral dissertation). Grenoble Ecole de Management, France.

May, W. F. (1999). Money and the professions: medicine and law. *William Mitchell Law Review, 25*(1), 75–102.

Schein, E. (1999). *Process consultation revisited*. Boston, MA: Addison Wesley New.

8   Emotions in coaching

Introduction

As a change process, coaching is inherently an emotionally loaded intervention for all the stakeholders involved. For the client, fear, shame, anger (Turner & Goodrich, 2010), anxiousness, and emotional detachment (Cox & Bachkirova, 2007) can either support or hinder transitions to new ways of being and doing. In their role, coaches are constantly facing both the felt and expressed emotions of their clients or various stakeholders, as well as their own. These difficult emotional situations will give coaches a "bad feeling" and make them "feel uncomfortable in some way" (Cox & Bachkirova, 2007). They can be linked to a particular situation, such as feelings of helplessness, frustration, vulnerability, or anger in complex and difficult situations. Or they can be experienced towards a particular person, whether the coachee or other stakeholders, such as sorrow and compassion (Louis, 2015). It is worth noting that negative emotions can turn into positive ones, such as excitement, satisfaction, and happiness, once the complex and difficult situation has been successfully dealt with (Louis, 2015).

Despite their centrality, the coach's own emotions are often neglected, with coaching portrayed as an essentially rational process. And the coachee's emotions can be under-examined, their importance in the change process underestimated. This neglect leads to missed opportunities to tap into the informative power of emotions – both negative and positive – when not impeding the coach's decision-making process and actions (Cox & Bachkirova, 2007; Louis, 2015).

The first case, "*Stress mode*," introduces Susan, an executive coach with over 15 years of coaching experience, who is contacted by a telecommunication company to provide developmental coaching to one of the executives. In the three-way meeting between the coach, coachee, and organization, the frustration of the line manager is quite visible as he talks about the coachee's performance issues, which causes the coachee stress. Susan feels the emotions of both the coachee and the line manager, and the conversation quickly becomes uncomfortable for all three of them.

In the second case, *Feeling with your body*, we examine the situation of David, an executive coach with a professional background as a marketing executive.

Early in his coaching career, David notices that he is experiencing all sorts of emotions and intuitions during coaching sessions. He is not sure whether he should ignore them in order to remain neutral and objective or acknowledge them and take them into account. He goes to his supervisor for advice.

Case 8.1. "Stress mode"

As a coach, Susan avoids remedial coaching because she thinks it's a "losing proposition." She prefers developmental coaching, when coaching is used as a tool "to accelerate a person's career" instead of "retarding the fall." Over her 15-year career as a coach, she has found it difficult to change the trajectory of a career or performance issue when it's already on a downward slope. She's found that, unless there's something glaringly wrong and easily fixable, achieving change can prove too challenging. Furthermore, in developmental coaching, everyone is usually involved with – and committed to – the process. While in remedial coaching, people are trying to mitigate risk, and are, therefore, less engaged.

Given Susan's stance, she was excited to get a call to do some developmental coaching with Kevin, a junior executive in a telecommunication company. In the initial two-party meeting with the commissioning manager, he spoke very positively about Kevin and explained that the coaching sessions were intended to support Kevin in his career progression. Susan then asked to have a three-party meeting with Kevin and the commissioning manager. In that meeting, she was very surprised to hear the manager saying a lot of negative things about Kevin and his performance right in front of his face.

Susan could see that the situation was making Kevin uncomfortable, and she understood why: he wasn't expecting to hear such negative feedback in this meeting, in front of a stranger, no less. He was clearly in "stress mode." Susan was feeling the stress, too! It became clear to her that there was an issue between Kevin, her coachee, and the manager, her client. And to make matters worse, the manager seemed insistent upon blaming the relational problem on Kevin.

Susan was caught off guard, and the atmosphere in the room became heavy and uncomfortable. To protect himself, Kevin shut down completely, his body language was all closed off, and he didn't utter a word. And Susan found herself in a difficult, stressful situation that she needed to handle.

Reflexive questions

- How would you interpret the commissioning manager's actions?
- Have you experienced a situation similar to Susan's? How would you have felt if you were in Susan's position? What would you have done?

In that three-party meeting, Susan tried, as much as she could, to tease out the real issue, encouraging the manager to translate it into a concrete, clear message. She also tried to re-establish communication between them, giving Kevin the opportunity to respond. The conversation was difficult, and it got heated as a result of bottled-up emotions. However, at the end of the meeting, the questions Susan asked opened their eyes to the larger issue of their relationship. She suggested that they go through conflict resolution instead of coaching and recommended a specialized consultant. The manager said that he would think about it, but decided not to go for it after all.

Reflexive questions

- What do you think of the way Susan handled the meeting? Do you think her recommendation was the right call?
- Have you ever recommended another type of support, either in complement or as a substitute for coaching? If so, what were the circumstances? If not, when might it be appropriate?

Commentary 8.1.a

Tony V. Zampella

Introduction

The outcome of this case was a stressful situation that occurred in a client meeting scheduled by Susan, the coach. I employ an ontological inquiry that focuses on the period between that initial client call and the first stressful meeting. Specifically, I examine the effect of assessments on outcomes.

In an ontological inquiry, how we observe and assess our being requires an awareness of how emotions manifest in our bodies and inform our listening as spaces of possibility, narrative structures, and predispositions for action (Sieler, 2007).

Here I consider that Susan's "stress mode" foreclosed her possibilities of making a difference as a coach. Stressful situations by themselves need not foreclose possibilities, but for this a coach must be prepared.

1 The being of being a coach

When confronted, Susan seemed to assess stress as a "difficult situation" that "she needed to handle." Perhaps Susan had only regarded "conflict" as a problem from a psychological viewpoint, to be fixed or solved.

- If we view coaching through a psychological or normative lens to diagnose and solve problems, we concern ourselves with *what works*, what's wrong, and how to fix it. Normative ideals precede problems that should not exist, so we offer prescriptions.
- If we consider an ontological perspective into the nature of being, we are concerned with *what's missing* or essential for a designated possibility or commitment, and how to create it. Freedom precedes problems, which are inevitable and universal, so we invent possibilities (Koestenbaum & Block, 2003).

The normative view avoids unsolvable problems; the ontological view expects perceived problems as inevitable in the face of change. Our views affect our observations and conversations – a coach's two primary resources. What if Susan regarded "conflict" not as a problem to solve but as an essential ingredient for "accelerating a person's career?"

In sum, from an ontological inquiry, we are concerned not with what's right or wrong but with what is missing – what does not yet exist that is essential for a designated possibility to become a reality. Problems may be evidence of breaks in predictable patterns that support the creation of an emerging future.

2 Worldview: fix-it or future

Fundamentally, Susan's performance as a coach is related to her capacity to observe and communicate. Many of Susan's beliefs reveal assumptions that form her assessments about the reality of "developmental" or "remedial" coaching, her profession, and this client.

These beliefs shape the scope of her work and horizon of possibilities.

- Is Susan approaching this client from a problem-solving or psychological model to fix problems? If so, this reduces "open" possibilities to "closed" probabilities, based on predicting the future from the past and improving upon that past.
- Or, is she approaching clients from an inquiry or ontological model that allows for discovery to view an emerging future and shape the coaching from expanding possibilities?

All of these issues point to the beginning: how Susan came to be in that room. For that, we examine the intake process.

From the start, Susan took on this client with an important expectation: a "call to do some developmental coaching." By her own account, Susan "found remedial coaching a 'losing proposition,'" and preferred developmental coaching when used as a tool "to accelerate a person's career."

This is a common theme among some coaches: Is the employer using coaching to "fix" an employee, avoid a problem, or ease someone out?

With very little information, it appeared that Susan listened for and confirmed her expectations in the initial two-party meeting with her prospective client, who spoke "very positively about Kevin and explained that the coaching sessions were intended to support Kevin in his career progression." This was a perfect match for Susan's expectations, without any more information or conversation. It influenced her to schedule a meeting with Kevin and her client, the commissioning manager.

Susan went into this initial client call without an intake process that allowed for discovery of the unexpected. She seemed more inclined toward diagnosing the need or fit: to "support Kevin's career progression" without conversations to bring forth some future possibility to which all could be mutually committed (Flores, 2012).

The effects of the lack of intake process were evident in the session with Kevin. Susan was "caught off guard" at the stressful moment. The effects were evident in the "heavy and uncomfortable" atmosphere and in Susan's expectations about what should or should not be occurring in the room, and about what she "needed to handle." This last concern included a normative worldview that assumes stress or conflict needs to be fixed or even avoided, rather than seen as necessary to expand possibilities.

3 Observations and assessments

This client confirms Susan's beliefs about coaching and clients, beliefs that had already formed strong expectations for that first meeting.

For this very reason, any coaching intervention initially involves an assessment process for client fit. Coaches, being human, are influenced by concealed assumptions, and implicit or explicit interpretations as we assess reality; these influence how we listen and observe. The *being* of a coach (the way we internalize experience) can become fixed by self-assessments that can govern our minds: our worldview and beliefs about what we deserve and about what's possible (Labarre, 2000) that shape the observers we are, and the conversations we have (Sieler, 2003).

These unexamined, untested assessments can also prevent us from observing possibilities beyond those views; or, more intractably, we believe the views that automatically occur to us must be the facts.

From a psychological perspective, assessments are reports on past behavior or events; from an ontological perspective, assessments are critical declarations about what kinds of possibilities for action are opened and closed for us in the future. The future is paramount as a commitment and as a possibility. In addition to saying something about what we observe, assessments reveal who we are as observers, and shape how we declare action for the future.

As coaches, we can mitigate getting swept up in assessments, and refine the observer we are for future possibilities, by testing our assessments through an *intentional intake process*, and by *grounding assessments*.

INTENTIONAL INTAKE

Generally, the intake process is often overlooked or reduced to a minimum of steps before the "real work" begins. However, if we view the intake as the real work of expanding discovery versus narrowing by diagnosing problems, we can expand possibilities for all parties to bring forth a future possibility to which all can be mutually committed.

For example, "being involved and committed to the process" is important to Susan, yet it was never addressed, explicitly or intentionally, in the intake process, nor was it a condition of that first meeting.

The intake gives clients the important choice of whether to commit or not, and creates the relationship space for engaging difficult conversations to leverage unpredictable issues in the face of stress. In Susan's situation, it was unclear when that choice occurred between all three participants.

Instead, Susan left that initial interview with an implicit understanding and unexpressed expectations about the goals and direction of an engagement, yet without having tested them with each participant invited to the upcoming meeting. She did not see the potential for confusion in such a meeting with two colleagues from the same company, each with their own observations of the organization, and each with their views about how they see themselves in the organization's future.

Moreover, what led Susan to forego the same meeting with Kevin that she had with his manager? Did she assume facts about Kevin, which led her to assess that she was prepared to have a three-way meeting without first interviewing Kevin? Did her assessment of a client-fit cause her to forego questioning the manager's expectations about Kevin's "career progression" or inquire after any concerns?

In sum, the lack of intake found Susan influenced by assumptions and assessments that became *automatic* predispositions to *action*. Failing to take account of them by means of an intake process limited her possibilities for action as a coach.

BEING GROUNDED

Another option to refine who we are as observers involves grounding assessments, to test the underlying assumptions, evidence, and beliefs that form our assessment about ourselves, others, and reality. From the beginning Susan seemed guided by her assumptions about the "developmental coaching client," which had already determined her client profile preferences. They also influenced what she listened for and directed her course of action. For instance, she:

1   found *remedial coaching* a *"losing proposition"* involving people trying to *mitigate risk* who are *less engaged*;
2   preferred *developmental coaching* when used as a tool "to *accelerate a person's career*" instead of *"retarding the fall"*;
3   believed that unless there was something *glaringly wrong* and *easily fixable*, *achieving change* can prove *too challenging*;
4   found it *difficult* to change the trajectory of a career or performance issue when it was already on a *downward slope*;
5   expected that *everyone was committed to* the process of developmental coaching.

It is unclear whether Susan's specific (underlined) assessments were formed long ago, and/or whether they were tested against recent evidence. Further, it is not clear whether Susan was aware of the ways assessments shaped her viewpoint or capacity to listen, or, generally, whether she related to assessments as grounded or ungrounded, or the degree to which they affected her self-assessment (being).

What is clear is that her assessment about coaching, the manager, and Kevin placed her inside a small space of possibility, listening for narrow and predictable expectations, and perhaps missing other cues until stress was obvious in the participants' verbal and body language.

Susan was thus left at the mercy of any automatic assessments in the meeting. She tried "to tease out the real issue . . . and re-establish communication between them, giving Kevin the opportunity to respond" but seemed caught off-guard by her own assessment of a "difficult" and "stressful" situation.

Our influence as professionals is correlated to whether our assessments are grounded or ungrounded. To ground an assessment, Flores (2012) offered the following questions that lead to action:

1   What is my *concern* for making this assessment? (What do I want to *accomplish* with this assessment? To what end am I making this assessment?)
2   Which *domain* of action am I restricting it to?
3   Which *assertions* can I provide to support or refute this assessment?
4   What *standards* am I committed to?
5   What *actions* are now possible?

Grounding assessments is "an extremely useful procedure in coaching, if [someone] seems 'caught' in a strong negative assessment about someone else, and/or in a core negative self-assessment. We [also] can be blinded by our positive opinions and may lack prudence . . . about people with whom we have had little previous experience" (Sieler, 2003).

4 Possibilities and next steps

Susan can still intervene. She can inquire into why the manager didn't raise his concerns earlier or she can re-engage him privately.

More effectually, Susan might view this break in a predictable pattern as evidence of an emerging future. She might suggest pausing this session and meeting with each person individually. A pause offers time to secure important information, and perhaps an opportunity to reset the engagement.

Without the freedom to explore a commitment from the future, and the courage to ground long-held assessments that form our beliefs, "problems" can limit what is possible in addressing difficult conversations, and thereby lead to stressful situations.

Commentary 8.1.b

Nadine Theimann Mendelek

This case involves three protagonists under mounting stressful conditions following the negative feedback of the commissioning manager to the leader, in front of the coach no less. What could have triggered such reactivity on the part of the commissioning manager? How does a coach interpret such a situation and more generally deal with differences of perceptions, opinions, judgments, expectations, and subjective realities in order to know how to intervene and restore a semblance of calm and serenity? Neuroscience studies have shown that the same area of our brain (the amygdala) that detects physical dangers also detects social threats. When we feel physically or socially threatened, stress hormones (cortisol and adrenalin) flood our autonomic nervous system to tell us something important is happening, and we have three instinctual reactions to survive: *fight, flee,* or *freeze* (Siegel, 2010, would add *faint*). *Fleeing* is tempting, using avoidance and distancing tactics. *Fighting* can be alluring, too, becoming angry or defensive to avoid taking responsibility. *Freezing* is another option, feeling frightened, unable to utter a sound, and shutting down. Such somatic intelligence is tightly linked to emotional intelligence, and both will inform one's cognitive intelligence and, therefore, the quality of one's interpretation. The coaching situation herein showcases these three instincts as will be shown further down. Interpreting the stress mode is therefore more complex than meets the eye. To make informed decisions, a coach needs to take into account context, processes, and relational dimensions. We develop each in turn.

Contextual Understanding integrates structures that exist prior to the coaching intervention, which could refer to physical space, rules and regulations, organizational culture, national culture, etc. One could view the commissioning manager's actions in the context of a social threat as closer to a remedial coaching situation than a developmental one. The manager's *fight* reaction to the threat is clearly expressed through a judgmental attitude that involves blaming the executive, seeing him as the entire cause of the issue, and being angry at him, while Kevin's reaction is to *freeze* by shutting down and remaining silent. Susan's reaction to her own discomfort and that of the others involved could be interpreted as *fleeing* since she suggests "they go through conflict resolution instead of coaching."

An **Understanding of Processes** facilitates a smooth coaching flow, whereas insufficient preparation or misunderstanding of the developmental steps could explain the "venting" from Kevin's manager in the absence of a conversation that should have taken place beforehand. When someone requests coaching, the commissioning manager and the executive outline a number of developmental goals following performance reviews (two-party meeting), communicate them to the coach, and arrange an introduction to the executive. Once the chemistry meeting has taken place between the coach and the executive, a first goal-setting meeting occurs between them to further understand the executive's goals and current work environment, to set expectations and agreements, and to develop a plan and timeline for this process. It is good practice to set up a 360-stakeholder interview or online report to further tease out a number of developmental goals, and oftentimes some additional assessments are requested. Then an initial alignment meeting with the coach, executive, and commissioning manager takes place (three-party meeting) to ensure alignment of expectations, goals, support, and timeframes. In such an alignment meeting, the coach facilitates the conversation between the manager and the executive. In Kevin's case, if this process had been followed, the coach could probably have identified earlier on the negative feelings of the commissioning manager towards the executive, and could have reevaluated and circled back to re-establish the flow of the coaching process and set healthy boundaries.

An **Understanding of Relationships** is crucial to iron out potential conflicts. The commissioning manager's reaction could very well reveal social or emotional issues, so a courageous conversation needs to take place, and this is what I develop next.

What would I have done to facilitate a courageous conversation?

A hallmark of leadership skills is stakeholder agility, which revolves around understanding stakeholders and resolving differences (Joiner & Josephs, 2006). I would seize that opportunity to encourage and facilitate a dialogue between the executive and the commissioning manager using the Internal Family Systems (IFS) methodology (Schwartz, 1997) to create a trust space for the two actors to express themselves in a non-judgmental and non-critical mode.

In IFS terms the mind can be conceived of as subdivided into a number of sub-personalities or parts, each with its own perspective, interests, memories, and viewpoint. Everyone has a Self, and the Self can and should lead the individual's internal system. As Schwartz (1997) says, sub-personalities are aspects of our personality that interact internally in sequences and styles that are similar to the ways in which people interact. Parts may be experienced in any number of ways – thoughts, feelings, sensations, images, and more.

A core tenet of IFS is that every part has a positive intent for the individual, even if its actions or effects are counterproductive or cause dysfunction. This means that there is no reason to *fight* with, coerce, or try to eliminate a part; the IFS method promotes internal connection and harmony by welcoming and listening with an open heart and mind to every part's intention and agenda. Changes in the internal system will affect changes in the external system, and vice versa. The implication of this assumption is that both the internal and external levels of the system should be assessed. Conflicting parts may be experienced in any number of ways: thoughts, feelings, sensations, images, and more. All parts want something positive for the individual and will use a variety of strategies to gain influence within the internal system. As a result, polarizations (inner tension and conflicts) are created as parts try to gain influence within the system, and more often than not they can spill over externally and affect individual exchanges, thus reenacting polarized positions, leading to stress and emotional arousal.

Concretely applied to the case, it means that having noticed how triggered both the executive and the manager are, I would invite both of them to slow down and mindfully observe the state of energy in which they find themselves right here and now (mindfulness is a powerful self-awareness state). Then I would ask them to notice where in their body they find that tension or energy activated. Energy follows attention, so such focus on the body helps the person be present and centered. I would inquire as to how they feel toward that sensation and if any thought came up with it. That would surface eventual polarizations or inner conflicts that spill over into conflict with other people. I would ask questions to help them explore, feel toward, and befriend in a non-judgmental way their thoughts or limiting beliefs to tease out the intention or agenda. Finally, I would ask what is it they are imagining or fearing, pointing to the origin of their limiting beliefs and emotional reactions. The inner critic part of the commissioning manager may well be behind his negative feedback toward Kevin, and the befriending part would allow him to recognize its positive intention to protect himself by blaming his subordinate. The Self can ask this part to relax, step back after seeing and hearing it to allow compassion and curiosity toward Kevin. This approach constitutes a far better option to giving feedback, so the other party can then respond likewise, centering on his own activation. Both partners could then own their triggers and responsibility for their defensiveness, thus restoring calm and curiosity in their dynamic interaction.

In the process I would help facilitate the exploration and focus on strengths to "feedforward" the undamaged core of each individual's Self, the ability of the parts to shift into positive, championing roles. The IFS powerful language opens a new path to look at the Self and others in a holistic way, and it encourages self-disclosure and behavioral responsibility, while providing a way to work with "resistance" and denial. When differentiated, the Self is competent, secure, self-assured, relaxed, and able to listen and respond to feedback. A self-led individual has one or several of the following essential qualities to use in interpersonal interactions: calm, curiosity, courage, creativity, connectedness, clarity, compassion, and confidence, to which we can add patience, perseverance, and playfulness.

Susan's method and support

We know from the case that Susan did not believe in remedial coaching, snatching the victory from the jaws of performance failure, or turning around a downward career slope. Indeed, change could prove challenging under such difficult circumstances. She suggested they go through conflict resolution instead of coaching and recommended a specialized consultant. She could well have suggested doing this in parallel and in support of the coaching process in the spirit of both rather than either/or.

On one hand, I would assume that after 15 years of coaching, Susan knows her own limitations and has the capacity to face bottled-up emotions, as well as the ability to handle conflicts in order to make such a call. On the other hand, Susan's ability to know her own triggers and defense mechanisms would have helped her recognize her limiting beliefs and instinctual reaction to threat – a *flight* reaction over *freeze* and *fight*, evidenced by her suggestion of a third-party conflict mediator. Further, it is useful for a coach to be supported by a supervisor, to address complex cases around context and processes, and by a therapist, to address challenging emotions encountered in coaching experiences.

Doing the inner work for a coach entails setting the following flow in motion to address triggering situations: self-observations lead to self-awareness and allow for self-corrections, which finally lead to self-generation through a constant practice. Practice makes masters. Models and tools for handling emotional stress exist in coaching and unless faced can result in serious mental health problems. I would recommend coaches to keep on learning and pushing against their growing edges and to seek support in their efforts to elevate their level of consciousness. There are rarely "difficult" clients, and coaches owe their clients coaching excellence by continuing to evolve and grow to their next stage of ego maturity. Another type of support would definitely be called for in cases of trauma and psychological hyperarousal instead of or in parallel to coaching. Coaching and counseling for change are possible with a clear process put in place and if the coach is equipped with such training. For any other case, it would be better to refer the client to a psychotherapist or even a psychiatrist.

Case 8.2. Feeling with your body

David used to be a successful marketing executive. Then, he decided to change his career, undergoing training and completing all his certification requirements to become a leadership coach. This career shift meant that he needed to develop new skills. When he was a marketing executive, he was essentially using his analytical and sales skills. But as a coach, he was experiencing all sorts of emotions that he hadn't anticipated. Because he wanted to remain "neutral" and "objective" – as he was told during his coaching training – he repressed his emotions and ignored his intuitions. Indeed, he was so obsessed with doing a "proper job" that he focused solely on factual observations during coaching conversations. He thus disregarded what he was feeling in his body, putting his emotions "into a container" during the coaching sessions.

David was struggling with the emotions he experienced as a coach. He wasn't sure how to deal with them: Was he right to neglect his emotions? Or was he supposed to voice them, be it inside or outside the coaching sessions? So, he took this issue to his coaching supervisor, asking for her advice.

Reflexive questions

- What role do you think emotions play in coaching?
- How can a coach deal with his or her emotions, as well as those of the coachee?
- Have you ever had a coaching intervention where you had to ignore or repress your feelings?
- If you were David's coaching supervisor, what advice would you give him?

David's supervisor told him that it was important to acknowledge his feelings, without voicing them in the coaching sessions. She also told him that he needed to be aware of his coachees' emotions and try to understand where they were coming from. Basic knowledge of psychology would be helpful in understanding these emotions.

Following his supervisor's advice, David decided to take psychology classes. He now has a certificate in psychology and counseling, as well as an Neuro-linguistic Programming certificate. Today, David puts a lot of emphasis on understanding and dealing with the emotions of his coachees. For him, the psychological contract is the most difficult contract for any coaching journey. Although he doesn't consider himself a psychologist, a psychotherapist, or a psychoanalyst, he tries to stay mindful of any psychodynamic behaviors he observes in coaching conversations, looking at inferences and counter inferences, what the coachee is projecting, and what he, as a coach, is projecting back onto the coachee. Once these inferences have been identified, he finds the courage to voice them.

Reflexive questions

- If you were David's supervisor, would you have provided similar advice? Why?
- What do you think of David's decision and the actions he took?
- Do you think a coach needs some training in psychology to be able to deal with similar issues?

Commentary 8.2.a

Natalie Cunningham

I would like to start by acknowledging David's self-awareness to commit to supervision. While studies in the UK and Australia estimate that approximately 85% of coaches undertake some form of formal supervision (Passmore & McGoldrick, 2009; Lawrence & Whyte, 2014; Grant, 2012), this practice is by far underdeveloped in other countries (Bresser, 2013). In a discussion of this topic, Peter Hawkins shares a Chinese proverb that states: "The last one to know about the sea is the fish because they are constantly immersed in it." He likens the role of the supervisor to helping the coach become a flying fish so that they may reflect on and see the "relational water" in which they are swimming (Hawkins & Schwenk, 2011).

In this context it is important to be aware that just as a coaching client comes to a coaching session with their history, biases, assumptions, and background, so a coach enters the coaching and supervision relationships with their own scripts and background. A study looking at what influences coaching practice identified three different clusters of life experiences that have an impact on characteristics of coaches and coaching practices: stressful personal experiences influence empathy and self-awareness; field-specific coaching experiences influence practical skills and knowledge base; and previous professional training and experiences affect coaching practices and perceptions of the client workplace (Campone & Awal, 2012).

We see David's past background as an analytical marketing executive reflected in his desire to remain "neutral and objective." This is David's worldview or paradigm. A worldview is a lens through which we see, perceive, or view the world. David's worldview was that: "We need to be objective and neutral." Often, we are drawn to people who perceive the world in a similar way to how we see it. We resonate with these people and feel at one with them. David's supervisor advised him to be aware of his emotions but not to share them in the coaching session. This is the supervisor's belief or value system and reflects the supervisor's worldview. It echoes or supports David's worldview of neutrality in coaching in terms of emotions. A different supervisor with a different paradigm and lens might have suggested an alternative direction. It's important to note here that our worldviews are not necessarily bad or good, but more often a blind spot that we do not see. As coaches we need to become aware of these blind spots, these underlying assumptions and drivers, and we also need to become aware of our supervisors' worldviews.

Some good questions to ask ourselves as reflective coach practitioners are:

1   What do I believe about reality?
2   What do I believe about the nature of the relationship between coach and client?
3   What methods, approaches, or techniques do I use, and on what philosophy are they based?

These same questions can be posed to a supervisor.

My own answers to these questions are summarized below in brief. I disclose these to the coaches I supervise.

1   *My beliefs about reality* – I have been coaching for close to 20 years and in my experience people see their world from different perspectives, and their experiences influence the language that they use to describe their world. This, in turn, influences their world.
2   *My beliefs about the nature of the relationship between coach and coachee* – I believe it is an equal partnership with collaboration and co-creation of coaching processes. I thus believe that the coach needs to be genuine, authentic, and human. There is no need for artificial neutrality.
3   *My choice of methods and approaches* – I choose methods that resonate with the above two beliefs. I draw on the Narrative coaching approach, which involves creating awareness about the stories we form in our minds. The principles contained in Gestalt coaching, which speak about presence and enhancing self-awareness, also fit with my paradigm. The approaches I choose focus strongly on enhancing self-awareness and meaning-making – as opposed to sharing techniques and toolkits.

I believe that behavior change follows from self-awareness. The coaching process begins with understanding. Understanding encompasses many factors – understanding preferences, understanding context, understanding emotions, values, history, and multiple other considerations. Once understanding is present, the process moves to making meaning, which is personalizing the understanding of one's own identity and life choices. This leads to a person's thinking differently and only after that,

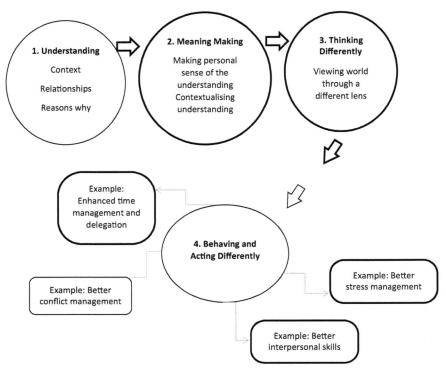

Figure 8.1 Diagrammatic overview of flow of process that leads to outcomes in coaching as described by coached executives (Cunningham, 2017, p. 108)

acting differently. This can be displayed in many ways – some of which are illustrated in Figure 8.1. The behavior examples such as stress and time management, as well as enhanced interpersonal relationships, are not an all-inclusive list of behaviors.

So the starting point of the coaching process is that we begin with awareness of our worldviews and those of our supervisors.

I will now look at emotions and the "feeling with your body" concept and share what I would have suggested to David as a supervisor. Some of these suggestions are informed by a study that I conducted on the lived experience of coached executives (Cunningham, 2017). When commenting on what made the coaching relationship valuable, the executives expressed an appreciation for who the coach was as a person. They spoke more about the coach's authenticity and presence than about the coach's qualifications and knowledge base. Presence is defined as "a state of awareness, in the moment, characterized by the felt experience of timelessness, connectedness and a larger truth" (Silsbee, 2008). Cuddy (2015, p. 25) confirms, "It is a state of being attuned and able to express true thoughts, feelings, values and potential. Presence is not about managing an impression; it's about true, powerful, honest connections that we create intensely with ourselves." So, while there are some behavioral components that demonstrate presence, it is more a state of being than actual behavior.

The "be" and "do" framework was originally developed in the United States Army as part of its Leadership model, which was known as the "Be, Know, Do" model of leadership. It was argued that because individuals influence others by their character, competencies, and actions, effective leadership development must focus on the type of person an individual is ("Be"), the kinds of competencies he has ("Know"), and the kinds of decisions he makes ("Do") (Campbell & Dardis, 2004). This model can be equally applied to coaches as it was originally applied to leaders. On the basis of what the coached executives were saying – that the "being" component was very valuable to them – I would have suggested that David focus more on the "being" component than on the "knowing" component. I do agree that psychological knowledge and acumen are a necessity, but the knowledge alone without the resonant, real presence of the coach will be limited in efficacy and application. I think David needs to let "himself," his essence, and his emotions be seen. Being appropriately human, real, and genuine in a coaching relationship is what makes the relationship so valuable.

In my study, one executive used the word "real" to describe his coach and combined it with the word "open." He stated:

> Her openness: She shared a bit about herself, her background, her family, challenges with her sister because at the time her baby was just over a year, and looking for schools for example, because her sister is in the area. So it made her real: sometimes you struggle when you have these facilitators and they sometimes have it altogether, you know?

Another executive used the word "*real*" but extended it to the idea that realness gives validity to the process. She stated: "Certainly I would say that my coach is very real, she doesn't bombard me with her stories about herself, which is just as it should be, but you know from just occasional things that she will say, that she has kind of been there, done that. So it is just that validity that you get." Authenticity and presence were closely related, as described by an executive, who said of his coach: "He was a very genuine person, that is the other thing – genuine and sincere – if I have to I would attach these kind of labels but they do not really describe the full story. . . . Obviously there [is] quite a bit of trust built up early on." It is interesting that both these executives comment on the trust they developed in relation to the genuineness and realness of the coach.

As David's supervisor, I would have explored with him how to be more present, authentic, real, and genuine, how to show up with his emotions. I would commend him for the times he had the courage to voice his inferences and encourage him to keep doing this. I would suggest he increase his awareness of his own contributions to coaching sessions. He could reflect on these questions: What is happening to my body as the client speaks? How could this awareness potentially help the coaching conversation? Should it be used or not?

As an illustration, I've summarized a case below where I used my own body's feelings in a coaching session.

Natalie was coaching a young manager, Paul. Paul tended to be verbose and overly detailed in his conversations. He would repeat himself and then digress. He would talk in a monotone. Natalie was an experienced coach but found herself struggling to listen effectively. She found herself fidgeting and shifting positions, looking around the room, and feeling a sense of impatience. Natalie shared with Paul her experience by saying: "Paul, I am finding my attention wandering and I am starting to feel restless. I am just wondering: If I as a person who listens as a career am struggling, how might others also struggle to stay focused and listen?" Paul said at a later stage that this was the most memorable conversation in the coaching process and that it shifted his behavior. In the end, he improved his conversational skills.

As the above vignette shows, I drew heavily on Gestalt coaching. Gestalt coaching is an approach that brings in a strong focus on body and emotions. Other approaches with a similar focus include onto-logical coaching, somatic coaching, and interpersonal neurobiology approaches. I believe that knowledge in these areas can always help us understand the role of emotions in coaching. We must balance who we are (**be**) with what we **know** and **do**. We need to do this with all aspects of coaching, including emotional awareness.

In conclusion, I would like to reiterate:

1   Coaches need supervision.
2   Coaches need to be aware of their own worldview, their preferences, assumptions, and biases that influence their coaching practice and choices. Increasing this awareness will lead to their making more mindful choices in terms of their methods and approaches.
3   Coaches need to be aware of their supervisors' worldviews, biases, preferences, and assumptions, which influence the supervision relationship, and subsequently to be mindful of these when reflecting on the supervision process.
4   Coaches need to recognize that their authenticity and presence are valued by coachees. They need to be mindful of how they show up at coaching sessions – how they are, not only what they do.
5   A range of different methodologies can enhance the knowledge component of emotional and somatic coaching approaches.

Commentary 8.2.b

Alison Pullen and Mojdeh Tavanayan

Since the 1970s emotions have attracted multidisciplinary scholarly attention. Emotions are an intrinsic element in the creation of management knowledge and the process of learning (Fineman, 1997). On the one hand is the common myth that work is the public domain of rational behavior while emotions are the domain of private life (Putnam & Mumby, 1993). In studies of managerial work, for example, we see this in the rational, disembodied manager, often viewed as the "ideal worker" (Roper, 1994; Acker, 1990). The repression of emotion at work has thus been recognized in the literature on emotions and management (Fineman, 2000). On the other hand, emotion work, emotional labor, and the management of emotions have become central to discussions of the labor process and management of people. Hochschild's groundbreaking work on emotion-management (1979) exposed the ways in which the instrumentalization and manipulation of emotions in the workplace across many occupations and industries have required people to perform their roles and demonstrate commitment to organizations by displaying positive emotions of love, joy, happiness, and so forth (Bolton, 2004). Further, we also know that negative emotions are part of the fabric of organizational life as fear, worry, envy, and anger are intrinsic parts of working life, and their manifestations depend on individual personalities and organizational cultures. There is an organizational demand for individuals who are emotionally intelligent and can read the needs of their clients, roles, and organizations and display the appropriate emotions accordingly.

Coaching requires high levels of emotional labor and emotional intelligence, but also the built-in self-management of emotions, so they are used appropriately through the facilitation process, repressing any unnecessary or inappropriate emotions. Coaching, emotion work, and the management of emotions can be a complex territory for professional coaches like David. If we consider a management learning perspective, the learning that David is displaying in the case can be characterized as a set of rational activities (reflecting, evaluating, integrating, and communicating), and these processes are informed by emotions and/or are affected by individuals' state of emotionality. Fineman (1997) articulates that management learning is not outside of the socially contextualized, socially constructed discourse on emotions, and offers the concept of "cogmotion" to explore the cognitive, rational elements of learning and emotions.

Coaching not only involves the management of emotions to perform the role, but also the reflexive knowledge that emerges not only from thought and cogmotion, but also the body. Alison's reading of *Feeling with your body* prompts several initial questions. First, the career change from marketing executive to leadership coach invokes a reaction that David is moving from a role characterized as disembodied to coaching, which requires interaction, engagement, and increased intimacy with clients. Central to the coaching role is the built-in tension of managing self and other (coachee). Therefore, coaching requires the coach to understand the complexities of the ways in which self-other relations inform the working relationship. Emotional reactions are ever present, and the coach is required to be aware of the emotions of others. However, emotional dissonance between self and other can affect the coaching relationship and also the well-being of both the coach and coachee. Second, because of the nature of coaching, the body becomes a source of knowledge and reflection (Ignatow, 2007), and the surfacing of unexpected emotions unanticipated by David is open and transparent. Third, the containment of emotions experienced during the coaching sessions raises questions about how to manage the emergent nature of coaching.

Given that David's supervisor "told him" to "acknowledge his feelings without voicing them in the coaching sessions," a question emerges about what to do with the emotions as they present in the moment and how to process, manage, and control them in the interactions with the coachee. Further, how can the coachee's emotions be read and used to enhance the coaching experience and outcomes? And, how can David's reflexivity about his own known feelings be used as a way to enhance the coaching relationship? Given that David turns to psychology classes to enhance his knowledge, he learned processes that he uses to read the psychoanalytic dimensions of the coaching relationship. However, whether David's psychoanalytic methods work with his emotions can be questioned, but this cannot be supported by the material presented in this case. Here, much emphasis is placed on David's ability to voice coaching behaviors. Some questions we can ask are: What happens to the emotions that surface after coaching sessions? What types of emotions are these? Positive? Negative? How does David manage his emotions after coaching sessions? Does he have a coaching mentor? In other words, what can David do with all these emotions after coaching? Are there emotions that remain either unknown to him or never surface? Do emotions go away or linger in the body?

The case prompts as many questions as responses. The types of emotions that surface in coaching are not made explicit. It would be interesting for David to reflect on the ways in which he privileges the management of some emotions over others because the acceptance of emotions are not equal, given the range from positive to negative that either coachee or coach might experience in the coaching interaction. For example, how would David respond to a charged environment in which unexpected emotions surface, given his previous career? Does David retreat back to practicing the containment of emotions when certain emotions are triggered?

Overall, emotional awareness and reflexivity as a coach are central to David's success. Reflexivity requires both cognitive and embodied awareness. Embodied knowledge is the means through which individuals feel and understand everyday life, garnered through emotions and seeping into the coaching space. Feminist writers such as Elspeth Probyn remind us that affect (as the consequence of being *affected* by another body, by something external) has the potential to make us question our ingrained assumptions about the people and organizations we experience and the roles we practice. In organization studies we have experienced an affective turn (Clough, 2007) and affect becomes the means through which organization are understood and conceptualized (see special issue by Fotaki, Kenny, & Vachhani, 2017). Affective relations between bodies and the constructs we use to think about, order, and evaluate bodies have received increasing attention in organization studies. Pullen, Rhodes, and Thanem (2017) demonstrate the containment of affect, and the desire for such containment in organizations:

> As I write this now, some years later, I still feel the deep sigh that emerged from my gut that evening. I remember the hard hit of a heavy, throbbing pulse. I remember too controlling my response and having to contain the visceral affects with which my body responded. What would the consequences be of giving in to these affects? Affective containment requires order, control, and organization of the body. Giving in to the visceral would be unprofessional, chaotic and, maybe, hysterical.

Given the privileged position that coaches occupy, there is an obligation to engage and work with the embodied knowledge that emerges from the coaching encounter, but also to contain it until the "right time." Probyn comments that there is a problem of "how to account for practical knowledge" (Probyn, 2004, p. 335) because it is ever present and we can now reflect that surfacing this practical knowledge becomes a platform for discussion, disruption, and change. To illustrate, self-reflexivity of the coachee during coaching can have greater, lasting effects organizationally, such as a senior manager realizing that she is an abusive manager of staff, or a senior executive acknowledging that his lack of moral decision-making in the organization has contributed to a recent scandal. Acknowledging and reflecting on emotions in coaching can facilitate individuals to become more responsible for their own self-reflexivity, as well as the embodied reflexivity required to coach. Reflecting on this embodied knowledge changes the conversation from emotions and how to manage them to the potential use of embodied knowledge as a coaching practice. After all, affects are the "visceral points" or "hunches" that move us (Hickey-Moody, 2013, p. 81) to act. The embodied affects live on well beyond the events in which we first experience them.

Conclusion

To address the issue of emotions in coaching through the cases presented in this chapter, our experts have taken different perspectives. The neuroscience perspective sheds light on the parts of the brain controlling our emotions, the stress hormones, the fight, flight, or freeze reaction when facing stress, and how these apply to the coach. The ontological perspective stresses the importance of awareness and assessment of one's being, which leads to identifying what is missing in order to create possibilities. And the Gestalt perspective offers a strong focus on the relationship between the body and emotions.

All these different perspectives ultimately converge and provide similar recommendations to help coaches tap into their emotions, as well as those of the client, and facilitate informed decisions. In fact, Cox and Bachkirova (2007) identified the ways that coaches currently deal with their own difficult emotions. These include reflection and self-examination, actively exploring the issue with the client, and taking the issue to supervision. Our experts, in their commentaries, have reiterated those ideas, and further built on them. They suggest that, when dealing with their own emotions, coaches are encouraged to do the following:

- Exercise self-observation, which leads to mindfulness and self-awareness, and follow with self-correction and self-generation.
- Embrace and cultivate qualities such as: calm, curiosity, courage, creativity, clarity, compassion, confidence, patience, perseverance, playfulness, authenticity, presence, true and honest connection, and openness.
- Seek support when needed whether by a coaching supervisor or a therapist to increase mindfulness and learn how to deal with emotions.
- Refine observation and interpretation skills by testing one's underlying assumptions, worldviews, and beliefs, which form our assessment about ourselves, others, and reality.

When it comes to dealing with the coachee's emotions, Cox and Patrick (2012) showed that coaching can be instrumental in helping coachees identify and regulate counterproductive emotional responses and gain power over their own feelings, resulting in increased freedom from previously experienced emotions. According to our experts, coaches can achieve this by applying to the coachee the same principles outlined above. In other words, a coach can support the coachee to exercise self-observation, identify the underlying assumptions and beliefs, and be honest, open, and present.

References

Acker, J. (1990). Hierarchies, jobs, bodies: A theory of gendered organizations. *Gender and Society*, 4(2), 139–158.

Bolton, S. C. (2004). *Emotion management in the workplace*. New York: Palgrave Macmillan.

Bresser, F. (2013). *Coaching across the globe: Benchmark results of the Bresser Consulting Global Coaching Survey with a supplementary update highlighting the latest coaching developments to 2013:* BoD–Books on Demand.

Campbell, D. J., & Dardis, G. J. (2004). The "be, know, do" model of leader development. *People and Strategy, 7*(2), 26.

Campone, F., & Awal, D. (2012). Life's thumbprint: The impact of significant life events on coaches and their coaching. *Coaching: An International Journal of Theory, Research and Practice, 5*(1), 22–36.

Clough, P.T. (2007). Introduction. In P.T. Clough & J. Halley (Eds.), *The affective turn: Theorizing the social* (pp. 1–33). Durham, NC: Duke University Press.

Cox, E., & Bachkirova, T. (2007). Coaching with emotion: How coaches deal with difficult emotional situations. *International Coaching Psychology Review, 2*(2), 17–28.

Cox, E., & Patrick, C. (2012). Managing emotions at work: How coaching affects retail support workers' performance and motivation. *International Journal of Evidence Based Coaching and Mentoring, 10*(2), 34–51.

Cuddy, A. (2015). *Presence: Bring your boldest self to your biggest challenges.* New York, NY: Hachette.

Cunningham, N. (2017). *A theory of the coaching process based on the lived experience of coached executives in South Africa* (PhD thesis), University of the Witwatersrand, Johannesburg, Wits Business School.

Fineman, S. (1997). Emotion and management learning. *Management Learning, 28*(1), 13–25.

Fineman, S. (Ed.). (2000). *Emotion in organizations.* London: Sage Publications.

Flores, F. (2012). *Conversation for Action and Collected Essays: Instilling a Culture of Commitment in Working Relationships.* CreateSpace Publishing Platform, South Carolina.

Fotaki, M., Kenny, K., & Vachhani, S. J. (2017). Thinking critically about affect in organization studies: Why it matters. *Organization, 24*(1), 3–17.

Grant, A. M. (2012). "Australian Coaches" views on coaching supervision: A study with implications for Australian coach education, training and practice. *International Journal of Evidence Based Coaching & Mentoring, 10*(2).

Hawkins, P., & Schwenk, G. (2011). The seven-eyed model of coaching supervision. In T. Bachkirova, P. Jackson, & D. Clutterbuck (Eds.), *Coaching and mentoring supervision theory and practice* (pp. 28–40). Berkshire: McGraw Hill.

Hickey-Moody, A. (2013). Affect as method: Feelings, aesthetics and affective pedagogy. In R. Coleman & J. Ringrose (Eds.), *Deleuze and research methodologies.* Edinburgh: Edinburgh University Press.

Hochschild, A. R. (1979). Emotion work, feeling rules, and social structure. *American Journal of Sociology, 85*(3), 551–575.

Ignatow, G. (2007). Theories of embodied knowledge: New directions for cultural and cognitive sociology? *Journal for the Theory of Social Behaviour, 37*(2), 115–135.

Joiner, W. B., & Josephs, S. A. (2006). *Leadership agility: Five levels of mastery for anticipating and initiating change.* San Francisco, CA: Jossey-Bass.

Koestenbaum, P., & Block, P. (2003). *Freedom and accountability at work: applying philosophic insight to the real world.* San Francisco, CA: Jossey-Bass.

Labarre, P. (2000). *Do you have the will to lead?* New York, NY: Fast Company.

Lawrence, P., & Whyte, A. (2014). What is coaching supervision and is it important? *Coaching: An International Journal of Theory, Research and Practice, 7*(1), 39–55.

Louis, D. (2015). *Complexity in executive coaching: Toward a theoretical framework to analyze the nature and management of multiple stakeholders and agendas* (PhD thesis), Grenoble Ecole de Management.

Passmore, J., & McGoldrick, S. (2009). Super-vision, extra-vision or blind faith? A grounded theory study of the efficacy of coaching supervision. *International Coaching Psychology Review*, *4*(2), 143–159.

Probyn, E. (2004). Everyday shame. *Cultural Studies*, *18*(2–3), 328–349.

Pullen, A., Rhodes, C., & Thanem, T. (2017). Affective politics in the gendered organization. *Organization*, *24*(1), 105–123.

Putnam, L. L., & Mumby, D. K. (1993). Organizations, emotion and the myth of rationality. *Emotion in Organizations*, *1*, 36–57.

Roper, M. (1994). *Masculinity and the British organization man since 1945*. Oxford: Oxford University Press.

Schwartz, R. C. (1997). *Internal family systems therapy* (The Guilford family therapy series). New York, NY: Guilford Press.

Siegel, D. (2010). *Mindsight: The new science of personal transformation*. New York, NY: Bantam.

Sieler, A. (2003). *Coaching to the human soul: Ontological coaching and deep change* (Vol. I, pp. 3–35, 350–357). Melbourne: Newfield Australia.

Sieler, A. (2007). *Coaching to the human soul: Ontological coaching and deep change*, (Vol. II, pp. 111–121). Melbourne: Newfield Australia.

Silsbee, D. (2008). *Presence-based coaching: Cultivating self-generative leaders through mind, body, and heart*. San Francisco, CA: Jossey-Bass.

Turner, R. A., & Goodrich, J. (2010). The case of eclectism in executive coaching: Application to challenging assignments. *Consulting Psychology Journal: Practice and Research*, *62*(1), 39–55.

9   Codes in coaching

Introduction

Most, if not all, coaching associations have a code of conduct, i.e., a text describing the dos and don'ts of so-called "quality" practice (Cloet & Vernazobres, 2011 p. 39). Codes stand as key references for training and accreditation purposes, and overall, they legitimize the service provided. However, referring solely to codes of conduct can prove limited – even dangerous – when it comes to solving ethical dilemmas (Fatien Diochon & Nizet, 2015). Indeed, in the specific case of coaching, Fatien Diochon and Nizet (2015) have identified three major restrictions to the use of codes to solve ethical dilemmas in coaching: 1) the code is not relevant to the situations at hand or does not represent a legitimate authority for the other party, 2) the code has shortcomings, such as being too cognitive, too simplistic, or too timorous, and 3) the code is an obstacle to the ethics of the coach who does not see him or herself in the code, for example in terms of personal values, whose role is specifically discussed in Chapter 4.

More generally, critical studies in organizations show that codes prove limited in reducing an ethical decision to a compliant issue, i.e., the application of an externally imposed frame of reference, neglecting the emotional and reflexive process inherent to an ethical decision (Mercier & Deslandes, 2017). In this chapter, the two cases explore some challenges that stem from departing from the application of the code. Bob provides an example of a coach who *Followed the code and fled*, as his rational decision to follow the code contradicted his emotional intuition to take distance from it. Second, Flora's case exposes us to the challenge of what she frames as *Embracing one's freedom* when questioning the code.

Case 9.1. I followed the code and fled

Bob is an external coach, with a background in clinical psychology and more than 30 years of coaching experience. One day, he was called on by a pharamaceutical company to help Alex, a doctor, better manage his team. The initial three-party meeting with Alex's manager went relatively well. He noticed though that Alex's manager was the standard Nurturing Parent in Transactional Analysis terms: "She was very caring but never passed up the opportunity to underline your errors in red."

Bob was satisfied with his first coaching sessions with Alex, who seemed very engaged in the beginning. But to Bob's surprise, at the fourth session, Alex told him: "I've been thinking a lot, and our coaching work has helped me see that, in the end, it's better for me to leave the company. I have no future here with this manager or in this department." Thus, Alex explained, he wanted to focus the remaining coaching sessions on preparing for his new career.

Immediately, Bob felt deeply uncomfortable. On one hand, he understood the motivations of his coachee and the rationale behind his decision. He even found them legitimate, given the dysfunctional relationship between Alex and his manager; Bob also confessed to identifying with the client, who seemed young and brilliant. He said to himself: "After all, this poor guy is the one who's trapped, and I can't leave him alone or let him down." On the other hand, from a deontological point of view, Bob had to stay within the boundaries of the contract. He summarized his discomfort as follows: "My ethics tell me to protect the weak and oppressed. But from a deontological standpoint, I am supposed to meet the needs of both parties."

Reflexive questions

- How do you understand Bob's dilemma?
- What situations, if any, could lead you to "take the side" of the coachee? Or the organization?
- What would you do if you were Bob?

Bob solved his dilemma by sharing his feelings with his client and asking him to renegotiate the coaching contract with the HR manager. Given the refusal of the client to do this, Bob put an end to the contract, not without pain, and estimated that he made a deontological decision, but not an ethical one. Indeed, he said,

> Ultimately, my decision was rational, based on the code. I followed my reason, not my emotions. So the deontology overrode the ethics.

But physically, I was not fine at all with that; I felt like I was flee-ing. I was really looking forward to the end of that assignment. And stakes were so high that I didn't even look my coachee in the eye when I told him my decision. . . . I think that, symbolically, I wanted to show him the inner conflict I was dealing with personally.

Reflexive questions

- Bob differentiates between deontology and ethics in explaining his reasoning. To what does he associate deontology? Ethics?
- Do you make a distinction between deontology and ethics? If so, how?
- Do you think Bob made the right decision?
- What, in your experience, are some limitiations to using the code of ethics to solve dilemmas?

A shorter version of this case has been published in: Fatien Diochon, P. and Nizet, J. (2015) "Ethical codes and executive coaches: One size does not fit all" *Journal of Applied Behavioral Science*, 51(2) 277–301.

Commentary 9.1.a

Gilles Amado

This case illustrates for me a variety of issues in the coaching practice from which I have selected five to discuss: the nature and effects of the contract, "reality and truth," the coach/coachee relationship, the reso-nance processes, and deontology and ethics.

I will present and discuss them in relation to several aspects of this case.

A contract or a simulacrum

It is very common, when a coach is called by an organization, to have a three-party meeting – between the future coachee, his/her boss or HR manager, and the coach – where a contract is established about the mis-sion, generally the improvement of the coachee's skills/behavior.

A series of problems can occur here:

- First, regarding the objectives of the mission, focusing on the improvement of individual skills and behavior might leave in the shadows the potential responsibility of the boss and/or the organization in the problems the coachee is facing.
- Second, related to the process, and this is what I will mostly address here, there can be a type of simulacrum, mostly from the coachee, during this contractual phase for a few reasons:
  - The coachee may have no other choice than to agree because of power issues or economic motives.
  - He/she may agree formally but try to use the coach for his/her own benefit, different from the boss' objective.
  - Nobody knows exactly how the coach works (even if precautions are taken on that issue) or what can really happen in the interaction, which can lead to all sorts of misleading expectations.
  - Such a three-party contract, when one of its members (usually the coachee) does not follow its initial purpose, should ideally be renegotiated.

In the present case, we are unable to assess precisely the quality of the coachee's engagement, or whether a three-party renegotiation will take place.

While it is not unusual to see the agenda shifting over the course of the coaching – and any coach can easily identify with Bob's dilemma – the request Bob makes of Alex to renegotiate the objective of the coaching in order to help him leave the company brings challenges:

  - It puts pressure on the coachee, where the responsibility of this "new" desire is also dependent on the interactions that take place with the coach.
  - It bypasses Alex's manager and the initial contract.

- It creates a challenge for the HR manager who would probably wish to avoid bypassing Alex's manager.

Therefore, given the possible simulacrum during the contractual phase and the emergence of hidden agendas over the coaching engagement, I would recommend having a private interview early on with each of the parties before having a three-party meeting. This modality may lead to an understanding from the beginning of the possible discrepancy between expectations and to anticipation of any difficulties and drawbacks.

Reality and truth: forget about them

The coach never has access to the "reality" of the work situation (reality testing does not exist), or to the "truth," i.e., the validity of the analysis of the situation by his/her interlocutors. The coach deals mainly (only?) with the perceptions of the so-called reality and the necessary subjective analyses that are offered to him or her for a variety of reasons and purposes, some conscious, some less conscious. The coach's job, therefore, means working with perceptions and intersubjectivity, which also means, of course, being aware of the coach's feelings and thoughts during the sessions and outside them in order to make sense of the impact of what psychoanalysis calls "countertransference" (Stefana, 2017) issues (i.e., here emotions and ideas stimulated by the coachee's discourse, which need to be worked through).

In this case, Bob sometimes gives the impression that he takes for granted the descriptions and analyses of his interlocutors without giving us sufficient data about his own feelings and analysis. For example, if the initial three-party meeting, according to him, went "relatively well," what does "relatively" mean?

Isn't it because Bob experienced within himself ambivalent feelings about Alex (caring but judging)? Isn't it dangerous to find the decision "legitimate" to leave a company on the basis of a perceived "dysfunctional" relationship? Isn't there a risk that such an experience will happen again elsewhere if the coach gives credit to his feeling that his coachee is "weak and oppressed"?

Protecting or colluding?

Because one can't have access to "reality" and "truth," the only way to practice deontological work as a coach is to maintain a reasonable distance from the feelings and thoughts of the interlocutors. This requires empathy, not identification: empathy as a permanent effort to grasp something of the inner reality expressed by the coachee while avoiding the collusion of identification where the distance is abolished. "Because it was him, because it was me," the French writer Montaigne said of his friend La Boétie.

One has to recognize that the dual situation of coaching often stimulates protection and identification processes. One of the reasons is that the personal success of a coach may depend on the success of his/her coachee. Another one is that the coach may wish (sometimes even dream of) achieving the status position of the coachee.

In the present case, Bob confesses to identifying with his client, a "young and brilliant" guy, "trapped" by a manager who was "the standard nurturing parent" (a qualification that does not seem positive in the coach's mind). Undoubtedly, Bob's identification with his coachee and a possible counter-identification with his boss did not help him to maintain the appropriate distance.

The unpredictability of the resonance process

Individuals differ from one another in that situations and words resonate differently in each person's mind, guts, and psyche, even if similar collective resonances happen sometimes (Amado, 2010). Most of the time, resonance processes cannot be anticipated, as their effects are generally unpredictable. Even if we don't want to hurt another, this can happen to our surprise.

Here Bob does not seem to have anticipated Alex's decision. Is it because Bob identified too much with Alex's success in the firm? Is it because the information he got during the sessions misled him? Alex's decision may be simply the result of unpredictable resonances produced during the sessions.

Because of such unpredictability, my personal view is that coaches should be careful when signing contracts: the coaching situation may reveal hidden meanings and wishes, and awareness of these may free coachees from inhibitions. This possibility should be acknowledged and accepted in order to protect the coach who wishes to truly help his/her coachee.

However, one way to "control" the mysterious resonance processes is by making time to review at the end of each coaching session and check regularly where we are in relation to the initial coaching objective.

Deontology and ethics

In this case, it is difficult to follow Bob's reasoning with his dilemma. Most of the reasons are linked to the above observations. Indeed, such a dilemma, which led to Bob's strong sense of guilt (he couldn't even look

Alex in the eyes), depends both on the insufficient care taken in the contract negotiation and on Bob's emotional and "irrational" collusion with the coachee. Here, we may point out a mechanism of "projective identification" (Roth, 2005). After all, leaving the company may not be such a bad option for Alex. It may even be the best solution, who knows? Coaching may have been the transitional, safe space (Amado & Ambrose, 2001; Amado & Vansina, 2005) Alex needed to make the best decision, "making the right accident happen," as Harold Bridger (one of the founding members of the Tavistock Institute of Human Relations) would have said. One indication for such a hypothesis is given by the coachee himself who declares that – thanks to the coaching – he has been "thinking a lot," which has helped him realize that it is better to leave the company. Therefore, the coaching may be considered a success from the point of view of the personal and professional development of Alex, even if Bob can't go on to help him achieve the goals of the coaching contract.

By some aspects, Bob's attachment to his coachee resembles that of a mother. But Alex is not a child; moreover, he grew through the coaching experience and may be well aware that the early contract is already over if he chooses to leave the company. I think Bob may have projected his own fears (to be mistreated, rejected, even abandoned), identifying himself in an imaginary "weak" Alex. Such anxiety, mixed with the feeling of betrayal towards the firm, may have been the source of Bob's "inner conflict."

More generally, I wish to say that the clearer the personal ethics of the coach and contract are made, the easier the decision can be made when ethics and deontology seem to be conflicting. This does not mean that such a tension is easy to manage. Even a very experienced coach with a clinical background in psychology, exploring his own behavior honestly, may become trapped in such dilemmas. This is one of the lessons of this case, which deserves our great thanks to Bob for his generous "transparency."

Commentary 9.1.b

Alyssa Freas

Bob's dilemma is one that many executive coaches face. Bob felt that from a deontological point of view he had to stay within the boundaries of the contract to which he had agreed upon with the organization (his client). Even if Bob empathized with Alex (his client) and understood the motivations and rationale for Alex's decisions, Bob felt he was "supposed to meet the needs of both parties [or clients]," and so his actions followed deontological ethics.

Bob's dilemma and others like it are often defused by clear contracting with "the client." Understanding who the client is may be complex in a coaching situation. The more upfront work done with "the client," the easier it is to have congruence between legitimate decisions about coaching and adherence to the "boundaries of the contract." While Bob may have 30 years of coaching experience, he was caught up in a dilemma that is often cleared up during the contracting phase. Clear contracting is essential because:

> Coaching creates a triangular relationship between the coach who provides the service, the coachee who receives the coaching, and the client that pays the coaching bills. The client actually is a collection of interested parties, usually including the coachee's boss – a key player – and the human resources department. The work succeeds when all the people involved agree on explicit goals that genuinely further their own interests as well as the common good.
>
> (Sherman & Freas, 2004)

When contracting, we discuss possibilities such as these:

- What if the coachee is fired?
- What if the coachee gets a new job?
- What if the client needs to move the coachee to another position?
- What if the organization is desperate to have the coachee succeed in the current position, but the coach doesn't believe that will happen and says "It isn't possible"?
- What if the board wants something that isn't part of the CEO's coaching?

While contracting can't predetermine every possible situation, clear contracting does establish well-defined boundaries, identifies the client and decision-makers in the process, delineates roles, and gives the coach more opportunities for clarity.

While Bob wanted to "take sides," his adherence to the deontological decision helped him to see that he had a "perceived duty" to excuse himself from helping Alex prepare for a role in another company. A coach must consistently do the honorable thing – clarify objectives, make clear who the client is, ensure everyone knows who is accountable for the success of the coaching process, and gain agreement on the measures of success. This must all be a part of the initial phase of the coaching process.

This isn't a game. We are not cheerleaders or advocates. There is no "taking sides" since, as executive coaches, we serve the system. We coach leaders, teams, and organizations to be the best, to inspire others to achieve top performance, and to go beyond what they thought they were capable of doing.

While it was uncomfortable for Bob, he did stick with the contract and the commitments he made to the organization. He navigated through the process with integrity. It may be that if Bob had made his personal ethics clear prior to undertaking the work, he could have said, "I am going to coach Alex in confidence," and not had any concerns that Alex would soon be leaving because he told the organization who he thought the real client was – Alex.

In our experience, a coach's self-awareness can help prevent personal vulnerabilities, perspectives, political beliefs, philosophies, or opinions from complicating the contract with the organization. A coach must be explicit with the organization upfront so as to avoid difficulties during the process.

For example, initial conversations among the parties might also include the duty to inform, e.g., if the coach becomes aware of a situation that could cause material harm to the organization or to an individual. That conversation might also include some examples of situations where the coach may feel it appropriate to terminate the relationship, e.g., being asked to do something unethical. Describing what an executive coach is and is not is also a good idea – not a psychiatrist, an employee, a management consultant, or an outplacement firm, etc.

Acting with integrity, knowing the right thing to do, and behaving with a high level of ethical integrity are universally important for the client organization and coachee, and, no less, for the executive coach. Those north stars guide the coach as unanticipated situations arise, for example:

> Together, the three parties should choose goals that maximize mutual interests. If the client has a strategic objective and the executive has a career objective, for example, they must identify a goal that integrates both aims. . . . Coaching contracts should reflect the sensitive nature of the task. Ours usually include a no-fault escape

clause, permitting any party to terminate a coaching relationship that isn't working. When we find ourselves in an engagement that isn't working for one reason or another, we exit. That's awkward, but it saves the client's money and improves results.

(Sherman & Freas, 2004)

We follow these "rules" so that well-intentioned clients don't make unintended mistakes or ask for things we can't do or won't do on their behalf. Our firm has experiences with these concerns. For example, one organization told us they were going to fire an individual we were coaching and asked us to keep that plan confidential yet continue to coach the individual for another three months while they searched for a replacement. We negotiated a much more transparent process that yielded better results for the individual, the organization, and the coach.

In another instance, a venture capital (VC) firm hired us to coach a CEO they had brought in – from the opposite coast of the US – to turn around one of the companies they had invested in. We found out early in the coaching process that this new CEO was perceived to have serious behavioral issues that were not likely to be resolved in coaching, e.g., he was viewed as untrustworthy and uninformed about the business. We had serious ethical reservations about the VC firm's plan to move the new CEO's family across the country in light of our sense that the CEO was not going to last long in the company. The deontological challenge was: do we "honor" our contract and coach, or do we surface our perception that this CEO would not perform well in the role? Given the new CEO's resistance to much of the feedback, we felt an obligation to bring our awareness of the low likelihood of his success in this company – with or without coaching – out into the open. Despite our strong concerns, the VC firm invited us to stay on, saying they would increase our fee even though we made clear that it would have no impact. We declined the offer and persisted in setting up a three-party clarifying conversation with the coach, the CEO, and the venture capitalist. Prior to that meeting, we coached the venture capitalist about their obligation to do the right thing regarding their plan to move the coachee's family across the United States. This had become a coaching opportunity not just for an individual, but for the entire system. In the end (after two sessions), they agreed that they had to make a change in their choice of CEO. The end results were: a humane disengagement of the CEO from the company, no cross-country move, a more suitable job for the executive, and an opportunity for the company to find a better fit for the CEO position.

In yet another organization, we were asked to coach a president who was viewed as a rising star and part of the C-suite succession plan. He was promoted, but he was not successful in the new role. The organization asked our opinion about his potential for future success in that role. Instead of answering that question directly we put the accountability for answering it back onto the client organization. We engaged the executive's manager and HR in thinking through what the executive and the organization needed long term. And, what would the impact be of removing him from his current role? Our contractual commitment was to ensure the organization received value from our coaching. Rather than simply answering their question – which coaches should never do anyway – we had interactions with the manager and HR that provided a deeper level of reflection on the strategic moves they needed to make in order to achieve the best possible outcome for the entire system.

It all boils down to having the courage to do the right thing. In the end, the contract outlines much of what is right and what is wrong. Sometimes, however, you have to use experience to distinguish between the two and to act accordingly. This may be a particularly difficult choice for a coach just starting out. However, not only may it be the right thing to do, but if a young coach makes a bad choice, from a purely pragmatic standpoint, that choice could have serious career consequences down the road. It is also important to hold the system accountable, and that should be done upfront, not afterwards as a reaction. To do that, a coach must have the experience required to develop an effective coaching process and the courage to do what is right.

If we were in Bob's shoes, we would:

1   Go back to the basics and make it clear to Alex that we weren't in a position to coach him on how to prepare for a role in a different company while being paid by his current employer. We believe Bob likely said to Alex something like, "As much as I'd like to help you with your transition, I can't because I believe both you and the organization are my clients and your goals are in conflict." Perhaps Bob could add, "If I have permission to coach you under those conditions, I will happily do so."

2 Offer to Alex, "If you want to pay my coaching fee directly, and with the permission of your current company, I will consider working with you after you leave the organization."

3 Suggest to Alex that he use the current budget to learn how to work effectively with difficult and challenging bosses. We would recommend to Alex that he ask himself, "What can I learn? Why do I really want to leave?" Then we would engage him in a consequential conversation with his boss. We would coach Alex to define for his boss (and himself) what would need to be different for him to be more comfortable. We would get Alex focused on keeping his commitment to growth and would deflect the opportunity to help him leave. In so doing, we would feel that our personal ethical interests were consistent with the deontological "adherence to the rules."

4 Engage in meetings with Alex and his boss so that Alex learns specific techniques that will generalize to other situations and improve Alex's performance.

We would not ever view our clients as victims of their boss' behavior. Rather, we look at tough boss situations as opportunities to learn. We never want to find ourselves in a position as coaches where we are going to "protect the weak and oppressed." Indeed, we wouldn't want to set our coachees up to believe they needed protection. Our role as coaches is to enhance the growth of the coachee, not to protect him or her.

In the end, the practical reality is this: As coaches, we cannot predict the future success of our coachees, but we hope to build success for the organization and the coachee. In order to do so, we must start with clear contracting. We also have to ensure clear roles and accountabilities in the coaching process. All the pieces work together to ensure success.

Bob used adherence to the contract to make a decision that he was not personally comfortable with, yet it was "rational and based on the code." If Bob continues to have concerns over such decisions, he could use this experience to redefine how he contracts with organizations, stating that the coachee is the primary client. In our experience, most organizations invest in coaching for the betterment of the *organization* not just the individual, so Bob's decision to create a new form of contracting could impact his client list. Still, it's an interesting choice to consider.

Case 9.2. Embracing one's freedom

Flora was working as a sub-contractor for a company that she knew well, for which she had mostly provided training. But this time she'd been hired for a coaching assignment. This situation caused two issues for her. First, because she was in a situation of subordination with this company she had to follow the coaching process, methods, and tools that they had sold and were providing to her. This included using a certain coaching model (based on behavioral and cognitive theories). She was familiar with this method because she'd used it in training, but applying it to coaching constrained her, making it difficult for her to determine her own "zone of freedom."

Second, Flora progressively worried that her coachee might be the victim of mistreatment by his boss. She told herself, "This guy might be in a situation . . . I will not say it's active harassment, but it seems like his boss doesn't really trust him and is progressively pushing him aside. And my coachee is totally blind to what's taking place."

Flora felt very much at ease because of what she called "her principle of neutrality." She believed that there were two major schools of thought: neutral coaches and engaged coaches. Given her psychoanalytical background, she believed in neutrality. At that time, her philosophy was to base her intervention on what the client brought to the coaching. In this situation, if she were to speak up, she would do something that departed from what her coachee had told her. Her dilemma was the following: "Should I warn my coachee of a worrisome situation, between him and his manager, when he isn't asking me to work on that? Who am I to 'shake the tree,' taking on this issue over those agreed upon in the contract?" Indeed, this action was totally outside the scope of the predefined contract. Flora continued, "I feel guilty using time paid for by the organization to work on something they didn't ask me to . . . but I realized the barn was on fire while we were enjoying a cup of tea!"

Reflexive questions

- How do you define your coaching philosophy?
- In forming your coaching intervention, how much comes from you? From the paying organization or the subcontracting company? From the coachee?
- Under what circumstances might you share your analysis with the coachee?

Flora dealt with the situation by talking to her supervisor. "He first comforted me in my analysis of the situation, saying that given all the elements I had gathered, I could legitimately conclude that the coachee might be the victim of moral harassment. Second, he helped me take distance from the situation and avoid falling into the deontological trap that was threatening me." The supervisor explained to Flora that while neutrality was indeed important and represented "a certain commitment, there was a higher commitment." In this situation, given her psychological background, she was able to make an informed analysis, draw some conclusions about the coachee's well-being, and speak up. Today, she feels that in a similar situation she would not be so skittish. She would speak up more easily and "embrace [her] freedom." "But," as she said, "this is an ethical choice, not to explicitly follow the code of conduct – and the expected neutrality. And embracing one's freedom is scary."

Reflexive questions

- Like Flora, have you ever experienced a "superior commitment" or "duty alert"? If so, what brought you there?
- Have you ever voiced your concerns or analysis about a coaching situation to a supervisor or other party? If so, how and when?
- How do you understand Flora's statement: "Embracing one's freedom can be scary"?
- What factors might discourage you from voicing your concerns to your coachee, the organization, and/or other stakeholders? What factors might encourage you to do so?

Commentary 9.2.a

Tatiana Bachkirova

I found this case interesting on many levels. First of all, it is about the coach as a person, working on the self during coaching supervision, a topic that is close to my heart. Second, it touches on a fundamentally important philosophical issue concerning what coaching is for, something that I currently explore. It also clearly touches on psychological issues about human nature that we all hope to understand, at least to some degree, in our coaching work. On a personal level, it was also interesting to observe and moderate myself commenting on this case as I have a tendency to contradict "the obvious."

It would be fair to say that there is much more to this case than this brief account makes available to us, and it is possible that some points which I will be raising could have been sufficiently considered by both Flora and her supervisor but were left unaddressed here. Nevertheless, this is a commentary on what seems to be missing for me in this case rather than on what has been described.

Being a coaching supervisor, my particular concern is about the quality of supervision on the case that Flora quite rightly brought to discuss. It is possible that Flora's supervisor had good reasons for thinking that "embracing the freedom" was the most important developmental step for her, but I want to argue that staying doubtful, if not "skittish," for a sufficient amount of time might be useful in these types of cases, probably more useful than "embracing one's freedom." Cases such as these "ask to be explored" systemically, in light of the potential consequences for all parties involved.

In terms of these potential consequences, my first concern is whether sufficient attention has been paid to the client's "blindness" to what Flora identifies as "moral harassment" and to what the client's role is in relation to the matter. This "blindness" is an important element of the picture, but is not explored in this case. "Blindness" may indicate a self-deception for protection or a defense mechanism that a client uses in a situation that might need to remain as it is at that stage of life. "Revealing the truth" of the situation as it appears to the psychoanalytic coach may be the last thing the client needs, creating disequilibrium in his life when he may not be ready to confront that particular problem (Vaillant, 1992). Defenses may be about an important issue for the client that could indicate a developmental theme in its own right, which needs to be dealt with in an appropriately sensitive manner in order for the client to be able "to see more" (Fingarette, 2000; Bachkirova, 2016a).

Another more serious concern is with the assumption that Flora makes that her freedom to "reveal the truth" may solve her client's problem. Unfortunately, it takes much more than the coach "speaking up" for a client to be able to recognize manipulation or oppression, let alone to empower that individual to deal with this and to grow (as has been shown in an excellent study by Shoukry (2014) on coaching for emancipation). I am also concerned with how small the role of the client is in this dilemma for the coach. It is the coach who has "made an analysis" and decided on the focus of the process. This seems more like the practice of an expert social worker who comes to assess the case rather than a coach who should intend to explore together with the client a complex situation that might be seen differently from different perspectives. I wonder what now remains for the client to do, having been "rescued" (Newton & Napper, 2010) by the coach.

Now, about the coach. It might seem obvious to act according to one's personal values. As I look at this case from the position of an educator and supervisor, a question that I want to ask is: what has Flora learned from this situation? I am afraid that "embracing one's freedom" might be something of a limited outcome. The problem seems bigger and starts much earlier for Flora. I wonder if she understands that her freedom is restricted at many different points. At the point of becoming professional coaches, we all sign up to following certain expectations. At the point of taking the contract with an organization, we commit ourselves to a certain standard of conduct. If what is asked of us does not fit with our principles then contracting is the point at which we must exercise our freedom to walk away or challenge these expectations. If we have "a higher commitment" that overrides all others, it has to be part of our professional code of conduct and/or be identified through explicit discussion with the sponsor and clients.

Another important feature of this case seems to be about regaining the freedom from the code of "neutrality" that Flora has chosen according to her psychoanalytic background. I am not sure, however, that Flora was in any "deontological trap." This code of neutrality was of Flora's own choosing and not imposed by the rules and norms of this particular organization. I am also not sure in what way a division of coaching into "two major schools of thought" is particularly helpful. A lot would seem to hang on Flora's subjective appraisal as to what would count as "engaged" and what would count as "neutral" coaching, and whether such categorical assertions are anything more than somewhat arbitrarily imposed statements of preference. It is also not clear whether she realized "higher commitment" has now made her an "engaged" coach. Above all, I am concerned that she calls not choosing to follow the code of conduct an ethical choice. Why does she need a code of conduct that does not fit with her ethics?

My personal view is that *value-neutral instrumentalism* (Bachkirova, Jackson, Gannon, Iordanou, & Myers, 2017) is a philosophical position that creates more problems than it solves, not only in relation to the education and assessment of coaches as has been argued, but also in relation to assessment of ethical decisions in complex situations. According to this view (and what Flora might have meant by neutrality), coaching is seen as "a professional service provided to clients in order for them to achieve their goals, whatever these goals might be" (p. 36). If the coach is almost a value-neutral holder of useful tools professionally applied, there seems to be no place for ethical dilemmas in coaching practice. The alternative, as I see it, is not what is called in this case an "engaged school," but *developmentalism*, in which development of the client is seen as both the means and the end of coaching. According to this position coaching is a "meaningful dialogue in which new ideas, values and actions are conceived with an overarching aim of developing the overall capabilities of clients to engage with their environment" (Bachkirova et al., 2017, p. 36). This dialogue may happen in ways that are not specified at the start of the coaching process, thus requiring flexibility of approach with openness and ethical maturity on the part of the coach (Bachkirova, 2016b).

Going back to this particular case, Flora might benefit from understanding that "embracing one's freedom" sounds very attractive, but it does not free her from the need to:

- create a coherent rationale for her model of coaching (the Why, What, and How of her approach) (Bachkirova et al., 2017);
- reflect on each situation, considering as many perspectives and discourses as possible (e.g., Western, 2017);
- consider the effect of her decisions on the developmental process of the client (Bachkirova, 2011);
- explore her role as an instrument of coaching (Bachkirova, 2016b).

In this case, if "speaking up" means being open about her perception of the situation, there is nothing heroic about this, especially if she acknowledges that her inevitably "second hand" perception is limited and might be simply wrong. If "speaking up" is about "protecting the client" against this "evil boss" under the flag of "embracing her freedom," then it may be merely seen as being little more than an act of self-aggrandizement on the part of the coach.

Finally, my most serious concern is about the quality of the supervision on offer and how easily the supervisor was able to "comfort" Flora for her analysis of the situation on the basis of the "three-times removed" perception of the situation. Although it is very important to support the coach at a time of serious concern, one of the most important forms of assistance that can be provided is to explore the various consequences of potential coaching interventions from as many angles as possible. Among these angles, exploring the potential for self-deception by the coach (Bachkirova, 2015, 2016a) and the employment of defense mechanisms by the client (Vaillant, 1992) may not only be effective in securing beneficial outcomes for the client, but may prove to be developmental also for the coach.

Commentary 9.2.b

Melvin L. Smith

It is important for coaches to have a clearly defined coaching philosophy. This may entail things such as fundamental beliefs regarding adult learning and development, the potential role of coaching in the individual development process, and the responsibilities and boundaries of both the coach and coachee in the coaching relationship. Additionally, a coach should be clear about the methods, processes, tools, and codes of conduct that frame any coaching intervention in which they are engaged. And finally, I believe that a coach should also have a good sense of the amount of variability with which they are comfortable when it comes to the process, methods, and codes to which they adhere.

In Flora's case, she seemed to be clear about her coaching philosophy, methods, codes of conduct, etc. However, she was facing an issue regarding her perceived inability to deviate from the process, methods, and tools of the subcontracting company by whom she had been hired. This led her to question her "zone of freedom," or the degree of latitude she had in interacting with the coachee. Once the coaching began, Flora also faced an issue regarding whether she should be willing to deviate from a specific code of conduct (the principle of neutrality) to which she adhered, which in this case would also require her to break the code of staying within the boundaries of the initial coaching contract. I suggest that this is more appropriately described as wrestling with her "zone of comfort" relative to her perceived need to adhere to (or her willingness to potentially deviate from) specific codes of conduct.

In the most straightforward and simplistic scenario for a coaching engagement that is nested within a subcontracting arrangement, the coaching contract and resulting coaching that takes place fall cleanly within the intersection of the coach's and subcontracting company's process, methods, etc. (see Figure 9.1a). If that had been the scenario for Flora, she would not have encountered either of the issues that she

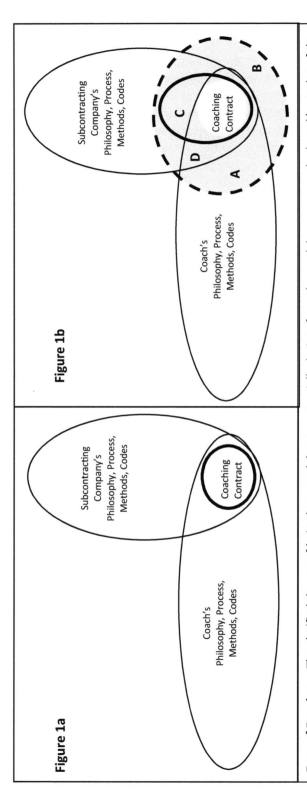

Figure 1a

Coach's Philosophy, Process, Methods, Codes

Subcontracting Company's Philosophy, Process, Methods, Codes

Coaching Contract

Figure 1b

Coach's Philosophy, Process, Methods, Codes

Subcontracting Company's Philosophy, Process, Methods, Codes

Coaching Contract

A B C D

Zone of Freedom – The clarified degree of latitude a coach has to potentially deviate from the model, process, methods and/or codes of the subcontracting company in service of the coachee (area A in Figure 1b above).

Zone of Comfort – The extent to which a coach is willing to operate outside of their normal coaching approach and/or to potentially deviate from strict adherence to one or more codes of conduct to which they normally adhere, when doing so would serve a higher commitment or moral obligation (areas B and C above).

Figure 9.1 Zones of freedom and comfort in coaching

experienced. As we see in this case, however, in life (and in coaching) things are often not that neat and tidy.

In coaching, things are not always black and white. As illustrated by the shaded area in Figure 9.1b, gray areas often emerge in doing coaching work, especially within a subcontracting arrangement. In these cases, the coach may need to navigate through those gray areas by 1) having a clarifying conversation with the subcontracting company regarding the latitude the coach has in the engagement, 2) exercising the use of moral reasoning and personal judgment rather than strict adherence to codes of conduct when faced with an unclear ethical dilemma, or 3) engaging in some combination of these two things. I will use this figure to discuss the issue that Flora experienced around understanding her *zone of freedom* to engage with the coachee in her preferred manner, as well as the issue she experienced around her *zone of comfort* (as defined above) in deviating from strict adherence to both the principle of neutrality and the code of staying within the boundaries of the coaching contract.

Flora's initial discomfort stemmed from not being clear on how much latitude she had in the manner in which she engaged with the coachee, given that the coaching process and methods of the subcontracting company were different from her preferred approach. Rather than sitting in that discomfort, Flora could have openly discussed with the subcontracting company the differences between the contracted coaching process and her preferred approach to reach an understanding around the degree of latitude she had (if any) to deviate from their process and methods in favor of her own. In other words, a simple conversation may have enabled her to gain greater clarity around her *zone of freedom* for this engagement (see area A in Figure 9.1b).

As the coaching progressed, Flora felt additional angst as she sensed that the coachee was blind to the fact that he might have been the victim of mistreatment by his boss. She felt handcuffed by the principle of neutrality, even though she realized that saying nothing in this case might leave the coachee exposed to a potentially harmful situation. Flora worried that proactively exploring this issue would require her to violate the principle of neutrality, and doing work with the coachee on the issue would also require her to break the code of staying within the boundaries of the coaching contract (see area B in Figure 9.1b).

Flora's discomfort relative to this second issue was driven largely by the fact that she wanted to be true to the codes to which she felt bound as a coach, even though doing so in this case might not have been in the best interest of the coachee. I believe that she could have at least somewhat alleviated this discomfort by recognizing that, while codes of coaching conduct are useful and in fact necessary to advance the professionalization of the field, coaches need to exercise some degree of moral reasoning and personal judgment in applying them. Codes cannot be written to capture every possible ethical dilemma a coach might encounter, so coaches need to be comfortable with their responsibility to use interpretation in the application of the codes to specific situational contexts (see Fatien Diochon & Nizet, 2015 for a discussion of applying ethical codes in executive coaching).

In working with the coachee in this case, Flora picked up on something that, if not explored, could have allowed the coachee to experience professional and/or personal harm. This caused her to question whether she had a moral obligation that superseded the strict adherence to the codes of neutrality and working only within the bounds of the established coaching contract. Situations such as this shed light on the fact that strict adherence to codes without an understanding and consideration of specific contextual circumstances can potentially lead to a moral absolutism that can ultimately do more harm than good.

Given her discomfort with this situation and her lack of clarity regarding how she should handle it, Flora did the right thing in going to her supervisor for guidance. While that act itself could be seen as a potential violation of some codes regarding the confidentiality of the conversation between the coach and the coachee, speaking with her supervisor helped Flora to see that there is sometimes a commitment higher than the one to the code.

I have had coaches who I was supervising come to me with similar dilemmas. In some cases the "higher commitment" has involved looking out for the coachee's interests (success, personal well-being, safety, etc.). In other cases, that higher commitment has involved looking out for the safety and/or well-being of others around the coachee, however, such as in the case of a coachee who made statements to a coach sparking fear that the individual may be at risk of doing harm to himself or others. In cases like this, there are other moral obligations that outweigh adherence to the code of confidentiality between the coach and coachee.

Being able to operate in these gray areas is not always easy. In fact, as Flora stated, "Embracing one's freedom is scary." I offer, however, that having a clear understanding of one's zones of freedom and comfort (as defined in this commentary) when dealing with gray areas in coaching, and having a strategy for dealing with those potential situations, can actually be liberating. Table 9.1 provides suggested actions for dealing with the various gray areas from Figure 9.1b that may test coaches' understanding of the latitude they have in the coaching engagement and/or may challenge them to go beyond the boundaries of their normal processes, methods, or coaching codes to which they adhere.

Table 9.1 Strategies for dealing with coaching contract dilemmas

Area from		
A	The coach sees a need or opportunity to utilize a process and/ or methods other than those specified by the subcontracting company in the coaching contract.	Before the coaching engagement begins, the coach should discuss any differences between their preferred coaching process/ methods/codes and those established by the subcontracting company and determine the degree of latitude they have in choosing their approach.
B	Through engaging with the coachee, the coach senses the need to go beyond the boundaries of the coaching contract and deviate from their normal coaching approach, including potentially violating one or more coaching codes of conduct in service of a higher moral obligation.	The coach should assess the specific situation and exercise personal judgment in determining the ethical implications of either strictly adhering to all coaching codes or potentially violating one or more codes for reasons they deem to be justifiable. The coach should also discuss the situation with a supervising coach at the subcontracting company to reach agreement on the latitude they have in operating outside of the established coaching contract and codes.
C	The coach is specifically asked by the subcontracting company to utilize processes/methods other than those that they would normally use, and/or adhere to codes of conduct other than those to which they normally adhere.	Before the coaching engagement begins, the coach should evaluate the request and determine their level of comfort in following the approach and codes of the subcontracting company rather than their preferred approach. If the coach is not comfortable doing this, they should decline the coaching engagement.
D	Through engaging in coaching work with the coachee, the coach sees the need to go beyond the boundaries of the coaching contract while staying within the processes/ methods/codes of both the coach and the subcontracting company.	As long as the coach is doing the work with the coachee as established in the contract, going slightly beyond the contract while staying within the process/methods/codes of both the coach and the subcontracting company may not necessarily require any additional action. The coach may have to exercise personal judgment, however, to determine if and when any work beyond the coaching contract becomes significant enough to warrant a discussion about recontracting.

Growing more comfortable in dealing with these types of situations in coaching comes in part from experience. Establishing and being clear about your personal coaching philosophy can also help. For me, one of my beliefs or fundamental tenets is that I will always attempt to privilege the coachee's interests and agenda over all others (e.g., me as the coach, the sponsoring organization, a subcontracting company, etc.). If doing so requires going outside of the boundaries established by the coaching contract, then I use personal judgment and have conversations with all appropriate parties regarding any potential deviations of significance as described in the process above. Being clear on my basic philosophy and having a clearly articulated process for dealing with challenging exceptions has given me comfort in handling almost any situation that might arise.

The same holds true when I am in the role of the supervising coach of the subcontracting organization working with hired coaches. While I expect that coaches will exercise a certain zone of freedom in utilizing their own coaching style in the contracted engagement, I also expect that any significant deviation from our established process and methods will be discussed and agreed upon beforehand. Similarly, if the contracted coach experiences a situation that would require them to go outside of the established coaching codes of conduct, I would expect them to use personal judgment regarding what the right thing to do might be, but also to have a conversation with me regarding the situation to make sure that I am aware of it. Then, we are in alignment regarding the approach to be taken.

Conclusion

These cases and commentaries have helped us further delve into "ethical complexity" referred to as "grey areas" by our experts, or situations where actors are unaware of or unsure about which norms and values should prevail (Reinecke & Ansari, 2015). Codes can certainly help reduce uncertainty about what norms, rules, and interests should prevail, but their application often results in an oversimplification of the situation and the objectification of the client. Indeed, as discussed by the experts, the so-called "reality" portrayed in codes often appears conflicting with the embodied, intersubjective, and interpretive nature of reality as experienced by the coach. Codes, and more generally normative approaches to ethics, tend to portray individuals as abstract categories to be managed (Pullen & Rhodes, 2014) rather than as Others to be acknowledged in their difference. Additionally, this approach to ethics often frames dilemmas as "out there," independent of the actors experiencing and even constructing them. In fact, if we embrace a sensemaking approach to ethics rather than the prevalent objectivist accounts, dilemmas do not have an exterior existence independent of subjects but rather result from their construction and interpretation (Brown, 2015).

Consequently, ethics are not "an objective feature of reality" or "something . . . moral (vs. amoral) when a particular thinker interprets a situation as such" (Parmar, 2014, p. 1108). If we embrace the socially and emotionally constructed nature of ethics, our experts encourage delving into the positivity of so-called "incidents" to articulate their meaning. In this vein, Fatien Diochon and Nizet (2015) bring forth the idea of dilemmas as signals – of coach's history, maturity, and even symptoms of a larger organizational or industrial issue. Therefore, according to this transformative approach to ethics, the coach's role is to tap into the dilemma to diagnose and use it to inform her decision rather than reject it as a default or an error to correct.

Still, codes definitely have a role to play: rather than imposing fixed action through compliance, they potentially enable "ethical progress" when "interpreted and appropriated with practical wisdom" (Mercier & Deslandes, 2017, p. 781). This shows the potential political dimension of ethics (Pullen & Rhodes, 2014), when through the dilemma the coach will likely challenge the status quo to generate organizational change. That said, our experts also caution us to be mindful of whose interests are really served when coaches "embrace their freedom": those of the organization, the coachee, and/or their own?

References

Amado, G. (2010). Subjectivité limitée, travail et résonance psychique. In Y. Clot & D. Lhuilier (Eds.), *Travail et santé, ouvertures cliniques* (pp. 65–77). Toulouse: Erès.

Amado, G., & Ambrose, A. (Eds.). (2001). *The transitional approach to change.* London & New York, NY: Karnac Books.

Amado, G., & Vansina, L. (Eds.). (2005). *The transitional approach in action.* London & New York, NY: Karnac Books.

Bachkirova, T. (2011). *Developmental coaching: Working with the self.* Maidenhead: Open University Press.

Bachkirova, T. (2015). Self-deception in coaches: An issue in principle and a challenge for supervision. *Coaching: An International Journal of Theory, Research and Practice, 8*(1), 4–19.

Bachkirova, T. (2016a). A new perspective on self-deception for applied purposes. *New Ideas in Psychology, 43,* 1–9.

Bachkirova, T. (2016b). The self of the coach: Conceptualization, issues, and opportunities for practitioner development. *Consulting Psychology Journal: Practice and Research, 68*(2), 143–156.

Bachkirova, T., Jackson, P., Gannon, J., Iordanou, I., & Myers, A. (2017). Re-conceptualizing coach education from the perspectives of pragmatism and constructivism. *Philosophy of Coaching: An International Journal, 2*(2), 29–50.

Brown, A. D. (2015). Making sense of sensemaking in organization studies. *Organization Stud* ies, *36*(2), 265–277.

Cloet, H., & Vernazobres, P. (2011). Le marché français du coaching: Zoom sur les conven tions de qualité. *Revue Internationale de Psychosociologie, 42*(XVII), 37–69.

Fatien Diochon, P., & Nizet, J. (2015). Ethical codes and executive coaching: one size doe not fit all. *The Journal of Applied Behavioral Science, 51*(2), 277–301.

Fingarette, H. (2000). *Self-deception: With a new chapter.* Berkeley, CA: University of Californi Press.

Mercier, G., & Deslandes, G. (2017). There are no codes, only interpretations. practical wis dom and hermeneutics in monastic organizations. *Journal of Business Ethics, 45,* 781–794.

Newton, T., & Napper, R. (2010). Transactional analysis and coaching. In E. Cox, T. Bachki rova, & D. Clutterbuck (Eds.), *The complete handbook of coaching* (pp. 172–186). Londor Sage Publications.

Parmar, B. (2014). From intrapsychic moral awareness to the role of social disruptions, labe ling, and actions in the emergence of moral issues. *Organization Studies, 35*(8), 1101–112(

Pullen, A., & Rhodes, C. (2014). Corporeal ethics and the politics of resistance in organiza tions. *Organization, 21*(6), 782–796.

Reinecke, J., & Ansari, S. (2015). What is a "fair" price? Ethics as sensemaking. *Organizatio Science, 26*(3), 867–888.

Roth, P. (2005). Projective identification. In S. Budd & R. Rusbridger (Eds.), *Introducin psychoanalysis* (pp. 200–209). London: Routledge.

Sherman, S., & Freas, A. (2004). The wild west of executive coaching. *Harvard Business Revieu 82*(11), 82–90, 148.

Shoukry, H. (2014). *Coaching for emancipation: A framework for coaching in oppressive environmen* (PhD thesis), Oxford Brookes University, Oxford.

Stefana, A. (2017). *History of countertransference. From Freud to the object relations school.* Londor Routledge.

Vaillant, G. (1992). *Ego mechanisms of defense: A guide for clinicians and researchers.* Washingtor DC: American Psychiatric Press.

Western, S. (2017). The key discourses of coaching. In T. Bachkirova, G. Spence, & D. Drak (Eds.), *The SAGE handbook of coaching* (pp. 42–61). London: Sage Publications.

10 Violence in coaching

Introduction

Over the course of their interventions, coaches are potentially exposed to a wide array of violence. It can originate from aggressive behavior and/or personalities on the part of the coachee, the sponsor, or even their peers. For example, an "abrasive" personality characterizes individuals who are selfish, competitive, and insensitive, alienating those around them. This behavior is often perceived as acceptable because of the perpetrators' associated expertise and competence in a specific field (Hicks & McCracken, 2009). Other types of difficult personalities include the narcissistic leader, the manic-depressive, the passive-aggressive, and the emotionally disconnected leader, who all create a toxic workplace (Kets de Vries, 2014).

Despite their apparent negative connotation, aggressive personalities are sometimes implicitly sought after in organizations, leading to violence at the organizational level. The organization might encourage aggressive personalities with their focus on profit and performance at any cost, which develops a corporate culture that encourages "management by fear and intimidation" and ignores, or even worse, rewards arrogant and abusive leaders (Daniel & Metcalf, 2017). This results in more complexity for the coach to manage.

Our two cases engage us with personalities and cultures that contain a certain form of violence, resulting in challenges for the coach.

In *Why didn't I see it coming?*, Kat feels guilty about a violent conflict that emerges during a team debriefing between a doctor and a technical assistant. She wonders what she has missed to allow such violence to take place within the coaching space.

In the second case, *An aggressive manager*, Frank is hired to coach Karl, a recently promoted manager, who used to be a top salesman known to be "aggressive," and outgoing, even pressuring people to attain goals. Frank's challenge, as he sees it, is to help Karl raise his awareness and accept that the same "aggressive" behavior that got him to his leadership position is now a problem for the organization, as he is alienating his team members and constantly in conflict with them.

Case 10.1. Why didn't I see it coming?

Six years ago, Kat was engaged in a team coaching intervention at a hospital where she had been coaching for a while. The goal was to increase "team cohesion," and the group was engaged in a debriefing. While Kat was showing the group slides on the 360-degree feedback she had conducted over the past month, a conflict emerged between a doctor and a technical assistant. She heard a chair falling and looked up to see the doctor grab hold of his assistant's arm roughly. Two coworkers intervened, separating the doctor from the assistant.

Kat was in shock. Naturally, she was averse to violence, but more importantly as a coach, she hadn't seen this coming. She felt guilty, as if she'd failed in her role. She wondered: "How did I allow this to happen? What did I miss?" Following the session, a colleague who was friends with the assistant told Kat that this incident was just "the tip of the iceberg." The assistant had been the victim of other acts of violence by the doctor, but this often occurred behind the scenes. Today, the conflict emerged in front of many colleagues, including the team's boss who was equally shocked.

Reflexive questions

- Have you ever faced similar violent situations in coaching?
- What might be some potential sources and forms of violence in coaching?
- Do you understand Kat's guilt?
- If faced with a similar situation, what would you do?

After reflecting on the situation through two sessions with a senior coach and advisor, Kat realized that the team coaching intervention had allowed the emergence of a latent conflict. Her intervention had in a way offered the receptacle for this violence to be revealed. And it had also allowed the team's manager to observe an unhealthy relationship in the organization and to take action to solve it. Further, Kat felt she had no choice but to embrace the conflict. She could not pass it on to anyone else. After all, she had been chosen to intervene in this specific context – in a way, the context chose her. Thus, Kat worked hand in hand with the team's manager to help him deal with the violent situation. Most importantly, they worked on "how to neutralize the violent doctor without stigmatizing him."

Reflexive questions

- What do you think of Kat's interpretation of the conflict that emerged during the coaching session?
- Do you think that coaches choose the context they intervene in, or rather that they are chosen by the context?
- This event took place during a team coaching intervention. Do you think that continuing coaching is the best way to proceed? Would this type of violent incident call for HR disciplinary action?
- In addition to helping the manager deal with the situation, should Kat have played a role in conflict resolution between the doctor and the technical assistant after the incident? Why or why not?

Commentary 10.1.a

Pascale Répécaud

The situation that Kat has had the courage to describe is interesting, as it involves a topic that is often avoided in organizations and coaching, namely violence and what causes violence. This is a crucial, difficult, and complex issue, not least because it questions our capacity, as coaches, to recognize it in ourselves. The instinctual is expressed, and sometimes erupts in a sudden and unexpected manner; it is a life force and has an aspect of destructiveness (Bergeret, 1984). The struggle to live and defend oneself can result in acting out, as occurred in the scene recounted by Kat.

On reading the case, it is clear that the title is related to the length of the intervention. "Why didn't I see it coming – six years ago?" There is always a limit and an end to an intervention in an organization, whether thought out or not, whether chosen or imposed, or even caused by fatigue. Can we sustain our "third party" objectivity throughout the entire duration? This is not by any means sure . . . long-term relationships with clients are likely to make us drop our guard. This is a point on which we must remain vigilant. Coaches working in pairs are able to maintain a critical viewpoint in team coaching sessions, which are more complex and likely to reveal "attacking" defensive movements. Are we prepared to "pass over" an assignment and say no? "Calling it a day" or working in pairs both have a significant economic impact. This also involves leaving what we know to move towards a blank space, the unknown . . . and towards the discovery of new areas of intervention, facilitating the renewal of our practices. We are challenged on how we handle change, absence, loss, and separation and questioned on our position as external third parties, we are "passing through."

The environment in which the intervention took place is not inconsequential. The primary task of the hospital environment – namely to provide care – needs to be taken into account. Hospitals are places of care and "repair," but are also places where anxieties are reawakened and losses are borne, as well as being places of suffering. Healthcare workers that are "supposed to heal" are worn out working in a corrosive environment. The healthcare sector is where the notion of burnout first emerged and has been extensively studied (Maslach & Leiter, 2011). Behavior identified as signifying that healthcare workers' limits have been reached includes irritability and aggressiveness – towards both patients and other healthcare workers. And this does not take into account aspects relating to the context and occurrences in their private lives that affect their relationships with others.

Prior to a team coaching, listening to those involved in the context of individual interviews generally reveals situations of strained interpersonal relations and individual or collective malaise. Relational difficulties are not necessarily revealed through use of 360-degree-type tools. Interviews remain an excellent tool for establishing the situation of the team. Although not "everything" emerges, interviews give an idea of the submerged parts of icebergs and can prove useful, providing the coach dares to question the participants' fears regarding group sessions.

Details of the context. Questions arise regarding systemic details of the context which are not apparent in the case and which should be taken into account in the intervention program, in particular for team coaching. These include the institution and its characteristics, the department's activity and background, how it functions and is managed, the composition of the team and relations between professionals, as well as relations with patients, families, etc.

Events in this case took place during the 360-degree feedback phase. Use of 360 degree makes an impression and this needs to be taken into account: 360-degree feedback is group feedback and, as such, has a widespread impact. A group of people testify, and the production of the group may be interpreted by some members of the group as a "judgement," similar to that of a court, the voice of the group makes law. A series of opinions are expressed on each and every one. Individual monitoring of people ill-at-ease in their work demonstrates this, especially when people are vulnerable or having difficulty with forming part of the group.

Acting out in the middle of a debriefing. What was Kat saying in her debriefing? What subject was she discussing when the violence broke out? What rules and protections had been implemented upstream of this collective feedback session? How had the group been working with Kat prior to this phase?

Feedback is a form of interpretation. It is a sensitive phase in itself, which may lead to violence and for which we do not always sufficiently consider what may be provoked (Aulagnier, 2007). Speaking in a capacity as an outside third party or observer involves giving critical feedback about a group to which the individuals belong. It involves talking to each person, and potentially causing hurt, unintentionally, by provoking a defensive movement related to the anxieties triggered by unveiling the actual or supposed elements of the life and intimacy of the group and its members. One can subconsciously feel persecuted or intruded on by a third party who is "meddling with" ones lives. An intervention is upsetting. The way in which the group is "contained" and made secure by both the coach and manager is essential. As a team coach, it is important to acquire basic skills regarding defense mechanisms specific to group functioning (Bejarano, 1975). Understanding how a group functions and what can go beyond our understanding due to subconscious mechanisms enables us to think out and develop our practices, on the basis of technical and theoretical references, and no doubt feel less guilty. A group is a "moving entity," that is reactive, vibrant, and driven by instinctual movements that are sometimes violently defensive. Through the many feedback sessions I have conducted in companies, I have experienced the "negative effects" linked to my own approach. Feedback sessions may "violently harm" individuals and the group, or even the organization itself. Defensive reactions can reflect a sensitive situation, as can the "over" – overspoken, overly quickly – to the detriment of the development of the group by itself, at its own pace, trusting in its collective analytical ability supported by the accompanying third party. Listening to a group is a skill that needs to be learned and is not always straightforward.

Taking the time to allow the group itself to express its difficulties, using mechanisms that foster emergence, ensures development that respects the rhythm of the group and its members. It is tempting to forge ahead, to demonstrate, to want to solve issues quickly, at the risk of causing harm and providing responses in situations where the responses would gain from being produced for the benefit of transformations that are longer, yet go deeper and lead to longer-lasting team cohesion. Taking the time for a group process means that you build trust and a sense of security. This then enables you to develop the capacity of group members to hear and tolerate diverse opinions and feelings, listen to each other and develop the ability to self-regulate, as well as to be able to express and deal with potentially problematic issues. In this case, the third party is no longer there to reveal, but rather to help the group to reveal itself.

Effects and reflection on practice. Expression of violence often generates a sort of shock. It is difficult to apprehend what is happening without stepping back from the situation. Indeed, it is this meta-position with respect to the sight experienced that comes into play in the context of supervision or intervision, as Kat has done. When there is more than one person, thought processes are more operative and more open (see the principle of this book). For interventions involving groups and institutions, it can be very insightful to jointly lead sessions. The interventions are dissipated between the two coaches and it is easier to take a step back and have more than one perspective – while presenting other forms of limits to be worked upon. Jointly leading sessions enables the upstream-downstream development of interventions and develops plasticity during interventions. Working in pairs creates confidence and strength, as well as enabling the coaches to better contain compulsions during group work.

Acting out violence and the non-developed. The acting out of violence in this case is like the unutterable being expressed, the non-developed, the non-considered that "blows up" and intrudes into real life. Certain contexts can cause situations to "flare up" – and feedback may be an example. What couldn't be expressed differently? What was it that couldn't have been held back? For the doctor and for the assistant? For the group and for the institution? The feedback session revealed an obstacle encountered by the group when performing its joint task. The unsaid "jumped out" and called for regulation that had not been able to occur prior to this moment. This situation questions the work rules and functioning of bodies that potentially listen to healthcare workers experiencing difficulties, including healthcare managers, staff representatives, and unions. It also calls into question the capacity of managers and the work collective to listen to weak signals and take them into account in terms of responsibility in their teams. What prevented the problem from being expressed? How does the coordination of work processes operate in teams? The acting out of violence could signify difficulty in encouraging listening and welcoming group emergence in teamwork. Indeed, the situation was known to at least one colleague. This is a source of working scenarios.

The role of the manager or leader of a group process is indeed to "deal with the negative" and facilitate its development and transformation. In her position as coach and as part of her assignment, Kat needed to act as a third person and overcome her guilt – with the help of her own third-party supervisor – in order to facilitate the work of the organization and the group on the "undeveloped" that had emerged. However, each person must keep to their role and not substitute for the institutional roles. The text shows that she was able to cope with the situation and build on it, but a situation could have arisen where a coach was unable to do this. It happens . . . and it happened to me. It can be painful. Dead-end situations are also a source of learning, providing they are worked upon in the appropriate areas of reflection and training. We all do what we can with obstacles encountered, both with what actually happens and with what escapes us. It may be going too far to say that we choose the situation or that the situation chooses us. . . . But whatever the case, I think that it helps to believe this.

Where is violence located? Who carries it and expresses it? What non-perceptible elements does it theoretically express? We mustn't prejudge the source of violence and analyze the situation on different levels. Something happened in the interpersonal relationship between the assistant and the doctor that needs to be explored. The assistant-doctor pairing can however reveal or be a "voice-bearer" (Pichon-Riviere, 2004) for violence that can be expressing something else, such as the situation within the team or relations between doctors and assistants in general. The expression "the violent doctor" in some way raises the issue of a relational persecutor-victim game which forces us to question the responsibility of each person, over and beyond the obvious. The institution, tasks performed, work procedures, and other people can all drive us mad.

Commentary 10.1.b

Andie Pendel

In focusing on the challenging situation that this case study presents, I am aware that I bring my particular voice, perspective, and professional identity to the analysis. I am a UK-based coach, therapist, and academic, so my understanding of workplace violence is from a UK perspective. At the university where I work, I teach coaching and train counselors within the humanistic-integrative tradition. My coaching practice tends to have a social dimension (I often work with those involved in social enterprise, education, and the UK fire service). I am aware that this means the experience I have and the pressures I am subjected to vary from those of the self-employed coach seeking contracts in the corporate setting or life coaches working solely with individuals outside organizational contexts. Inevitably, I expect this means that many readers will find themselves diverging from the perspective I offer here. I am also aware that internal contradictions, ambiguities, and conflicting perspectives can surface within the narratives that I generate, e.g., the desirability of Rogerian unconditional positive regard (Rogers, 1951) juxtaposed with the necessity of organizational protocols that challenge persecutory and bullying behaviors (ACAS, 2014).

A survey of a number of general coaching texts (e.g., Cox, Bachkirova, & Clutterbuck, 2014; Palmer & Whybrow, 2007) show that violence, harassment, and bullying do not feature in the indexes, suggesting that the issues raised in this case study are thankfully uncommon in coaching. While I have not come across violence in my coaching practice, sadly I have seen it among graduate trainees. In that setting the tension exists between caring for the protagonists and ensuring that attention is paid to the question of fitness to practice. Gillespie, Gates, Miller, & Howard (2010) note that violence and harassment are increasingly present issues in health settings. Citing DuHart (2001), they observe that in the States the rate of violence against physicians was 16.2 per 1,000 workers. Against nurses, it was 21.9 per 1,000 workers, and against healthcare workers, generally it was 8.5. In a study conducted in South Korea, Park, Cho and Hong (2014) have discovered that nurses are most likely to experience sexual harassment and bullying, and the main perpetuators of workplace violence and harassment after patients are physicians. Manier, Kelloway, and Francis (2017) have established that the consequences of workplace aggression are far-reaching and hugely damaging for the organizations within which they occur. My own sense is that the highly challenging situation that Kat has encountered at the hospital does not have a single resolution, but there are more-or-less informed ways forward. Kat's way forward, while clearly well-intentioned, can be questioned on a number of levels due to her apparent disconnection with the wider organization (which was paying her fees).

It is curious that the colleague who discloses that this assault is "the tip of the iceberg" is also a friend of the assistant. One wishes that Kat questioned what could have led the assistant's friend to stand by passively while violence occurred. It would appear that at some level there is a culture of collusion among the team (possibly arising from fear and intimidation). The team leader is as shocked as Kat by the outburst leading one to conclude that he does not have a grasp of the dynamic within the very team that he is supposed to be leading. The fact that the other acts of violence occurred "behind the scenes" suggests an element of premeditation on the part of the doctor, leaving the question as to whether this incident is symptomatic of abusive and violent behavior that might extend beyond the assistant to include patients and other vulnerable people in the doctor's personal life. There is no mention of whether he is either remorseful or unapologetic for his actions, which might impact the decision as to whether Kat would work with him. It is also puzzling that Kat and the manager's perspective seems to be characterized by a lack of curiosity regarding the impact of events on the assistant who has been victimized. As a member of the coaching division of the British Association of Counselling and Psychotherapy, I am bound by the ethical principle of justice, which states we are committed to "the fair and impartial treatment of all clients and the provision of adequate services" (BACP, 2015). This does not appear to be what is occurring here. Such a lack of engagement with the assistant could lead to negative consequences for the hospital further down the line should the assistant wish to argue she is the victim of constructive dismissal.

Team coaching has the potential to be a highly positive practice where individuals can share their learning with peers, and change can be instituted on a systemic level (Clutterbuck, 2014). Skiffington and Zeus (2000) have also noted that facilitating problem-solving and managing group conflict in that setting are also reasonable expectations of the team coach. However, it is questionable if working with violent individuals and actual violence in the workplace is an equally reasonable expectation. Both the ICF (2015) and EMCC (2016) ethical codes make clear that coaches should be working within the limits of their competence, and unless she has received specialist training, I question Kat's capacity to embrace this particular conflict. The UK General Medical Council has a fitness to practice policy (GMC, 2016) for doctors that would classify this doctor's actions as "misconduct," and in all likelihood this would be pursued in that setting. It is also possible that once the violence became openly acknowledged, the assistant might wish to pursue a legal action of her own against the doctor, the hospital, and any others deemed to have contributed. I know of counselors who have been prevented from working with witnesses in upcoming criminal trials because their interventions might subsequently be deemed to have impacted the testimony. Kat might wish to pause in the short term before intervening in this situation and reflect on whether she might be professionally vulnerable to a similar accusation. Additionally, it is a valid concern for the practitioner to consider her personal safety (Reeves, 2015), and I wonder how safe Kat is working one-on-one with someone who is violent "behind the scenes." Valley and Thompson (1998) have noted that team behaviors and norms can be employed as the means to resist change and consolidate the group culture. The group culture that Kat finds herself enmeshed in appears to be a toxic one that conceals violence and harassment towards a junior colleague. My sense is that Kat would do well to take these factors on-board when considering her future work in this context. I also find her decision to work hand-in-hand with the manager and the "violent doctor" questionable. It is possible that this individual would be better served by specialists experienced in working with the perpetuators of violence in the workplace. I do not know Kat's level of experience, but in light of this decision, I wonder if she is new to coaching at this point. My own experience in facilitating group supervision is that new practitioners' worries about their personal experience and competence can often lead to compliance with unreasonable requests made by authority figures in their placement setting.

I am unclear as to what Kat means by "embrac[ing] the conflict." However, the term suggests that the conflict is being seen as a distinct entity separate from the context in which it occurred. It also suggests that she understands her role as that of holding and containing this troubling dynamic alone, rather than in partnership with the wider organization. Kat's belief that she has no choice is not a sustainable position existentially and suggests that she is making decisions from a position of disempowerment. This is not in keeping with the quality of individual empowerment that I perceive to be characteristic of positive coaching. It suggests that despite the reflective sessions she had with the more experienced coach, she continues to be driven by guilt and self-blame. Similarly, being "chosen to intervene" and believing she is chosen by the context suggests a sense of fatalism or pre-destination. When confronted with an ethically challenging situation, it is important to reflect on the relevant ethical frameworks, come to an informed decision, and act with agency. Kat should also review the contract for her work at the hospital and consider how the unfolding situation relates to the brief she was originally given. Does it cover this work? I am also concerned that Kat agreed to work closely with the team manager and the physician, suggesting that this is being managed at a local level. Given that the manager is slow to realize the problem within the team, by keeping things at this level, it could be that there is a tacit agenda of concealing his shortcomings from the eyes of senior managers. Ethically, Kat needs to ensure that events are fed upwards in the organization to senior HR level managers who can take an informed (and documented) view on whether disciplinary action is appropriate. Given that the violence was ongoing and known, it is possible that such action could extend beyond the doctor to both the manager and those who were complicit in concealing the violence. By not being active in ensuring that this is fed upwards, Kat herself becomes open to allegations of complicity. It is only when you are confident that issues are being addressed at an organizational level that you can begin once more working within such a troubled team. If I were Kat, I think that ongoing work with the assistant might be informed by trauma work (Rothschild, 2000), assertiveness, and the narrative approach to coaching (Drake, 2015). To work with the manager, it would be helpful to draw on the Full Range Leadership Model (Bass & Riggio, 2006) and consider ways that he could move his leadership behavior from one characterized by a laissez-faire style to one based in a transactional style. An element of psychoeducation might enter the coaching field through discussion about the transformational leadership approach. Any work that was undertaken with the doctor would be informed by the other considerations outlined above. A final thought on this issue: I am curious about how I might avoid stigmatizing someone I have already labeled as "the violent doctor."

Case 10.2. An aggressive manager

Frank had been working for many years as an external trainer for an office equipment company, mainly training their sales staff, when they asked him to coach Karl. From the different cohorts he'd trained, he remembered Karl very well; he stood out from the group for his outgoing personality and assertiveness. His colleagues described him as an "aggressive" salesman who was not afraid to pursue potential clients or "pressure" them in order to make a deal.

Because of his excellent sales record, Karl was promoted to team leader. However, the very same "aggressive" behavior that got him the promotion suddenly became a problem, as he was alienating his team, often in conflict with them. That's when Frank was called in to coach Karl on how to manage his behavior while dealing with his team members.

At their first meeting, it became clear to Frank that Karl didn't recognize his behavior as "aggressive" or problematic. On the contrary, Karl thought that his personality was exactly what made him good at his job and the reason for his success in the company. He also felt that it was the responsibility of his team members to adapt to his leadership style. Karl was very clear with Frank: he didn't want to be coached and didn't feel he needed help. The only reason he accepted the meeting was because it was a request from management, and he felt he had no other choice.

Karl's attitude and blatant resistance made Frank wary of this assignment, especially as he normally didn't accept a job if the coachee showed resistance. While he'd faced more latent or passive resistance in the past, this was the first time he'd been confronted by such upfront and direct resistance. Frank started to notice his own emotional reaction in the face of Karl's resistance. Frank felt both irritated and challenged, and he wanted to make sure his assessment of the situation wasn't getting skewed as a result.

Reflexive questions

- Do you agree with Frank's concerns regarding this coaching assignment?
- How should Frank have handled Karl and his "aggressive" personality?
- How would you deal with such upfront resistance?

Frank considered himself a coach with high emotional intelligence, which he hoped would help him navigate such situations. So, despite the resistance, Frank accepted the coaching assignment. He wanted Karl to realize that the skills that got him to the top wouldn't keep him there; in his new position, he would need a different set of skills. But after a couple sessions, Karl still didn't get it. And he was furious that his manager believed his aggression was a problem in need of solving. He wasn't able to recognize his responsibility in any of the conflicts he had with his team members. Frank encouraged Karl to have these conversations with his manager. But he refused. Instead, he decided to look for an opportunity elsewhere, "where he didn't need to deal with these issues," and he left the organization.

Reflexive questions

- What role does emotional intelligence play in coaching? On the part of the coach? The coachee? The organization?
- What do you think of Frank's approach to coaching Karl?
- What do you think of the final outcome of this coaching intervention? Did Frank fail as Karl's coach?

Commentary 10.2.a

Carlos Davidovich

In my career as a coach I've had the opportunity to work with many clients labeled as "difficult" or characterized as "bullies" as in the case of Karl. And it was often the reason why the company decided to offer a coaching intervention as a potential solution.

As seen in Karl's case, we need to recognize and accept the double messages that some companies send to their employees: "We like a salesman/executive with an outgoing personality, which shows determination, initiative, assertiveness and drive and will not give up easily, mainly achieving sales, and achieving results." In general, they mean responsible, hardworking, and knowledgeable perfectionists. While this sounds reasonable for a company's expectations from their sales force, these same behavioral traits can have a dark side: impatience, the inability to hear criticism, and a domineering, competitive, and self-centered personality. As Whitney Johnson (2012) comments, "There can be a very thin line between a bully and a leader." Through many years of trial and error I've developed a seven-step process to deal with this type of situation in my coaching practice. I will delve into the first two and go more rapidly over the last five.

1 Self-awareness

At the beginning of a coaching intervention, it is crucial to investigate the level of the client's self-awareness. It isn't necessary for the coach to be an expert in psychology in order to identify a pathological mental condition. At the same time, this is a determining factor which helps a coach decide whether to take on an intervention. Perhaps we are dealing with a psychopathic personality, and in this case any coaching approach will be a waste of time and money. In some cases, we can leverage the power of personality assessment to identify a pathological situation. Yet most of the time we don't have an assessment and need to rely on our professional experience. If no positive response derives from the coaching process, should it continue? In these situations, we must rely on the level of professional experience possessed by the coach.

The case that we are discussing sheds light on the basic "tacit coaching contract" that should be in place from the beginning. The coachee must understand and agree on the coaching objectives. When the coachee doesn't initially understand or accept why the company calls him "aggressive" or why he is supposed to change, he must at least show some level of commitment or interest in diving into the situation and finding out what exactly the organization is requesting of him. A coaching process is a contract where both parties agree on the terms and objectives. Karl was convinced that his behavior was fine, and his manager mistakenly delegated the task of explaining the coaching goals to the coach. This is not correct. Without Karl's decision to work and collaborate on this issue, there is no sense in starting the intervention. As the coach, Frank's concerns are justified.

We must have accountability from Karl. This is not present in the case.

One anecdote from my experience involved coaching a high-level executive who was without a doubt a bully. His level of self-awareness was very low, but at least he understood that the coaching process was a must in order to stay in the organization. In one session he commented about one of his direct reports from the French part of the country. He said: "You know how emotional the French people are!" In that moment I felt a unique opportunity to bring an often-unrecognized topic to the session. My comment was: "Yes, you are right. They are as emotional as you." A long silence followed my comment. And then I added: "Well, not as emotional as you, you excel at that." Complete silence again. It took me several sessions to help him understand that his personality was driven mainly by strong emotions. He was focused on his rational arguments, not the negative emotional charge behind his communication style.

2 Defining a motivation, a purpose

In my first meeting, the "chemistry meeting," where the coachee meets the coach and decides if it's the right match, I make clear that I'm also in a decision-making process. This makes a huge difference in the mindset of the coachee. Bullies are in general type A personalities and behave like alpha males or alpha females. This kind of personality will not accept or respect coaches who are unable to set limits, openly disagree, or send the subconscious message that they do not have a high level of self-respect. A coach who presents as too kind could be perceived by the coachee as weak. I don't mean to recommend impolite or rude behavior; rather, it's important to be clear, firm, and determined. Coach and coachee must be seated at the "same table."

This is another paradoxical situation. This type of personality loves to be challenged and confronted in their opinions. But most people don't like to do it because they are afraid of the reaction. At the same time, it's true that coachees often have substantial levels of knowledge and skill, and their arguments are not easily defeated. Furthermore, the inherent quandary is that the personality elements, which have contributed to the coachee's career success, have now become an Achilles heel. This is hard for the coachee to digest. Here is where a level playing field must be established, and the coach must gain credibility.

During my initial chemistry meeting with a coachee who is a bully I look for an answer to a very specific question:

Why would you change your behavior or personality at this time in your successful career?

I normally add: "You need to convince me with a very good reason that you want to make a change."

This is the fundamental question; without a powerful motivator, there is no sense in starting the coaching process. Karl must be motivated to make a change; this is the key driver for a positive outcome.

I can recall several situations in my coaching practice when I've asked this question. In one of my cases the coachee was the CEO of a US-based manufacturing company. He had worked at the same company for 30 years. I must admit my surprise when the company requested a coaching process to "fix" his bullying personality after 30 years. I raised these concerns in my first phone call with the company's CEO, my coachee's boss. He spent more than half of the conversation telling me how good, efficient, and clever my potential coachee was. By that time, I was even more confused. Then he told me that they knew about his personality, and they were managing it, but now a new employee was being bullied by him and was threatening to sue the organization. I was sorry to hear that the goal was not to benefit or help the coachee but to protect the organization. Despite this, I decided to move forward to the chemistry meeting. In the meeting I asked the coachee the same question: "Why would you change your behavior after 30 years of a successful career?" His answer was clear and concise: "I'm three years away from retirement; I don't want to end my career in this way." For me, that response was more than enough to start the coaching process: he had a powerful motivator to generate a change. And ultimately, the intervention was a success.

Another of my cases involved a young executive with a few years of experience living in Canada, who came from Eastern Europe, a cultural context where an abrasive or aggressive boss is not always perceived as negative. Personally, I've worked in Central Europe, coaching executives from similar backgrounds and was able to understand and metaphorically speak his language. In his mind, his personality was his key success factor and he was right, but he was not able to separate this from his abrasive behavior.

Canada became the wall against which he would be crushed, but because of his value to the company, they decided to offer a coaching process to "fix" him before taking a more drastic step to resolve the situation.

We had an outstanding and challenging chemistry meeting. I was mirroring him, and he was clever enough to understand my strategy. His answer to my question was very interesting: "I'm young and ambitious.

I want to succeed in Canada as an executive. I've moved my family, and I don't have any room to fail. You understand my experience. Let's start now."

However, building trust with this kind of personality doesn't always necessitate having had similar experiences in life. First and foremost, in our professional work we need to be attentive, practicing empathetic listening, and waiting for the word, comment, experience, emotion that we can connect with in order to build the bridge for success.

3 Intention vs. impact

Once the process starts, my main goal is to support my coachee in his understanding of the difference between intention and impact.

Their intentions may be correct, but their blind spot is their impact on others.

4 Let's be compassionate

Inside a bully there hides a helplessness. It's beyond our scope as coaches to analyze or bring roots from the past to our sessions. But at least we can keep in mind that if we understand the underpinnings, our work will be easier and more effective because we will be connecting through compassion. This is a doorway to solutions.

5 Small steps, big changes

This is a general maxim in the coaching practice, but when the client is defined as a bully it becomes even more important. Remember they have a very short attention span and most of the time they look for instant gratification: "Let's solve it now" or "Faster is better." At the same time, this is one of the reasons for their failures.

I define with my coachees a concrete action plan with small steps for success. These steps should not be too numerous and must lead to outcomes that my client can measure in the short term.

In my experience this is the only way to maintain their motivation.

6 Walk faster, be flexible, and plan periodic breaks

If the session is not moving quickly, or there are too many long silences, it's best to end the meeting early and arrange for the next one. Be flexible with scheduling. Give them a break from time to time. I normally meet with my clients periodically every 2 to 4 weeks, depending on the situation. When my client is a bully, from time to time I allow for longer periods of time between meetings. They need to feel that we have let them go and will follow-up later.

7 Be mindful and accept the facts

This step is directed at us as coaches. We need to be mindful of how the process is moving forward. If the small changes are not there, we need to be respectful of our clients and accept that they have decided to continue with their behavior. In the end, it is their choice alone.

Wrap-up

Returning to our case study with Karl, we observe the loss of a huge opportunity, not only in the company, but also in his career. He will face the same situation in the future.

The organization was not able to predict his behavior with his team members, and in fact, such behavior is often hard to predict. In two other cases I worked, my coachees' aggressive behavior was directed only at peers, whereas they were great at leading their teams. In certain situations, this is understandable; continuing with the concept of alpha males and females, we can understand their behavior with their tribe or better to say their "packs." It's always "us vs. them."

It's impossible not to be emotionally impacted by Karl's attitude. In my view, Frank did well in trying to work with Karl despite his original position – he gave it a try. Sometimes we can work with our client through reframing the situation and opening a window for potential change. However, although it's impossible to predict whether it's going to work or not, it's worth a try.

As the coach, Frank's perception of failure is understandable, but we need to accept that bullies are perhaps the most challenging coaching clients.

Still, such clients are a powerful source for learning, and in those cases where we attain a positive outcome the reward is enormous. They become great leaders, eager to help others going through similar situations.

Commentary 10.2.b

Oliver Plazza and Florence Daumarie

A first read of this coaching case may prompt a focus on the issue of the coachee Karl's aggressive behavior. Indeed, this is identified as Karl's issue. The damages of such behavior are now well documented in management and leadership research (Ashforth, 1994). Despite a potential "expected" outcome of compliance, tyrannic management undermines engagement, performance, team cohesiveness, and well-being. It lowers self-esteem and increases stress, frustration, and work alienation. So, how do you help someone missing the point or lacking the basic skills in emotional intelligence to reconsider his worldview?

We don't share the same values

For a coach who lives and often incarnates empathetic competencies, who honors respect as a key value, it is not an easy affair to coach someone who has opposing views. In such a demanding situation, a threat for the coach is to damage his capacity to unconditionally accept his coachee. This may lay the ground for a potential judgment of the coachee. Yet, we know judgments prevent empathy to grow and create distance in the relationship. Coaching has emerged out of humanistic roots, among which Carl Rogers brought structuring contributions (Stober, 2006). This is the very special, safe, and privileged relationship between coach and coachee that helps the latter truly be authentically who he is, and increases awareness of his own experience. Thus, coaches need to cultivate a high sensitivity to these damaging patterns and raise their ability to exit them, for instance through coaching supervision. A way to escape the current double bind that Frank is experiencing is to explicitly share with the coachee what is at stake. This could help Frank maintain an authentic position, where his words would reflect his inner state. Such an honest conversation also brings with it a kind of chaos where new behaviors may emerge for the coachee. A second and even more important way to avoid this double bind is to proactively design a different landscape from the very beginning of the coaching relationship. We'll explore this later.

Beware how the coaching offer is introduced

The way Karl describes his acceptance of the coaching offer shows a safe enough ground has not been established. He feels "he has no other choice." This is unfortunately alienating him. The organization considers this coaching as a way to fix Karl, which is a dominating way to deal with people's issues, mirroring Karl's behavior with his team. Coaching is neither about changing people, nor fixing them. More than 40 years of research on self-determination theory has made it very clear (Deci & Ryan, 2017). When an authority figure tries to control someone, this damages the latter's well-being, his access to his inner creativity, preventing a truly integrated motivation to flourish. Unfortunately, this is a common habit in organizations. On the other hand, choice and autonomy are key roots of coaching. Emphasizing personal choice and control is one of the best ways to roll with resistance. As Harakas (2013) puts it: "Persistent resistance is not a client problem, but a counselor skill issue." (Harakas, 2013) The more Karl resists this change, the more Frank may push for it. This classic reactance doesn't produce results (Miller & Rollnick, 2002). Rather, it hurts the coaching alliance and prevents true coaching from occurring. At this starting point, Karl is not considering change, a precontemplation state in the Transtheoretical model (Prochaska & Norcross, 2001). It means that the initial coaching process may first help him to get to the next stage, an intention to change. Expecting behavioral change is an unrealistic goal at this moment.

To change or not to change

When a coachee doesn't want to change, a vicious cycle may soon appear. If Frank confronts Karl and asserts the opposite view – i.e., aggression is not welcome in the organization – he breaks a coaching border by exerting power over his coachee. When the coach wants more than the coachee ("He wanted Karl to realize"), this should ring an internal bell in Frank's mind. On the other hand, if Frank accepts the coachee's worldview – i.e., aggression is not a problem; it is the way to perform – he may feel a voice is missing in the conversation, the normative one (*you must change*) or the caring one (*please, realize*). Persecutor and rescuer are not as different as they appear. This kind of double bind means impotency for the coach.

The solution then is neither to accept nor to confront. Coaching is about co-creating a reflective and experiential autonomy-supportive space that helps the coachee reach significant, meaningful, and challenging goals he or she is aiming at. As long as Karl doesn't want to change, then his coach is triggered in a wrong role, one that requires explaining to Karl that his behaviors are not suited to his new position. However, it is not the coach's job to express the limits and set the boundaries between what's expected and what's considered inappropriate or even deviant. More specifically, it is not the coach's responsibility to assert that aggressive behavior is not suited to management, nor is it his responsibility to align the coachee's behavior with the organizational culture of the company. Karl's manager has the responsibility to assert this, potentially with HR's additional voice. They represent the authority, the ones who know where the boundaries are and make sure they are known and respected. The responsibilities need to be held by the right person or people for the coach to play the right role. And it is the coach's role to make sure this conversation happens.

Setting the right stage

In order to frame a safe and fruitful container, Frank needs to set up an initial three-way meeting where management explicitly states its concerns and expresses the need for a change, while Karl finds a space to express his needs. If Karl's awareness doesn't reach a state where he feels a need to improve, other kinds of feedback could be brought to his attention. In some cases, a 360-degree feedback – even a simple one like collecting feedback from Karl's team members and colleagues – may help. In this case, Karl's tendency to be dominant over his employees may prevent him from listening to their views. However, his respect for authority and his love of performance should make him more sensitive to a strong statement from his superior. The intention would be to give Karl a chance to gain insight into the consequences of his behaviors. Learning from experience requires a loop feeding back on what works and what doesn't. In this case, it looks like Karl either is not receiving this feedback or he is denying it.

Frank also needs to clarify how coaching works, to underline the differences between the role of a coach and that of the training role he had when they first met, and to listen to Karl's own goals for this coaching. Karl needs a safe space to express his own view of the situation, to have it acknowledged, as long as he feels a desire to change something. This is where a true need for help may emerge. The way the coaching is set up is unfortunately reenacting the same aggressive behavior. An efficient coaching intervention would involve Karl contributing to defining the goals. What could be valuable for him? What could he get out of the coaching? In which areas would he want to improve? The contracting phase involves co-creation; it is not a unilateral push.

Zooming out

There might also be an interesting lesson in the initial three-way meeting: acknowledging that the organization itself plays a key role in this situation. There is no such thing as an individual problem in organizations.

Trying to act on an individualistic worldview is a promise for failure or a sub-efficient solution. Any problem is a systemic one (von Bertalanffy, 1969). Uncovering the interactional loops inside the system – between individuals and their environment – will help open new areas for improvements and fruitful efforts. In this case, what could be learned about pushing others to behave differently?

As a conclusion, we may outline that quite often in coaching and other organizational matters, the problem is rarely located where it seems to have manifested. This case is less about dealing with aggression than setting the right conditions to coach in a safe container so as to let the powerful coach shine.

Conclusion

To address the issue of violence in coaching and strategies for dealing with it, it seems important to first understand the reasons behind it, as suggested by our experts. This can be diagnosed in terms of the personality and characteristics of the individual, the organization, and/or its corporate culture (Daniel & Metcalf, 2017).

As far as the individual coachee is concerned, our experts' advice is aligned with Kets de Vries' (2014) in that coaches should recognize the different types of personalities and know how to address them. The coach doesn't need to be a psychotherapist or psychology expert, but a basic understanding of psychology and personality dynamics is very helpful for the coach in these situations.

In addition to recognizing the different personality types, our experts encourage coaches to acknowledge the emotions behind the aggressive behavior, as well as the emotions experienced by the victim(s) and the witness(es) of the violent behavior. The issue of emotions has been addressed in detail in Chapter 8. Moreover, the coach should also reflect on the coachee's ability to change. Reasons for the coachee's inability to change include a pathological personality, lack of self-awareness, refusal to acknowledge the problem in the behavior, or refusal to change.

When facing the coachee's resistance to change a violent or aggressive behavior, Hicks and McCracken (2009) suggest some ways that could help the coach. These are aligned with our experts' recommendations and include:

- Helping coachees see how their behavior is perceived and the resulting impact on their environment. In this scenario, recognizing the need to change is essential.
- Playing to the self-interest of the coachee. With this type of personality, having a "selfish" reason to change could be very helpful.
- Taking advantage of the competitive nature of the coachee to maximize his or her motivation and commitment to change.

When it comes to the organization, coaches can reflect on the corporate culture: to what extent is violent or aggressive behavior – and its associated characteristics – tolerated? Are they more tolerated in specific settings or for specific roles/jobs? With what other characteristics are these behaviors/personalities associated? For example, assertiveness, competitiveness, leadership, etc.

More generally, our experts have suggested several approaches that could be helpful in situations involving violence, aggressive behavior, and cultures. They include the humanistic approach, the narrative approach, psychodynamics, the transformational leadership approach, and the systemic approach. We could add to these approaches, conflict coaching in cases similar to *Why didn't I see it coming?* Conflict coaching involves a coach working with a client on developing an understanding of conflict, interaction strategies, and interaction skills. It can be used on an individual or team basis (Brinkert, 2013).

Finally, coaches should examine their own capacity and competence to handle conflict and violence. Do they have the relevant knowledge? Have they received any specific training? They should be able to recognize the limits of their responsibility and role. As mentioned in one of the commentaries above, they need to take care to avoid acting as prosecutors, judging or stigmatizing, or as rescuers, feeling the need to help at any cost. This is an issue that we have addressed in detail in Chapter 3 where we discuss boundaries in coaching.

References

ACAS (2014). *Bullying and harassment at work: A guide for managers and employers*. Retrieved from www.acas.org.uk/media/pdf/c/j/Bullying-and-harassment-in-the-workplace-a-guide-for-managers-and-employers.pdf

Ashforth, B. (1994). Petty tyranny in organizations. *Human Relations, 47*(7).

Aulagnier, P. (2007). *La violence de l'interprétation. Du pictogramme à l'énoncé*. Paris: Dunod.

Bass, B. M., & Riggio, R. E. (2006). *Transformational leadership* (2nd ed.). Mahwah, NJ: Lawrence Erblaum Associates.

Bejarano, A. (1975). *Résistance et transfert dans les groupes, Le Travail Psychanalytique dans les groupes*. Paris: Dunod.

Bergeret, J. (1984). *La violence fondamentale, l'inépuisable Oedipe*. Paris: Dunod.

Brinkert, R. (2013). The ways of one and many: Exploring the integration of conflict coaching and dialogue facilitation. *Group Facilitation: A Research and Applications Journal, 12,* 45–52.

Clutterbuck, D. (2014). Team Coaching In E. Cox, T. Bachkirova, & D. Clutterbuck (Eds.), *The Complete Handbook of Coaching* (2nd ed., pp. 271–284). London: Sage Publications.

Cox, E., Bachkirova, T., & Clutterbuck, D. (Eds.). (2014). *The complete handbook of coaching* (2nd ed.). London: Sage Publications.

Daniel, T. A., & Metcalf G. S. (2017). How some companies unwittingly make bullying a rational choice. *Employment Relations Today, 44*(1), 15–24.

Deci, E. L., & Ryan, R. M. (2017). *Self-determination theory*. New York, NY: Guilford Press.

Drake, D. B. (2015). *Narrative coaching: Bringing our new stories to life*. Petaluma, CA: CNC Press.

DuHart, D.T. (2001). *Violence in the workplace, 1993–99.* Washington, DC: U.S. Dept. of Justice Office of Justice Programs.

EMCC (2016). *Global code of ethics for coaches & mentors.* Retrieved from www.emccouncil. org/webimages/EMCC/Global_Code_of_Ethics.pdf

Gillespie, G. L., Gates, D. M., Miller, M., & Howard, P. K. (2010). Workplace violence in healthcare settings: Risk factors and protective strategies. *Rehabilitation Nursing, 35*(5), 177–184.

GMC (2016). *Guidance to the GMC's fitness to practice rules 2004 (as Ammended).* Retrieved from www.gmc-uk.org/DC4483_Guidance_to_the_FTP_Rules_28626691.pdf

Harakas, P. (2013). Resistance, motivational interviewing and executive coaching. *Consulting Psychology Journal: Practice and Research: APA, 65*(2), 108–127.

Hicks, R., & McCracken, J. (2009). Coaching the abrasive personality. *Physician Executive* September-October, 82–84.

ICF (2015). *ICF code of ethics.* Retrieved from https://coachfederation.org/code-of-ethics/

Johnson, W. (2012). Bullying is a confidence game. *Harvard Business Review.* Retrieved from https://hbr.org/2012/07/bullying-is-a-confidence-game?referral=03759&cm_vc=rr item_page.bottom

Kets de Vries, M. F. R. (2014). Coaching the toxic leader. *Harvard Business Review, 92*(4), 100–109.

Manier, A. O., Kelloway, E. K., & Francis, L. (2017). Damaging the workplace: Consequences for people and organizations. In N. A. Bowling & M. S. Hershcovis (Eds.), *Research and theory on workplace aggression* (pp. 62–89). New York, NY: Cambridge University Press.

Maslach, C., & Leiter, M. (2011). *Burn out: Le syndrôme d'épuisement professionnel.* Paris: Editions Les Arènes.

Miller, W. R. & Rollnick, S. (2002). *Motivational interviewing.* New York, NY: Guilford Press.

Palmer, S., & Whybrow, A. (Eds.). (2007). *Handbook of coaching psychology: A guide for practitioners.* Hove: Routledge.

Park, M., Cho, S. H., & Hong, H. J. (2014). Prevalence and perpetrators of workplace violence by nursing unit and the relationship between violence and the perceived work environment. *Journal of Nursing Scholarship, 47*(1), 87–95.

Pichon-Riviere, E. (2004). *Le processus groupal.* Ramonville Saint-Agne, Erès: La maison jaune.

Prochaska, J., & Norcross, J. (2001). Stages of change. *Psychotherapy, 38*(4), 443–448.

PUFBACP (2015). *Ethical framework for the counselling professions.* Lutterworth: BACP.

Reeves, A. (2015). *Working with risk in counselling and psychotherapy.* London: Sage Publications.

Rogers, C. (1951). *Cient-centered therapy.* London: Constable.

Rothschild, B. (2000). *The body remembers: The psychphysiology of trauma and trauma treatment.* New York, NY: W. W. Norton & Co.

Skiffington, S., & Zeus, P. (2000). *The complete guide to coaching at work.* New York, NY: McGraw-Hill.

Stober, S. (2006). Coaching from the humanistic perspective. In D. Stober & A. Grant (Eds.), *Evidence based coaching handbook.* New Jersey: John Wiley & Sons.

Valley, K., & Thompson, T. A. (1998). Sticky ties and bad attitudes: Relational and individual bases of resistance to changes in organizational structure. In M. A. Neale & R. Kramer (Eds.), *Power and influence in organizations* (pp. 39–66). Thousand Oaks, CA: Sage Publications.

Von Bertalanffy, L. (1969). *General system theory: Foundations, development, applications.* New York: Penguin University Books.

Conclusion

On its way to professionalization, coaching is fast growing and maturing, its evolution partly shaped by the conversations and debates that question, challenge, and push the boundaries and forms of its earlier shapes.

This case-based textbook was designed to nurture such dialogues. The conversation organized into ten distinct but overlapping sensitive topics has hopefully strengthened the connections between theory, practice, and research in coaching. We hope that the multiplicity of topics addressed, as well as the diversity in the contributors' profiles, backgrounds, education, and approaches, has allowed you to gain awareness and understanding of the complexity of coaching, and find your own questions and voice.

As a way to continue the conversation, and building on a few key messages across the book, we ask the below questions:

- **What do you find to be complex about coaching?** Coaching is certainly a complex practice as it involves multiple stakeholders, each with their own personalities, needs, motives, culture(s), and values, in complex organizations with intricate webs of politics and power dynamics. Even the "simplest" coaching situation can involve underlying complexities. But, while some situations might be recognized as complex or raise an ethical dilemma for any coach, others are more contextual and personal. *What areas of complexity stood out to you in the book? Where does complexity specifically lie for you in coaching? Why?*
- **How can you make reflexivity an integral part of your continuous development and learning in coaching?** Continuous development and learning seem essential in the professionalization and maturity of a coach. In this lifelong journey, reflexivity (both on the self and about the larger context) should be recognized as an essential skill in competent coaching. It allows coaches to increase their self-awareness and sharpen their observation and analysis of the stakeholders and issues at hand in order to make more informed decisions. *How do you learn as a coach? How easy is it to detach yourself from ready-made solutions and tools? And what role does reflexivity play in your coaching practice?*

- **What resources (will) sustain your reflexivity in coaching?** Exercising reflexivity is challenging, as it implies going outside of one's comfort zone. *What resources, financial, human, and/or emotional, can you implement to support your reflexive journey?*

Let's keep on sharing, reflecting, and developing!

Index